"Nobody, *I'm Italian!*"

From Italy
to America,
the life story
of Armando
Polito......
his way.

Nancy Jo Polito

Outskirts Press, Inc.
Denver, Colorado

Edited by Peter Heyrman of Bear Press Editorial Services
Cover and Photography Design by Robert Tillotson

Outskirts Press, Inc.
http://www.outskirtspress.com

ISBN: 978-1-4327-6234-6

Outskirts Press and the "OP" logo are trademarks belonging to Outskirts Press, Inc.

PRINTED IN THE UNITED STATES OF AMERICA

In loving memory of my Dad and Mom
who always supported me in every endeavor.
They are the reason I'm here at all and made me who I am today.

To my daughters, Angela and Adrianna,
brothers, John and Armand Jr. and nephew, Armand III,
I love you and wish to thank you for bringing to mind all the
wonderful stories that grace these pages through the many
emails that were transmitted over the last year. I could not have
remembered every detail without your help.

This book was written for "La famiglia" and most importantly to
remember our history and humble beginnings.
As Dad always stated, "Don't forget where you came from."

Table of Contents

Foreword ix

Introduction to My Father 1

Armando Arnaldo Polito Tells His Story 3

Life in Bovino 7

Eight Long Years 15

The *Taormina* 15

Portland, Maine 18

Not Many Friends 22

Prohibition and favors 25

My introduction to great music 27

Naples 31

Back in America 35

A Trip back to Bovino 36

High School Graduation and College 37

Meeting Isabel 41

Starting a life together 43

Old Orchard Beach, Maine 48

Luigi's Spaghetti and Pizza Sauce 52

A Father's Daughter 55

The Polito/Lacivita Family 56

The Profenno/DiMatteo Family 57

Lettomanoppello 64

Move to America 64

Two Opposites.. 67

Napoli Restaurant... 68

Sunday Nights 70

Camp Sabia 72

Italian American Community Center.............................. 88

Arbor Street 92

Washington Avenue.. 107

And Then There Were Pets 117

Helping Others.. 124

Halloween... 126

Profenno Construction Company 129

Dinnertime.. 130

House Rules 135

The Couch/Sofa 137

Homework and School Projects.................................... 138

Deering High School, Portland High School & Wentworth .. 140

St. Joseph's Church 141

The Piano 144

Never You Mind.. 145

Pizziola 146

Bad Business 147

Pierre's School of Cosmetology.................................... 150

Scarborough Downs 159

John moves in, I move out 161

Dad's Favorite Movies/Television Programs 165

1974 John moves out again 167

Guitar Lessons, Bowling Leagues, Race Horses.............. 168

Crème de Cacao.. 173

The Gout 175

Dad Sells Me Down The River 176

First Grandchild... 177

Retirement... 179

Cooking and Rules 181

Sporca! 184

Sergio Franchi, Perry Como, Frank Sinatra, Dean Martin,
    Jerry Vale 186

Dad and His Music... 187

Insomnia 187

John Buys A Farm 190

Second Grandchild... 191

Armand Jr. Marries A Caterer 192

Grandchild #3 196

Thanksgivings 197

The Garage.. 200

Normajean, Chris & Racehorses 202

Christmases through the years.. 203

New Year's Eve Parties 210

Dad's Home Remedies 211

The Grandchildren's Relationship 215

Stella Doro, Hydrox, Fresca & Ice Tea............................ 222

The Zipper... 223

Driving 224

"Mom?" 227

Donations.. 233

Camillo's Bakery.. 238

1990-2001 243

Things One Just Knew... 253

2002... 256

The Big Move 260

Dad's 90th Birthday 261

Thanksgiving 2002 263

Christmas 2002 263

February, 2003... 266

Italian words one would hear Dad muttering to himself 269

Foreword
By Nancy Jo Polito

Wednesday, February 5, 2003, 11pm

I had just come in from visiting my father at Maine Medical Center, when the phone rang. I had a sinking feeling that it was the hospital calling. I put the receiver to my ear, and heard a voice. It was barely audible over my pounding heart. "Your father's taken a turn for the worse," it said. "You and your family should come back in." I hung up, not even knowing whom I'd been speaking to. At that moment it hardly mattered.

I found my mother getting ready for bed. I told her what the caller had said. She quickly began getting dressed. I called my two brothers, John and Armand, to tell them Mom and I were heading back in. "You should come too," I said. I followed that with calls to my two daughters, Angela and Adrianna.

Angela was living in Boston, attending Massachusetts General Hospital Institute of Health Professions. "I'll grab some clothes," she said, "and I need to tell my roommates and call school."

On the drive back to the hospital, I felt ill. This was the moment I'd dreaded. Mom sat beside me in silence. My mind veered from hospital to highway: my father in a room dying, and my daughter all alone on the road for the two-hour drive from Boston to Portland. Silently I prayed that she would make it safely, yet I also hoped she would be in time. Just before we'd hung up she'd asked that I tell her "Papa" to wait for her.

At the hospital I pushed my mother's wheelchair, rolling her through corridors to my father's room. Once I parked her at the foot of the bed, I hurried over, sat down, and laid my head on my father's chest. "It's okay, Dad," I whispered. "They're all coming in to be with you. I love you, Dad". A weak hand patted my back ever so softly, as if to say: "I know you do, and I love you too." I moved up closer and whispered in his left ear, "Don't worry Dad, I promise I will take care of Mom." A moment later I added: "Dad, Angela is on her way home from Boston, please stay with us until she comes." The weak hand patted, then faded, then stopped.

That was his last sign of consciousness.

From my father's room I kept a close watch on the doorway, and down the long corridor. Who would come next? Would they get here before he died? One-by-one, my siblings arrived with their significant others: John with Normajean, Armand, Jr. and Linda, my daughter Adrianna and her then-boyfriend, Gregg, followed by my nephew, Armand III and Merry. We only had to wait for Angela. Every fifteen minutes or so I would glance out to see if my eldest daughter was coming. This was the last time, and was sure to be unlike any other.

My brother, John, started reciting the Lord's Prayer and we all joined in, bowing our heads. John had questioned the fact that a priest was not called in for my father's final hours, but I'd told him that priests no longer left their beds at midnight to give people like our father the Last Rights. That was no more than a memory.

Instead I stood over my father, and though I was barely able to speak, I gave him the Last Rights then kissed his forehead. I don't remember what I said. I was desperate to do the right thing, and I knew the gist of what needed to be said, but I couldn't conjure up the exact words. How could this be? All that Catholic education and I was stumped.

We stared at one another, not knowing what to do or say. Usually when we gathered as a family it was to celebrate a holiday or birthday. We were accustomed to being loud, but now silence seemed to be our only option. Somehow that felt so very, very wrong.

Up until then, when faced with a problem, we'd always turned to Dad. He was the one that fixed things. He was the core of our family. Now here he lay, motionless. Dad could no longer hold our world together.

As I sat by my father's bedside, cradling his hand against my face, I began to think of all he'd passed on to us. He'd taught us through his actions and through his stories. He'd told us of his youth in Italy, and coming to America. He wanted us to fully appreciate the opportunity this country had given him. He knew that, if we could learn to see what he'd found here, we would appreciate our own advantages that much more.

For fifty-five years I'd asked my father questions, and whenever he knew the answers, he told them to me. I'd never stopped asking, nor would I, but I now saw that I would have to find answers on my own. My brain rebelled at the thought. I could still hear his voice saying: "Never forget where we came from. Never forget my stories." Now he'd run out of time. Whatever we remembered was all there was. Under my breath I muttered, "Dear Lord, what will we do without this man?"

That was the moment I realized that I must preserve his stories so that future generations could see how we came to this nation. Our children's children's children should understand their history, starting with the Italy my father had left. I wanted to put all this down on paper, but I also wanted to capture his voice, his gestures, and his excitement and wonder at the thought of it all. It was all those things together that made me feel that I was truly a Polito.

Now that all came back to me as we gathered around his bed for the last time. Every so often a nurse would come in to give him another shot of morphine. Each time she said: "It won't be much longer." Not much longer. My Dad's ninety years were running out. It was a matter of hours, or maybe even minutes. I knew this was what had to be, but that didn't mean I had to like it. I tried to think of all the things I would have to write down about him. The scope of it should have scared me, but how scary could it be after going through this?

Finally my daughter, Angela, arrived just in time to tell her grandfather she loved him. She kissed him goodbye. He passed away at three-in-the-morning on Thursday, February 6th 2003.

It took my mother and I over a year to pack up Dad's clothes. Many went to Goodwill, but they didn't get them all. John, Armand Jr., Angela, Adrianna, Armand III and I all took some flannel shirts and favorite sweaters. They weren't so much for us to wear as for remembering the man who'd worn them. Two of his flannel shirts still hang in my closet. Sometimes I find myself burying my face in them just to get the smell of him. That brings back so many memories.

Some of his favorite clothes are still in his closet, and a few of his hats hang on the old bent wood coat rack that came from the house where I grew up. That rack now greets people when they enter through my back hall.

Four years after his death, I woke up at two-in-the-morning, and could not get back to sleep. I got up and glanced at the old Panasonic tape recorder sitting on the floor in the corner. On top, covered with dust, were three tapes. At that moment it occurred to me what these were: recordings of my Dad telling of his Italian roots and how he came to America.

Both had been recorded in early 2001, one by my cousin Tommy at the dining room table, and the other with cousin Cammie. Four years had passed, yet I still hadn't worked up the courage to put in a tape and press "play." In the middle of the night issues of courage and grief can seem less daunting. Now I put one tape in and pressed the button. Tears welled up in my eyes as my father's voice filled my ears. There I sat, listening to stories I'd heard a hundred times. I paused the recorder several times to collect myself and get more tissues.

That was the beginning. Over the next week I listened to the tapes from start to finish, then I listened again. During this second round I began to write down all I was hearing. The following accounts begin with those tapes, and go on with the help of memory. These are the stories my father knew and lived. This is his book, and it is my family's.

Introduction to My Father
By Nancy Jo Polito

Armando Arnaldo Polito

Armando Arnaldo Polito was born in the town of Bovino on November 22, 1912. He was arriving in a place rich in history. Bovino is a hilltop town in the south of Italy. It's quite mountainous, in contrast to the flatlands of Foggia only 40 minutes away. For centuries its position has given it a strategic role in area conflicts.

The town's first settlements date back to the Neolithic age. Bovino itself was founded by the Daunians of Southern Italy. They fought the Romans in the Samnite Wars, losing in 323 BC. The Romans destroyed Bovino, then rebuilt it as Vibinum. For centuries it was a part of the Roman Empire. Two centuries after Rome's fall, in a war against the Lombards, the Byzantines nearly destroyed it. But Bovino came back. In the early Middle Ages it obtained recognition as a town of independence and self-rule. In 876 the defense walls, castle and streets were rebuilt in a narrow, winding configuration that still exists today.

In the last millennium Bovino survived wars, plagues, and disasters, always recovering. The Saracens and Emperor Octon I both razed it to the ground. When Frederick II came to power, Bovino enjoyed a period of peace and prosperity. From the 14ᵗʰ to the 16ᵗʰ century various noble families succeeded one another as rulers of the fief of Bovino. Don Juan de Guevara, a Spanish nobleman, was given the title of Duke of Bovino, by King Philip of Spain in 1575. The Duke added to the castle, making it seem a noble palace. To this day visitors from any direction see the massive Palazzo Ducale, as well as Earl Dragon's Norman tower as they approach Bovino.

It is here that my father's story began, so it is fitting that he spoke of it on the tapes, just as he had so many times with us. The following is what he said, lightly edited so that readers can get the fullness of his story.

Armando Arnaldo Polito
Tells His Story
By Armando Arnaldo Polito

Bovino is an ancient town with parapets rising from its stone wall. When I was six or seven I remember my Grandfather telling me stories of how Hannibal encamped on the mountain of Bovino during his campaigns in the third century BC. From his own lifetime he told of how Garibaldi brought unification to Italy. Italy had been divided into three sections. The southern part was ruled by the Spaniards, the middle region was The Papal States under Rome, and the northern part gave its allegiance to the Savoia family. For centuries various Italians had dreamed of a united country. In the 1800s many of these people supported Garibaldi. They were called Garibaldini. In the mid-19th century Garibaldi and his supporters fought and won the wars of unification.

Being in the south, Bovino had been governed by Spain through the auspices of the Duke of de Guevara. The people of the region were all either serfs or those we saw as villains. My ancestors were serfs. My grandparents worked the land for the Duke, growing wheat and vegetables. In return they were given a share of the crops, as well as a patch of land on the hillside outside of the town where they could live. The Dukes remained for a time after Garibaldi's triumph, but by the early 1930s the current Duke had moved on to become the mayor of Naples. He'd left a keeper behind to tend to the castle.

My earliest childhood memory comes from when I was about two years old. World War I was still raging, and Austrian troops were fighting our Italian army. Flour and bread were rationed, and kept under lock and key. In the night there were air raids, and I would be frightened. When the war ended we had a parade to celebrate the return of our soldiers. Among them were my uncles. People carried candles, torches, and as they were marching through the streets, they would yell out: "Down with Francesco II of Austria."

Then as now, the town was surrounded by hillsides, which sloped down into fields filled with wheat, wild red poppies and vineyards. The roads around Bovino were rocky, narrow and winding. Back then there were no cars, just mules and carts. Anyone with money had a horse and wagon, and everyone else had a two-wheeled cart with a couple of shafts and a mule to pull it. Once you arrived at the top of the mountain you had to go through an archway known as Porta Maggiore to get in to the town.

My father, Giovanni Polito, was born into a farming family on June 28, 1886. His father, my Grandfather, Angelo Polito, and my Grandmother, Maria Guiseppe Lofrano, were born and lived in Bovino. My mother, Giacondina Lacivita, was born in March, 1889. She was from the region of Marche, north of Apulia on the Adriatic side. I believe her home town was Ancona. Her father was Guiseppe Nicola Lacivita and her mother was Antonietta Masciotra. My mother was the oldest of seven. She was followed by Angiolina, Valleverdina, Grazzieta, Pietro, Michele and Emilia. When she was 13 she lost both parents, but I'm not sure how that happened. From that time on she and her siblings did not attend school. Instead they all worked as soon as they were able, pooling their money so they might continue to live together. Before she met my father she married another man named Negri, but he died of tuberculosis. He left her with a two-year-old daughter named Antonietta. My mother's family was in the charcoal business, and my father met her when he was working for them.

The family's charcoal business involved bringing workers to the south in the winter and then to the north in the summer. When the business came into a town they would buy all the local trees, but not the land. They would set up sheds to live in, then cut down the trees to make the charcoal. They would bag the charcoal in 100-kilo sacks, then deliver to homes and businesses.

My father told me how heavy the sacks were. He would fill a two-wheeled cart with these sacks, and his donkey would pull as my father delivered coal to the various towns. In those days people used charcoal for everything from cooking to heating their homes. He even supplied the local police station with charcoal.

My father married my mother on June 3, 1909. That was when she moved to Bovino, with her daughter, Antonietta. My sister Josephine (Giuseppina) was born on February 29, 1910, my sister Angela (Angiolina) on October 3, 1911 and I was born November 22, 1912. When my father left to come to America on June 11, 1913 my mother was pregnant with my sister, Mary (Maria). She was born late in 1913.

My father sailed here on the steamer, *Ancona*. At the time he was 27. I was only 7 months old. My sister, Mary, died from polio when she was four. My father never saw her. In those days polio took many lives. I was only five when Mary died, but I remember how beautiful she was. Unlike my sisters and I, Mary was fair-skinned, with light blonde hair. My sisters told me that the day she died she lay on my mother's bed, weak, yet like an angel. At the moment she passed, a white butterfly flew from under her pillow out the window. Josephine swore it was a sign she'd gone to heaven.

Like many others, my father intended to only stay in America a few years. His plan was to learn a trade, make some money and go back to Italy to rejoin his family, and use his trade to start a business. For eight years my father worked in America, sending home money to support his family. Always expecting his return, my mother never spoke of moving. When World War I started Italy allied with Germany. Because of that many young Italian men in the U.S. were faced with a choice: join the army here, or go home and fight alongside their fellow Italians. Many returned home. The Italians always seemed to be supporting the wrong people, and that's how it was with the Germans. As the war dragged on they reversed themselves, siding with the Allies. My father decided not to go home. He stayed in America, registered for the draft, but was never called.

Bovino, Italy, 1918
Back Row: Gioconda Lacivita Polito, Maria Polito, standing on table,
Antonietta Negri Polito.
Front Row: Armando Polito, Angelina Polito and Giuseppina Polito

Life in Bovino

In Bovino my family did not own their own home. Like others, we rented from richer people. We were on a first floor that today would be like a storefront. We had one large room with a fireplace, a little kitchen area with a small table, and a charcoal kettle for heat. Further back was a bedroom area with a cloth curtain strung on a wire for privacy. Above was a little loft where my sisters and I would sleep.

Above and around the fireplace were huge hooks for hanging pots. My mother cooked on a flat tiled slab built into one side of the fireplace. Under it was a grate for charcoal to heat up the tiles. Boiling water for pasta required plenty of time, and the sauce took all day. I've often been bewildered when people here in America, using old family sauce recipes from Italy, say that it has to cook all day. Once it comes to a boil (which happens quickly on a conventional stove top) it should take no more than an hour or two depending on the type of sauce.

As a child I used to run and play in the castle and on the surrounding wall of the town. Down one hillside were flat fields where the farmers planted their wheat in spring. They harvested it in the fall. That involved the whole town. In the same field they laid out all their wheat in large circular sections to dry. Once it was dry, a farmer stood in the middle of a circle in each section with a reined mule. Behind the mule was a chain wrapped around a huge heavy stone. The mules would slowly walk in a circle, pulling the heavy stone across the wheat to crush and break up the hulls. This took all day.

Every morning the men got together and decided whether the wind was blowing in the right direction and with enough strength for the "tossing of the wheat" to take place. The men would throw a shovelful into the air and the women would use the bottoms of their dresses. The wind blew off the crushed hulls, leaving the grain to fall to the ground. They would shovel grain into bags, then take the bags to the mill to be ground into flour.

Everyone helped with the wheat harvest. My mother and her

friends would cook all day feeding those who were working. We children would run through the town. It was a big celebration with music and singing.

The mill would grind the wheat into flour, bag it in burlap, and distribute it to all the families. This provided us with pasta and bread for the whole year. My mother made pasta by hand, hanging it on wooden racks to dry. Because we did not have an oven, my mother would make bread dough early in the morning and have one of us kids drop it off at the baker on our way to school, then pick it up on our way home. The baker marked the bread for each family showing which bread belonged to whom. We did the same with beans that had to be baked in an oven.

One day my sisters and I were on our way home with the loaves on our heads, when we encountered a farmer and his pigs in the middle of the road. The pigs crowded us, not letting us pass. As we neared them, they smelled the bread and charged us, pushing us down and grabbing the freshly baked loaves. We all ran off screaming while the farmer laughed. My mother was furious with us when we arrived home without her bread.

In the back of our house we had a small underground cellar-like area with a few steps down, and a door. Here we stored flour, vegetables, olive oil, and wine. The place was small, dark and cold, but it kept food away from animals and the heat of the day. We made provolone and mozzarella by putting it in a calf's bladder and wrapping it in string. We hung this on hooks from the ceiling to age. When we had cured meats like pancetta, pepperoni, and prosciutto (which wasn't often) we would hang them from the ceiling.

When I was a boy charcoal was our fuel, and when I went back to Italy in 1930, they still used it. Outside, or on the balcony they would fill a brazier or "brazelle" (a kettle that was large, round and shallow, about a foot off the floor) with charcoal, then place a canopy of wire over it so no one would fall in. It was then brought inside and placed in the middle of the floor to heat the home.

We had no running water and no electricity. We did have petroleum. The Romans had built an aqueduct that ran through Bovino to a fountain in the lower part of town about halfway down the mountain. This fountain was divided. One section was for horses while another was where we could fill wooden barrels. Everyday people took their donkeys and large barrels to the fountain to collect their water. Those without donkeys carried their water back on the tops of their heads.

Each home had a wooden stand to hold the barrel of fresh water. This was the water for washing, drinking, and cooking. It was always cold and refreshing. On the way to the fountain was a stone wall full of holes. These holes were from Garibaldi's wars when men had been executed there. We counted the holes, imagining ourselves shooting each other there at the wall.

We ate pasta, vegetables and bread. There was pasta e fajoli (pasta with beans), pasta e patate (pasta with potato) and pasta e pizzelle (pasta with peas). Then there was everything else you could put with pasta. The ingredient that changed was the vegetable. We only saw meat a couple times a year. Meat was mostly for upper class. For fish we went to Foggia, which was closer to the sea. Once we had it, storing it was difficult, because we had no refrigeration. Fish was common at Christmas, especially eels or "capitone". Foggia's fishmongers would bring live eels up to Bovino the day before Christmas so that we could cook it right away.

At Christmas time we celebrated San Nicola (Saint Nicholas) and the birth of Christ. We spoke of "Natale," meaning birthday. "La Festa di San Nicola" or the Feast of Saint Nicholas came on December 6th with a festival in honor of this patron saint of shepherds. On Christmas Eve we had another huge feast with baccala, a salted and dried codfish, pasta, and eel. People walked from house to house, bringing bread and sweets, and singing. My sisters and I would place a plate at the table before going to bed. We hoped San Nicola would leave a coin worth about five cents under the plate. I was never very good so I always worried a little.

The stone wall surrounding the Duke's Castle was used for laying out tomatoes to dry in the hot sun of August. This method kept them without any spoiling, the same way we preserve sun-dried tomatoes today. We could store them for the winter and make tomato sauce. My mother would walk down to the wall every day to check their progress. If the weather was hot it took a week. One particular day on the other side of the castle wall my friends and I were playing with hair cut from a donkey. We began to throw the hair up into the wind, not knowing where it was landing. It landed on the drying tomatoes above us. My aunt saw this and yelled that we must stop or risk a beating. It didn't matter who reprimanded us. We'd been brought up to respect all elders. When my Aunt yelled we ran like hell.

The mountainsides were covered with vineyards. Everyone made wine and we drank it with every meal, even children. When I would come home at lunchtime from school my mother had a glass of wine and a hard crusty piece of bread waiting for me. That was all I would have before going back to school.

Homes didn't have bathrooms. Instead we had a porcelain pot to use in the night. My mother used to take it down the street to the side of the road and empty it. When my friends and I were playing and one of us had to poop, we would just walk into the fields or anywhere out of sight and go. Urinating wasn't any big deal. You just turned your back to people and peed on the side of the street. It was common to see women walking along with their long black dresses to the ground, stopping by the side of the road and picking up their dress just enough to keep the hem from touching the roadside. They peed, then continued on their way. I suppose the rain washed everything away.

At the end of every month my mother would give each of us a spoonful of castor oil to clean us out. My sisters were allowed to use the "pot" and they would take turns running to the field to empty the damn thing. She made me use the nearby fields to go to the bathroom. That was good for me. I would play out there all day anyway.

I spent my childhood days running around hillsides and through narrow streets, climbing castle walls and usually getting in trouble. My friends were Guido Savino, Silvio Ricotta, Idolo Nicastro (we called him "Idoluccio"), Carlino Calucci and Raffaele Morsillo. Idoluccio and Carlino were cousins and lived above us. We had no toys, only our imaginations. Whenever we got our hands on paper, we spent hours folding and creasing it into different animals.

One endless source of fascination was the cemetery. There the grave keeper would take us into a large room where shelves were filled with the skeletal heads of people from our town who had passed on. Because the cemetery was so small, space was in short supply. The grave keeper could tell how long it took for a body to decompose from the weight. When the time was right-- usually after a couple of years-- he would dig them up and dispose of the bones except for the heads. He lined the skulls on the shelves, and he could tell us their names. He would go around pointing, saying: "This one is Mr. So-and-so, and that one is Mrs. So-and-so. Over here is a little boy." It was always a fascinating place to hang out.

Before we moved to America I attended school through second grade. The girls went to a Catholic school while us boys went to a public school. My teacher was a priest named Don Vincenzo Capriano. Don Vincenzo was a mean old bastard. He carried a long wooden stick with a piece of metal running through its middle. If we misbehaved he would snap it at our legs or across our shoulders. Back then you did not complain to your parents about such things. Your teacher was educated and well respected, and in matters of right and wrong, he was always right. He could punish us, and no parent would question his judgment.

My friends and I hated Don Vincenzo. He was tall, thin and very stern. He wore dark glasses, so we never knew where he was looking. Each day he came into the classroom, sat behind his elevated desk, and smoked his long clay pipe.

At lunchtime we went home to eat, then we went back for afternoon class. One day we got back before Don Vincenzo, and we noticed his pipe lying on his desk. My friend, Carlino pulled a shotgun cartridge from his pocket. Idoluccio, Carlino, Guido, Silvio and I removed the tobacco and packed the pipe with gunpowder, along with a covering of tobacco. Don Vincenzo walked in, sat down, leaned back and grabbed his pipe. I started shaking. I knew that we were in for big trouble. He struck the match and placed it over the bowl of the pipe, took a couple of puffs and ....BOOM!!! The pipe exploded pushing him back onto the floor. A tiny pipe stem protruded from his lips. That was all that was left.

We ran like hell. I jumped out of the window onto a balcony, then leapt to the ground. Carlino ran out the door and as I looked back, Idoluccio followed me. I don't know where Guido and Silvio ran to, but they caught up with us at the belfry of the church.

The churches were always open, so the belfry was the natural place to go. It was high with no guardrails. We climbed all around the big bells. We could've broken our necks. After awhile it started to get dark. We knew that we had to go home, but we hoped that no one knew what had happened at school.

Every evening after dinner it was a social ritual to go for an evening walk called a "passeggiata." Don Vincenzo did this, passing by our homes where he might stop, and talk with our mothers. On this evening he told our mothers the whole tale. Finally, very late, I walked into the house carrying my books tied in their leather strap and buckle. I acted as if nothing had happened. My mother grabbed my books, strap and buckle, and swung it up over my head. It hit my forehead, the buckle cutting me. Blood trickled down my face.

My mother wasn't impressed by the blood. She yelled, "I know what you did today!" I was sent to bed with no supper. My sister, Josephine, wrapped a white kerchief around my forehead, covering the cut.

The next day my sister, Josephine, brought me back to school. Don Vincenzo met me and my friends at the door. I still had the white kerchief tied around my forehead with dried blood stained on it. Don Vincenzo looked at all us and said, "Come with me". We followed him to the back of the room. He directed us to kneel down on the cold hard tile floor, and he placed three hard beans under each of our kneecaps. We wore shorts, like Boy Scouts. We had to keep kneeling until he told us we could get up. The pain became excruciating. When we tried to shift our weight the beans burned, like nails driving into our skin. Guido, Carlino, Idoluccio, Silvio and I knelt for hours. Tears streamed down our faces. My knees grew numb. When Don Vincenzo finally allowed us to get up, the beans were stuck deep in our skin.

Most people in Bovino were superstitious, including my mother and sisters. If you come across a cart full of freshly baled hay you were to make a wish. On nights of the full moon we were not allowed to let the moon shine through the window onto our bed. If you did something bad would happen. There was talk that a werewolf roamed the streets. Sometimes we could hear howling through the night. My sisters and I huddled together listening to the weird noises, wondering if this mythical animal was about to attack. We never saw anything, but the next day everyone would be talking about the howling, and other weird noises. My guess now is that normal wolves were howling at the moon.

Every Sunday morning we would walk to church to attend Mass. One particular Sunday it was just my mother and I. I happened to look back down a street, and saw the image of a small girl in the haze of the early morning dew. Telling my mother about this little girl we both turned to look together; she was gone. When I described the girl to my mother, she said that a little girl had died in an accident there a few years before. "You must have seen something else," she said, but still she pulled my arm and made me walk faster. I kept looking back to see if she reappeared. She had seemed very real.

Every month there seemed to be some type of festival or what we called "Carnevale." The largest and most celebrated festival was that of Santa Maria di Valleverde the patron saint of Valleverde, on August 29th. Valleverde means 'green valley.' The church of Santa Maria Valleverde is built on the site of an apparition of the Virgin Mary halfway up the mountain to Bovino. The festival started with a religious procession. There were horses, parades, fireworks, music and plenty of food.

After these festivals my friends and I would go around and collect any of the fireworks that had failed to explode. We would pull them apart to get out the explosive material. Then we put the explosives in a can, and made a paper wick. After that we dug a hole. We'd put the can in the hole, light the wick, and wait. Sometimes the explosive would sputter and die, driving us crazy and one, then another, would edge closer to see what was happening. Was there a flicker of flame? Or had it gone out? Sometimes it would explode when we were almost on top of it. Other times the hole would go up in flames and the only way to put it out was to pee on it. That was the fastest way to put the fire out before one of our parents saw what we were doing.

With no real toys of our own, we made up games ourselves. The wind on the mountaintop of Bovino blew strong, and we would spend hours up there catching sparrows in flight. To do this we cut a small hole in the middle of a piece of cardboard-like paper. We then tied a string to one end, sat on the castle wall, and flew it like a kite. Flying sparrows would get caught in the hole, then we would pull it in. We would always let them go, but it was fun to see how many we could catch.

Life on the mountain was communal. Families did everything together to survive. My sisters did all they could to help my mother. Once in a while they took time off and joined other girls their age in jumping rope. As they jumped, they sang, "pipa ponte tela ponte tela pi-, col lo scopo con ca ti fa...col lo ti ca ti...col lo raffa ne...pipa ponte tela ponte tela....pi, pi." This little singing rhyme did not mean anything other than it was rhythmic.

Eight Long Years

Meanwhile my father continued to work in America. Others had gone there too. We knew of a family that had gone before my father, and my father's brother, Antonio, had preceded him, and now worked in the quarry in Thomaston, Maine. My father followed his brother to the Thomaston quarry. My father lived in a shack. He hated the work, hated the shack, and after awhile he moved to Portland. He got a job with the Romano-Forgone Construction Company building the South Portland Bridge. Later he worked for the City of Portland building streets.

Tired of hard labor, in 1919 he opened the Napoli Restaurant at 102 Middle Street. It was small, just five or six tables. He'd always loved working with food, so when the opportunity came he decided to give up digging for cooking. Many Italian and Jewish people lived on Middle Street. My father made friends with them all, and did very well. Pasta was new to the neighborhood, and it became popular. He ordered pasta from Boston. His best day was Sunday, especially once people started driving cars.

Eight years had passed since my father had gone. One day my mother announced to my sisters and me that we were going to be moving to America to be with him. This upset my sisters. They did not want to leave their friends and school. I didn't mind the idea. I thought that America was just a couple of towns over. I had no idea what was in store for me.

The *Taormina*

On All Saints Day, November 1, 1920 at 6pm, we boarded a steamship, the *Taormina*, in Naples. The *Taormina*, a service ship from Italy to New York, had been built by D & W Henderson & Company in Glasgow in 1912. It was 520 feet long, 56 feet wide and held 2,680 passengers. There was room for 60 first class passengers, 120 second class, and 2,500 third class.

Once onboard, we were led down to the very bottom level to third class. It was open, almost the length of the ship, with hundreds of bunk beds stacked three high. We each chose a spot to call our own, then we huddled together, waiting. The ship started. The noise from the engines was deafening. The ship's rocking made many people moan and scream. We thought we would never see Italy again. We thought we were going to die. My mother showed no fright at all. If she was scared, we never saw it.

Through the 13-day voyage I clung to my mother, never letting her out of my sight. The food had no salt, and I couldn't eat it. Even the bread was flavorless. I couldn't stomach it. The food was salt-less to keep our thirst at bay. Water was rationed.

At the start of our passage we were given a small pot. Each day at noon an old woman from the crew came around with a big pot and ladle. She would yell, "Pastina per i bambini," meaning pastina for the babies. This was pastina soup for all babies. My mother would tell Antonietta to take our pot and see if she could get some pastina for Armando.

The woman serving the soup saw that my mother had no babies, just me, age 8, sitting on her lap. I was very small for my age, but I was no baby. Still without a word the woman would ladle some soup in our pot, and quickly walk away. She could see that I was sick and needed nourishment, and she probably guessed that soup was all I could keep down. Needless to say, for me it was a long voyage.

In one corner was an area where passengers could go to the bathroom. A couple of large blankets were strung on a rope for privacy. Behind them sat some knee-high barrels. One area was for men, the other for women. Men would take the barrels up to the upper level and empty them into the ocean every few hours. Young children used a small pot by their beds.

My mother didn't know much about our destination. She'd brought her copper pots and pans. For an Italian woman these were like a dowry given by her family when she got married. My mother kept these in pristine condition, getting the bottoms refinished with copper every few years. My mother assumed there wouldn't be any pots in America.

A few days before we arrived in New York, word circulated that the authorities at Ellis Island would confiscate all personal belongings. My mother feared that they would take her prized pots and pans, so she went up on the top deck at night and threw most of them overboard. She figured if she couldn't keep them, then no one would have them.

She also brought a bale of wool for bedding for mattresses. My father threw this out when we arrived.

As we approached New York we saw a woman standing straight up out of the water with her arm held high. At first we couldn't see anything else. As we neared shore we began to see the buildings. Then we realized the woman was a statue, the Statue of Liberty. My sisters and I thought this looked funny. Once we got into the harbor we had to wait a few days for there were several ships ahead of us waiting to be cleared.

A couple of days before we'd gotten there my mother had sent a telegram telling my father when we were to arrive. My father had a fellow named Bruni take over his restaurant so that he could take the train to New York to meet us. During those days of waiting tugboats full of family members would pull up to different ships, circle around, and call out names of families. My sister, Josephine, heard someone yell out, "Polito" and she looked down and said, "There's Papa". She recognized him right away. I remember saying, "Where? Where?" I hadn't seen him since I was 6 months old. I had no idea what he looked like.

Finally, after two days of waiting, we disembarked on Ellis Island. There they put families in different rooms, depending on where you were going. My mother was tagged to go to Maine along with us children. The authorities immediately took my mother from us and left us all alone. She had to pass a physical. We didn't have to—just her. We sat and waited. Finally, she came back and we all huddled together waiting for my father to appear. It was frightening not to be able to understand what anyone said. Finally, my father found us. He took us to Grand Central Station to board a train from New York to Portland, Maine.

Portland, Maine

We arrived in Portland at about 6am, on November 18, 1920. It was snowy, cold and damp. The city looked dismal. We took a horse-and-buggy taxi to our new home on Middle Street. The house was furnished, but the rooms were so small we thought we were in a shed. We'd been used to big rooms, high ceilings, marble floors, balconies, and windows as big as doors. My sister, Josephine kept saying, "I don't like this" and "I don't like America" over and over.

My father's Napoli Restaurant was at 102 Middle Street. Our home was across the street over the Naples Brother's Store. Looking out the window we could see the Pevarada Grocery Store, a shoe store, and Flaherty's Drug Store. We were near the corner of Franklin and Middle. We had the flat because the couple who'd lived there before had divorced and moved. Before they left, my father bought all of the furniture, bedding, and curtains from them.

We all had to adjust to American food. Angela said the butter tasted like wax. We did our best, eating food from my father's restaurant. That was just like being back in Italy. That part of my life was the same, which made me happy.

After a week we had to go to school. My father knew a family on Deer Street with a daughter about Josephine's age. This girl spoke just enough Italian that we could understand her, so she walked us to and from school. She got us registered at the Catholic school on Congress Street. In those days the boys and girls were in separate classrooms. My two sisters were placed in with the girls' class, while I was with the boys. We were all in second grade because we could not speak English. I was 9, Angela 10, and Josephine was 11. This was a setback. In Italy Josephine had already reached high school level. My stepsister, Antonietta, did not attend school. At 14 she worked with my father and mother in the restaurant.

Napoli Restaurant, est. 1919,
Portland's first Italian Restaurant., Middle Street.

My first day was cold and dreary. It had snowed more since we'd arrived. Back then there were no plows, so snow just kept piling up, making it difficult to walk. We weren't used to so much snow and cold. Snow had been rare in Bovino. The girl from Deer Street took me to my classroom, and explained who I was to the nun. The nun showed me where to hang my hat and coat in the coatroom, then put me in a seat in the back of the class. The only thing I recognized was prayers. We prayed in the morning, then at lunch, and at the end of the day. We always knelt to pray. I could do that. I might not know what they were saying, but I could pray in Italian.

When other children moved outside for recess, I followed. Outside no one would speak to me and I couldn't speak to anyone else, so I stood there. No one knew what to do with me. When the bell rang everyone lined up. I didn't know what to do. The nun came over and put me in a line. I followed the other children back in. Again we knelt and prayed. I was good at that!

In class the children were drawing pictures of Santa Claus to hang on the windows and all around the room. I could not draw Santa Claus; I did not know who he was. Instead I sat there all morning doing nothing. Noontime came and the bell rang. Everyone knelt and prayed and then proceeded to leave. I sat, still doing nothing. I was told that the girl would come back and take me home.

So I waited. The nun and I sat at our desks staring at each other. Finally she opened a book and motioned for me to come to her desk. There I saw that she had a book of stories with pictures. She pointed to a picture of a house. I figured that the other children had gone home for lunch, so I assumed she was signaling that she wanted me to go home too. I turned around, got my hat and coat from the coatroom and walked out the door.

There were two exits from the school. I picked the one that I thought I'd come in that morning. I walked up Congress Street past Franklin heading toward City Hall. I soon realized nothing looked familiar, so I turned around. I walked back past the school and headed for Munjoy Hill. After some time I realized I was lost. I began to cry. A man stopped me and said something. I looked at him and said, "Armando Polito, cente due Middle Street, Giovanni Polito." This was the address of my father's restaurant.

"Italiano?" he said.

"Si, si," I replied. "Italiano."

Just then a woman walked by. She stopped, said something to the man, and then spoke to me. I kept crying and muttering in Italian, "Armando Polito, cente due Middle Street, Giovanni Polito."

This woman knew an Italian family who lived nearby. We all started walking across from Washington Avenue and Congress Street near the cemetery. We saw a woman on the front porch of a house. The man with me said something to her.

She said to me: "Come ti chiami? [What is your name?]"

"Armando Polito, cente due Middle Street, Giovanni Polito, Napoli Restaurante," I said rapid fire.

The woman knew exactly who I was. She'd once lived above my father's restaurant. She spoke to me in Italian, then called to her two sons, telling them to take me home. So I went off with them. I spoke to them in Italian, but they only knew English. As we walked I kept looking for any familiar landmarks.

We went down Franklin Street toward Middle Street, and finally I recognized Flaherty's Drug Store, and took off running as fast as I could. I left the two boys behind. I never looked back. I ran straight to my home, up the stairs and right into my father. He'd just come back from the police station where he'd reported me as missing.

My father wasn't happy. At his busiest hour, lunchtime, he'd had to leave the restaurant in the hands of one of his cooks. He'd gone out looking for me, and when he couldn't find me he'd gone to the police. When I ran into him he looked at me and: Wham! I got a slap in the face. I'd created so much trouble and worry.

It was at that moment that the girl showed up to walk all of us back to school. Our lunch break was over. As I left my father yelled at me not to leave the school until the girl showed up to bring me home.

At school the nun who'd shown me the picture was visibly shaken. She knew how much trouble I'd caused. After that episode she didn't let me out of her sight.

Even after a week of attending school we didn't seem to be learning anything. The nuns didn't know what to do with us. Josephine and Angela complained to my father that we just sat in the back doing nothing all day. My father spoke to a well-educated friend and he said that he would enroll us in public school. This man took us to the North School where they placed all three of us in the second grade again. Here the boys and girls were together in the same class.

Ms. Donohue was our teacher in a class of about 30 kids. She would assign the rest of the class to do a project while she worked with the three of us. I will never forget Ms. Donohue's patience. She was the most wonderful teacher.

There were three Russian children, two girls and a boy, about the same age as us. They could not speak English either. Ms. Donahue would work with all six of us, having us go up to the chalkboard where we would write words out and repeat them. The hardest word was "the." None of our Italian words had the sound "th." To us it sounded like "da." We kept repeating, "da" and then "te," going back and forth, each of us trying to get the tongue to stay at the roof of the mouth. It was not natural for us.

My eldest sister, Josephine, caught on fast, and moved up to the fifth grade. We all could do math, even me. Long division was not a problem. In this we were ahead of the other children. My sister, Angela advanced to the third grade, while I stayed in the second grade for the rest of the year. It seemed that no matter what I did I was always in the second grade. In Italy, second grade, Catholic school, second grade, North School, second grade!

Not Many Friends

I had only been in this country a couple of weeks when I witnessed a shooting on Middle Street near my father's restaurant. Once a week farmers came to town and set up carts along the street. They sold produce from their gardens, and from the train from Boston. At the end of the day the carts would stand empty. I was running around between the carts playing by myself. A car sped past, which was unusual. Few people had cars in those days. I heard the screech of tires. As I turned toward the car two men jumped out and chased a man in a long trench coat down the middle of the street. They fired two shots at him and down he went. I jumped behind one of the produce carts to hide. I was afraid to even breathe for fear that someone would see me. One of the men got out of the car, turned around, and saw me huddled behind the cart. He stared directly into my eyes. I jumped up and ran as fast as I could back to my house. I did not look back.

I told my father what I'd seen, and how they'd noticed me. He assured me it would be all right, but it wasn't. The next day the sheriff came by and asked my father about what I'd seen. Apparently someone else saw the whole thing, and recognized me.

A few weeks later my father told me that I had to go to court to testify about witnessing the shooting. I remember my father telling me not to worry. "Remember," he said, "you saw nothing." I didn't realize that the two men who'd done the shooting would be in the courtroom. An interpreter was present when I took the stand. As I looked around the courtroom I saw the man who'd stared at me on the day of the shooting. When I was asked the question, "Do you see the man you saw on the day of the shooting in this courtroom?" First I answered, "No," Then I answered: "Yes."

"How can you answer in English when you don't speak English?" the judge asked.

When the interpreter translated this I didn't know what to say. My father took the stand and explained that I'd only been in America for two weeks, and "yes" and "no" were the only English words I knew. I do not remember what happened to the two shooters, but I remember how scared I was that the man that stared at me would come after me, but he never did.

In the North School's third grade I was assigned to be one of the tellers that did banking for all the students. Everyone had a bank card, and most of us banked three or four pennies a week. It was my job to collect the money for the whole school and tally it up. Most weeks this added up to $7 or $8. Our principal Mr. Parmenter chose me to write up the deposit slip. He would then put the money in an envelope, and I would walk down Congress Street past City Hall to deposit it at the bank. I was proud of this job. It was something important. That made a difference, because I did not have many friends and I got into a lot of fights because of the language barrier.

Over the next couple of years my sisters and I adjusted to American life and its customs. We were especially intrigued by Halloween, Thanksgiving and Christmas. These celebrations were far more extravagant than what we were accustomed to. One Christmas my father decided to bring home a Christmas tree for us to decorate. My mother had tiny candles that clipped onto the branches. There were no electrical lights for trees back then. My mother specifically told all of us not to light the candles. They were for decoration only. I decided to light the candles and as I reached the last one, the whole tree went up in flames. I ran out of the living room screaming for help. My sister grabbed a pot of water and dowsed the fire. My father was mad, but still went out and got another tree. I received orders not to go anywhere near it. My father was determined to have an American Christmas.

In the third grade I started to have a lot of colds, sore throats and earaches. The doctor said I needed to have my tonsils removed. Though I knew nothing about it, arrangements were made for my surgery. One morning I got up, and learned what was to happen. My father had my sister, Josephine, write a note for me. With the note in hand, I went to get my tonsils taken out. My family wished me well, saying they would see me in a couple of days. All by myself, I walked to the Maine Eye and Ear Infirmary at the corner of Bramhall and Congress Street. Inside I handed the note to the receptionist. She took me to a room where I got undressed, then they took me to get the surgery. I was scared to death. After spending a few days in the hospital, I walked back home.

Prohibition and favors

During Prohibition, when you could not have any wine or liquor in the house or restaurant, the sheriff's department kept close watch on all Italians. They knew we had always made wine at home, and while there was plenty of bootlegging going on, making any alcoholic beverage was illegal.

This made no sense to us. We'd grown up drinking wine with our meals. To us wine was like water. When we came home for lunch we each had a glass of red wine, along with crusty bread and maybe a piece of prosciutto or cheese.

People made wine by filling big basement tubs with grapes. You could smell the fermentation through cellar windows as you passed by.

With Prohibition Sheriff Dowdy started searching the homes. Every once in a while someone on Deer Street would be arrested. It was a hardship because this was the way people made their living. Italians thought the Sheriff was a bastard.

Friends of my father's came from Boston and New York on business, visiting his restaurant for the Italian fare. They often held meetings after hours. I remember hearing them all talking Italian, drinking wine, laughing and eating. With the help of these friends, the Napoli Restaurant did well. One of his friends was Joseph Faietta. My father helped him open a candy store. When Joe was starting out my father sent Antionette over to run the counter while Joe made candy.

A few months later my father learned that Joe and Antonietta were having an affair. Joe was in his late twenties; Antonietta was 16 years old. My father couldn't believe that Joe would do something like this after all he had done for him. My father considered Joe's actions to be dishonorable. As soon as he heard about it he ran across the street to our apartment. He came out of the bedroom with a gun, yelling to my mother: "Do you know what your daughter and that no good stronz [turd, no good bastard] are doing?"

"No, No," my mother screamed.

"I will kill that bastard," my father shouted, as he ran down the stairs, and up the street toward the candy store.

My mother sat down at the kitchen table and cried. I believe she'd already known, but she'd never told my father. My father returned, saying that Joe was not at the store. He told my mother that Antonietta was not allowed to come to our house or restaurant. He said he disowned her, and he forbade my mother to see her.

Soon after that Antonietta and Joe got married. They lived about a block from our home. For years my mother would sneak out to see Antonietta, sometimes giving her money. My sisters would visit her now and then, but they had to be careful. My father kept a close watch.

The candy store didn't do well. Antonietta got pregnant and could no longer work the long hours. My mother felt helpless, but we all kept our distance, respecting my father's wishes.

When I was in the 4th grade my picture appeared in the newspaper under the heading, "Child in the U.S. only two years, wins North School Award for Scholastics." The article said, "Armando Polito was chosen by the two graduating classes as the pupil who best exemplifies the principles of good citizenship and was given a medal by the Falmouth Chapter of the Society of the Sons of the American Revolution. The award was presented by Dr. Cecil P. Brown, secretary of the Old Falmouth Chapter." I was proud of this bronze medal, and I have it to this day.

While attending North School, I learned to play the flute. I also studied the piano on my own. I played in the North School Orchestra directed by Miss Gladys M. Morgan. Whenever there was any type of school presentation or gathering, the North School Orchestra would play. I was in my glory; music was the only thing that I excelled at and understood.

One day I came home to find my father cleaning out a space in the basement. He was making room for a cot and table. I asked him what he was doing. He said that we were having company for a while, and this guest would stay in the cellar. I was not to talk about this person or mention to anyone that he was living here. This mysterious man moved in and lived in the basement for over two years. He was about 30. We all took turns bringing food to him and collecting his plates. My mother did his laundry and tidied up his room. No one ever questioned why he was there. It was not our business.

My father tried to become a citizen but he could not. Back then Portland was run by Republicans. A Democrat had little chance. They always rejected him because he could not speak English very well and he could not read it at all. When Al Smith ran for President, my father went to City Hall to see him. He wore a Smith button hoping this might show he could read a little. It didn't work. They still wouldn't let him become a citizen.

Though she could understand it a little, my mother never learned to speak this country's language, and my father spoke broken English. We were allowed to speak Italian in our restaurant and in our home, but not outside on the streets. My father was adamant about all of us working hard to assimilate into our new lives in America.

My introduction to great music

My sisters, Josephine and Angela stopped attending school in the 8th grade to work in the restaurant. My mother always stayed in the kitchen making the antipasto. She took great pride in making sure that everything looked just right. My father would yell at her to hurry up. In Italian dining the meal was served in stages. Antipasto was the first of the four courses, and he was trying to time the preparation and serving of the other three: primo (first course), secondo (second course), and la dolce (dessert). My mother frustrated everyone in the kitchen, arranging the antipasto so it looked perfect. It was her only job.

My father played Italian music at the restaurant, especially opera. Its beauty fascinated me. In the fall of each year the owners of the Chapman Building would bring a travelling opera company into Keith's Theater in their building. Often the singers and musicians ate at my father's restaurant. Beniamino Gigli (1890-1957), a self-declared "people's singer," had a wonderful tenor voice. He was known for his sheer beauty of tone as well as his dramatic intensity. He walked into the restaurant's kitchen and asked my father to cook him "Linguine con poco aglio [linquine with a little garlic]." The whole opera company was Italian. They would eat, sing and joke around with my father, my sisters and me.

One of the best sopranos of the 20th century, Amelita Galli-Curci (1882-1963), came to eat at the Napoli. Heavyweight boxer Primo Carnera visited the restaurant too. Some said he'd been exploited by New York mobsters who fixed his fights leading to the heavyweight championship. Where else could those Italians go but into the Napoli Restaurant? We were the only Italian restaurant north of Boston.

On December 16, 1923, our family welcomed my brother, Angelo Luigi Polito, into the world. He was named after my Grandfather Angelo Polito. Though he'd been born here, Angelo was not considered to be an American citizen because my father didn't have his citizenship yet.

1928, Portland High School, 16 years of age.

I studied the flute and piano on my own, and joined an all-Italian band. Antonio DeCristofaro founded and directed it. He'd been associated with the Fifth Infantry Band at Fort Williams in the early '20s. We were called the Caruso Symphonic Band. At 13, I was the youngest of the 28 members. We made our first public performance in a hall on Cumberland Avenue. I believe that building later became the Jewish Center.

We only performed on a few occasions. Mr. DeCristofaro could hardly make a living from it, so it soon disbanded. Subsequently, a professional musician, Ricardo DeCarlo, reorganized it, but he ran into the same problem. In the late '20s Joseph Palermo revived it, and we rehearsed in the hall of the original St. Peter's Church on Federal Street. Joseph Romano was next, and with him it became Romano's Band. By this time it was no longer exclusively Italian. The band didn't permanently dissolve until the Second World War.

Meanwhile, in 1928 my father closed up his old location, moving to a bigger place at 230 Middle Street. His restaurant was doing well.

I wanted to become a composer and begged my father to let me pursue my dreams. After finishing the 8th grade, my father decided to let me go back to Italy to study. I would attend the Conservatory of Music, San Pietro a Maiella in Naples. San Pietro a Maiella was the same school that Giuseppe Verde, the famous 19th Century Italian opera composer, had attended. It would be a 9-year course.

In May, 1928 my father filled out papers for all his children to become United States Citizens. It took months to get all the paperwork, especially copies of our Italian birth certificates. Once he'd filed these, we waited.

Naples

August 18, 1928, when I was 14, I left for New York with an Italian passport. My father was still not a citizen, so the passport was only good for two years. I had a second-class ticket on the steamer, *Saturnia*, $150.00 plus $5.00 tax. My father had made arrangements with the "man in the basement" to accompany me to New York. Apparently, it was safe for him to leave now. My father had asked him, as a personal favor, to make sure I safely boarded the boat for Naples. After arriving at Grand Central Station, we went to an apartment building to stay the night with some of the man's friends. At one point when I looked out the window at the streets, the man told me not to. Standing in front of any of the windows was not a safe thing to do. He didn't have to tell me twice. I couldn't wait to get aboard the ship.

When I finally did I started a crossing that would take 14 days. I walked on deck, read, talked with other passengers, and practiced my flute. The food was terrible, bringing back awful memories of my first boat trip. I could not wait to be settled into my room in Naples.

In Naples my father had arranged to pay $10 per month for my room and board with a family my Uncle Antonio knew. Uncle Antonio also knew an accomplished pianist from Bovino who helped me prepare for my Conservatory audition. After hearing me, this pianist decided I was better at the flute than the piano. He advised me to play the flute for my audition, saying that I should apply for entrance with the woodwinds. I would stay with the woodwinds until I studied piano, composition and voice. My entrance tax to the Conservatory was $10.00 per year.

I passed my audition with the flute and started my courses that same week. Studying music came easily, and soon I was learning to compose for flutes, violins, and piano. I found studying voice and learning the piccolo just as exciting. By my second year I was learning to conduct an orchestra. I enjoyed this the most. My best friend among my classmates was Vicenzo Aita. On weekends we traveled together to nearby cities.

The train ride from Naples to Bovino was about four hours. My Uncle Antonio had returned to Bovino and my father had sent him money to buy a house. His sister, Aunt Valleverdina Polito lived in the house. When I would visit Bovino I would stay with her. My Uncle Antonio had a couple of daughters and a son whom I would spend time with, and I would also visit my Uncle Lawrence and Aunt Grazzieta Fattibene, and their daughter, Marina, Aunt Emilia, Uncle Pietro and Aunt Lucia, Don Peppe and Donna Maria, my Godfather and Godmother and their son Alfredo. I sometimes went to see family friends Giulietta and Bianca Ricotta and of course, my friends, Carlino Colucci, Silvio Ricotta, Raffaele Morsillo, Idoluccio Nicastro, and Guido Savino.

During vacation when school was closed there was not much to do, so my school classmate, Vincenzo and I traveled to Venice, Pompei, and Rome. We would also visit my mother's sister Aunt Angelina D'Alessandro and her daughter, Clelia who lived in Fano on the west coast in the region of Ancona. I saw Uncle Achielle and Aunt Valleverdina Lacivita Rocca on their honeymoon in Naples.

In Italy students went through to the fifth grade, which was considered high school. If you wanted to continue from there you would attend an institute or university, for which you would have to pay. Guido and Idoluccio went on to the university in Foggia.

In July 1930 I noticed that my passport would expire on August 18, 1930. I went to the American Consulate to see what could be done. I had one hell of a time getting past the Italian guard at the entrance. When I told him what I wanted, he said I would need permission to get through. While the guard and I talked, two American tourists came by wearing knickers. They spoke English to the guard. Though the guard kept saying "Si, si," I knew he didn't understand a word of what they said. Still he let them through.

I left the Consulate and waited a week. Finally I dressed in knickers and put a cap on. Looking like an American, I went back to the consulate entrance where I saw the same guard. Approaching him I spoke rapid English. The guard said, "Si, si" and let me through. *What a pazze!* I thought ("pazze" meaning "stupid one" or "idiot").

1930, Naples, Italy, Aunt Valleverdina, Uncle Achielle & Armando
They were on their honeymoon.

Inside I went to a woman at a desk. She spoke both English and Italian. I told her that I was from America and I wanted to speak to the Consulere about my passport. She got me in to see him. The first thing the Consulere asked was if I was an American Citizen. I told him I thought my father had completed our family's citizenship process two years before, about the time I left for Italy.

"Then you must write your father," he said. "Tell him to fill out an 'Act of Recall' form. You're a minor so your father can recall you."

"But I don't want to go back to the States," I said. "I just want to finish my schooling."

"You were born here," said the Consulere. "You don't have an American passport. Your father made you and your family American citizens just before you left, but you have no proof. That means your father must fill out an 'Act of Recall' before Mussolini drafts you into the Italian Army."

I knew he was right. If I was called into the Italian Army it would be years before I could return to the United States.

I wrote to my father immediately. My father spoke to a lawyer, Frank Preti. They took care of the paperwork, and soon I got a note from the Consulere to come in with a picture of myself. I would need it for my passport. I did that the next day. Once I had an American passport the Consulere told me, "Go to the Office of the Italian Navigation in Naples and set a passage date right away." I did what he said. When school closed for vacation, I would be going back to America.

School vacation started at the end of July. That was when I went to board the *Saturnia*. As I walked up the plank I saw two *calledere*, or police officers, checking passports. They could not understand how I'd entered Italy with an Italian passport, but was leaving with an American passport. I explained as best I could, and they let me board. Still I was nervous. Would they keep me in Italy? Would I ever see my family again? Finally we sailed.

Back in America

Because we were all either 18 or under my father's citizenship applied to us. On my father's Certificate of Naturalization it says he was 42, 5'6", white with a dark complexion, brown eyes and black hair. It lists Guiseppina, as 18 years of age, Angiolina as 16 years of age, Armando as 14 years of age and Angelo as 4 years of age. I never did get my own citizenship papers and my mother never became a citizen.

Now I was 16 years old. Having finished three years' worth of courses in two years, I still hoped to go back to the Conservatory in Naples, but Mussolini started a war in Abyssinia, and that was it. I went to Portland High School where I excelled in music and languages. I played flute and piccolo in the Portland High School Band where I had many featured solos. As a musician I participated in all Portland High School graduating exercises, including my own.

In 1931 my father closed his restaurant on Middle Street and bought the Clover Club nightclub in the State Theater Building on the corner of High and Congress Streets. The entrance on Congress Street had a huge marquee with our new name, "New Napoli Club." My father bought the Clover Club furnished. He had the whole floor upstairs. The State Drug Store was underneath. I was in my first year of high school and I would cashier at the restaurant and study my Latin at the same time.

The club had a huge dance floor down the middle with private curtained booths around the edges. It seated a couple of hundred diners. The dress was black tie, even the waiters. There was dancing and partying every night. Performers would come from Boston with their dance bands. On weekends my father hired an off-duty policeman to keep the crowds in line. We were the only club north of Boston. I remember one bandleader, a saxophone player named Napolitano.

Prohibition was a severe headache for my father. The club didn't sell alcohol, but the customers would sneak in their own flasks. Bootlegging was everywhere. The Sheriff watched the Napoli Club, thinking that we must be selling liquor. My father went to the Sheriff's Department, and said he was running a clean business. They told him that they knew customers were buying liquor at the club. My father could not figure this out. They weren't buying it from him.

Finally, he learned his waiters had an arrangement with the druggist at the State Drug Store beneath us. Like most drug stores, it had straight alcohol for prescriptions. The waiters would go down the back stairs and buy the alcohol, then bring it up into the club to sell to the customers, making big tips in return. When my father found out he fired all the waiters and hired waitresses. He sold the club after three years. It was too much work trying to keep things on the up and up.

After closing the club, my father worked as a chef for the Elks Club. One day, when I was there with him, two government agents came in and showed him their identification cards.

"Are you involved in a Fascisti Club?" one asked

"What is the purpose of this club?" asked the other.

My father explained that it was a social club that met once a month. "We are not involved with helping Italy," he said. "It's just a club where Italians meet and talk."

The club was named the Aldo Sette Club in honor of a young man who'd been killed during the Fascisti uprising. My father was President and members wore black shirts and black fezzes. I suppose this looked pretty mobster-like. The Aldo Sette Club lasted four or five years. The government men seemed to think it was something bad.

A Trip back to Bovino

On July 9, 1931, when I was 18, and my brother Angelo was 8, he, my mother, and I went back to Bovino. When we arrived at customs in Naples, I was pulled aside for an inspection of my steamer trunk. In my trunk the officer noticed a black shirt, and a black fez-like hat. This made him think I was someone of importance. He apologized, "Scuzi, scuzi," and moved me, my mother and brother along. My

Uncle Antonio had come to meet us, and he saw this encounter from a distance. When we got to him he wanted to know what was going on with the black shirt and hat. I explained to him that it was not anything official, just the attire for my father's social club. We all laughed.

We stayed in Bovino with Uncle Antonio and his two daughters and son for a few weeks, then we went to Naples to visit my mother's sisters and brother. My mother's sister, Angelina went with us on vacation to Capri, Algiers, Lisbon, Portugal and Africa. This was the last time my mother saw her family. After vacationing in Italy for more than two months we returned to America on September 11, 1931. My father never did get back to Italy.

High School Graduation and College

During summer breaks from high school I would work in the restaurant where I learned to cook all of my father's great recipes. I also continued to compose music. Music consumed me day and night and I never stopped thinking of melodies. In October 1932 I copyrighted one particular composition. The copyright states: "Title of Music, Araby, words and music by Armando Polito."

I graduated from Portland High School in June, 1934. My father had opened another Napoli Restaurant at the corner of Congress and State Street. At the same time the stock market had fallen even more. If I were to go to college my father would have to withdraw money that he had in the Bank of Italy. He'd sent money to his account there because he'd always intended to go back. Now things had changed, and he needed the money here in America. He had Josephine write a letter to Mussolini explaining that he was President of the social club, Aldo Sette, and he needed to take some of his money from the Bank of Italy to send his son, Armando, to college. Not long after, Mussolini granted permission to the Bank of Italy to honor this withdrawal.

That summer, while waiting for acceptance to the University of

Maine, I worked at my father's new restaurant. On August 4, 1934 I received a letter from Dean J. N. Hart stating:

"You will find enclosed a card admitting you to the College of Arts and Sciences as a special student. We are taking you as a special student to enable you to demonstrate your ability to carry college work. You will be allowed to register for the same studies as you would have if you had entered as a regular student. If at the end of the fall semester, your record is excellent, we will then transfer you from the list of special students to the regular list.

"A special student is not eligible to represent the University in any Intercollegiate competition."

Finally, I was accepted. Despite the fact that my grades were rather poor the University would let me attend, but I had to prove myself. English, math, biology and the sciences were very difficult for me to learn. In my mind, when I read English, I would translate it to Italian and back to English.

In late August I left for the University of Maine and settled into college life. My goal was to become a dentist but after two years of poor grades, I knew that the sciences were not my strongest suit. When I switched to romance languages everything fell into place. Finally here was something I was good at besides music.

On October 27, 1934, I received a letter admitting me into the Spanish club. I paid the 50-cent initiation requested from new members. By November 26, 1934 I was running around with the best of them in the Pajama Parade. The freshmen would strip the sophomores of their pajamas and strew these around the grounds outside of the dorms. I also was involved in the traditional freshman "panty raid" where we would steal all the girls' panties we could find. Besides studying, I was certainly enjoying myself. I joined the Theta Chi fraternity which used pledge week to give every newcomer stupid stuff to do.

I still have the pledge card. It reads: "Proceed to the Great Works Cemetery, get the description and the inscription of the grave stone that begins with 'I'm a little Angel'....Go to the St. Michael's Court and get names of all inmates..."

My partner in crime was Festus Watson. That poor bastard, Festus, had to measure Main Street with a 6" ruler. We also had to collect all the ashtrays in all the living rooms of all the dorms.

In January, during the Winter Festival, the University had an ice sculpture contest, always with a different theme. We spent days tinting snow different colors, building the sculptures, and pouring water on them so that they would freeze into a state of pure transparency.

I also joined the Delta Pi Kappa Honorary Music Society. Every year the University held a Music Night at the Little Theatre. My first performance was a solo on flute on March 8, 1935. I played the Concert Waltz for a flute on Airs from "Traviata" by Verdi. The Conductor of the Orchestra was Professor Adelbert W. Sprague and the Conductor of the Band was Roy H. Monroe.

Meanwhile, my sister Josephine, who was working at the restaurant, was dating Joseph Urbano. Joseph attended St. Peter's Church where we all went to mass each week. One Sunday he followed Josephine home to see where she lived. Upon arriving at our house, Joseph realized that he knew our father. He and Josephine were married on Mother's Day, 1935.

I had several important moments in the next school year. Among them was when I was playing in the 73-piece ROTC Band (Reserve Officer Training Corps: a training program to prepare college students to be commissioned officers), and we performed at the Bates-Colby football game in Waterville, where we won the State Championship. Another was March 13, 1936, at the Annual Music Night when I had a flute solo, performing Fantasie from "La Sonnambula" by Bellini. Again conducting the orchestra was Professor Adelbert Sprague. The Conductor of the Band was Charles Jacques.

R.O. T. C. 1937 – University of Maine, Orono

Meeting Isabel

In my last summer before senior year my sister, Angela, was dating Donato "Dinny" Profenno. She'd met him at the restaurant. One day he came in with his father, Camillo Profenno, a well-known contractor in the Portland area.

Camillo and his wife, Sabia DiMatteo Profenno, had come from Lettomanoppello, Italy. They had seven children. In 1929, not long after Angela met the Profennos, Camillo died. He'd only been in his early 50s. Donato, his eldest son, took over the family business. The Profenno clan consisted of Donato, Filomena, Domenic, Samuel, Isabel, Rose and Angela. When my father met Donato's sister, Isabel, he was taken by her, and kept telling her, "I have the perfect man for you."

The Profenno Family 1928: Left to right: Donato,
(Father) Camillo, (Mother) Sabia, Filomena and Domenic.
Front row: Samuel, Angelina, Isabel and Rose.

In that last summer before senior year Isabel and I started dating. She worked as a cosmetologist in the Roselle Beauty Shop on the second floor of the old Strand Building on Congress Street. We would meet at my father's restaurant after she got out of work. Sometimes we would go to the movies uptown, then I would walk her home all the way across town to Deering Center where she lived.

While I'd been in college my family had moved to Brighton Avenue so our new house was about a mile from Isabel's home. Isabel and I had fun and good times with both of our families. She got along with my siblings and I got along with hers.

She was a very attractive woman. She had reddish brown hair, not long, not short. She was a slender willowy statue with a hilarious personality. She was always telling jokes, and was the life of the party. My family just loved her.

All that summer I worked, composed music, and dated Isabel. In August I went back to finish my last year at the University of Maine. As I continued my studies, I wrote to Isabel, and sent resumes to schools in an attempt to get an internship in a two-year program.

On January 3, 1938, a son was born to Joseph and Josephine Urbano. They named him Anthony or "Tony." Early that same year, my father sold the Napoli Restaurant to a Chinese family who transformed it into the Pagoda Restaurant. My father took a chef's position at the Cascade Inn in Old Orchard. He worked there for many years after, and also catered jobs at the Elk's Club.

On the Annual Music Night on March 24, 1938 I was Conductor of the Band, which was also the job of first lieutenant to the Conductor of the Orchestra. I was proud. It was as close as I would ever come to my dream of conducting an orchestra. In May, 1938 I graduated with a B.A. degree in Romance Languages. I got a position at Howland High School as a student teacher, teaching Romance Languages. I lived with Frank and Frances McCluskey, a couple that rented out rooms in Howland.

On long weekends and vacations I went home to see my family and Isabel. I spent two years training as a student teacher, then another two years as teacher. Throughout this Isabel and I continued our long-distance relationship. Summer was the only long time we had together.

While at Howland I conducted the 40-member Howland Choral Club. In May, 1940, as Music Supervisor of the public schools, I conducted their Spring Event in the Town Hall. That June I was home for the summer for my sister Angie and Donato's wedding. There was great celebration among the Politos and Profennos. On August 7th of the following year, 1941, we all celebrated the arrival of my nephew, Camillo "Cammie." Our family was growing and that made us all happy.

In May, 1942 I became the instructor of the Art Club at Howland. That made me responsible for the Art Exhibit at the Legion Hall where eight or nine students displayed their art. When that school year ended I left Howland, moving back to Portland, where I applied for a job teaching Spanish at Deering High School.

In June, 1942, my brother, Angelo graduated from Portland High School. After graduating all the boys either had to enlist or wait to be drafted for service in World War II. Angelo joined the Army.

Starting a life together

A month before Isabel and I were planning to get married, Isabel went to City Hall for a marriage certificate. She left in tears because the clerk could not find her name on file. The clerk had birth certificates for Donato, Domenic, Filomena, Samuel, Rose, Angela and a girl named Sabia, but none for Isabel. Isabel kept telling him she had no sister named Sabia. At home she tearfully told her mother, who then started laughing. "Sabia," she said, "is you."

June 20, 1942, Armando Polito & Isabel D. Profenno Polito

Isabel's real name was Sabia Dorothy Profenno. She'd been named after her mother. When Isabel was little, whenever her father would say the name "Sabia" it was his daughter who came running. To end the confusion her father started calling her Isabel. From then on that had been the name she went by, and soon she could recall no other. The subject of her legal name had never come up. Now that she knew, she legally changed her name to Isabel.

On June 20th 1942 Isabel and I got married at St. Joseph's Church. Immediately following the ceremony we had a wedding breakfast and reception at the Elk's Club. After the reception we took a train to New York City for our honeymoon.

Back in Portland we rented a small apartment on the corner of Stevens Avenue and Woodford Street almost across the street from Deering High School. Few people owned cars then, and Isabel took a bus to and from Roselle's Beauty Shop. She now managed the place. In August, Deering High School hired me to teach Spanish. We felt blessed with the convenience of the proximity our apartment.

That October the Deering High School Paper ran an article welcoming eight new faculty members. It cited me as the Spanish Teacher and Music Director. Everything went well except money. My teaching salary was tiny. Even though Isabel and I were both working full time we could barely make ends meet.

I decided to speak to the Principal. I explained that I couldn't get along on $3000 per year, so I would have to look for another job paying more money. He said he would see what he could do. A couple of weeks later he told me I would get more money.

St. Joseph's Parish sponsored Minstrel shows. Many of Portland's finest local talent performed, along with just about anyone who loved to act or sing. I directed months of rehearsals. The shows had titles such as "Pan-American Minstrels," and " Merrytime Minstrels." Isabel would often perform slapstick or anything that would bring a laugh. She was always ready.

On October 16, 1943 we welcomed another son to Angie and Dinny, this one named Donato "Donnie" Profenno."

On March 27, 1945, my son, John Armand Polito was born. At that point we outgrew our apartment and moved to a duplex home owned by Isabel's mother at the corner of Stevens Avenue and Arbor Street. We were still only a half-mile from the high school. This house was perfect. I could walk to work, and Isabel had room to start a beauty shop in the house. Besides that, we had two extra bedrooms.

Armando, Isabel and John, 1945

Around this time my sister, Antonietta, sick with TB, was sent up to a hospital in Augusta. With her husband, Joseph, she'd had four children, Johnny, Teresa, Domenic and Maria. Johnny Faietta, Antonietta's son, was in the military at the time, but was called home so he could see his mother. I remember my brother-in-law, Josephine's husband, Joseph Urbano, drove Johnny up to see his mother for the last time. She died shortly after he returned to duty.

Armando's favorite picture of Isabel – 1944

Old Orchard Beach, Maine

In the summer of 1947 my father opened the Napoli Restaurant at 44 East Grand Avenue in Old Orchard Beach. The Napoli would be open only for the summer, to serve the tourists. It was small, with about a dozen tables. It had a well-equipped kitchen. My father rented the whole building including the upstairs as living quarters. My father and mother lived there all summer."

Old Orchard Beach, Maine
Napoli Restaurant, 1947

He also rented a space over a garage down the street where his waitresses could live for the summer. Most of them were college students working at the beach for the summer. I remember the McCann sisters, Mary Margaret and Dottie worked a few summers, as did Mary George and Elizabeth Cobb who went on to become nuns.

At the end of the summer came the annual ritual of closing the restaurant down. Every chrome table and chair had to be coated with Cosmoline, a rust preventive similar to petroleum jelly. It always took all day to wipe the grease off the tables and chairs the next spring. It was a terrible job, but it stopped the rust.

In the cellar at home my father began experimenting with his own recipes for what would become Luigi's Pizza Sauce and Luigi's Spaghetti Sauce. He packed it in a five-gallon home canner and sold it at the restaurant at Old Orchard Beach. I designed the label on the cans. He placed a few cans in local stores such as Shaw's, Columbia Markets, 20th Century, First National and the A&P.

1947 - Armando, Isabel, John , 4 1/2 years and Nancy, 3 months.

People enjoyed the sauce so much they would buy it to take back home. My father was canning and selling the first ever canned sauce in the country. He registered to patent the name: Luigi's Pizza and Spaghetti Sauce.

Soon stores began reordering, some doubling and tripling their orders. This was no easy task for a home canner. My father had to add more and bigger home canners, and he enlisted more family to help out.

On October 25, 1947, my daughter, Nancy Jo Polito, was born. Finally, a girl in the family! Isabel and I were delighted to have one of each, a daughter and son. I continued to teach and Isabel continued operating her home beauty salon. Our house was always full of women getting their hair done. The smell of permanents filled the air, sometimes before the children and I were out of bed. Isabel loved her profession and she worked hard to please her patrons.

*The labels used on the Spaghetti and Pizza Sauce by Luigi's.
Armando designed and drew the labels himself.*

Luigi's Spaghetti and Pizza Sauce

My brother, Angelo, married Helen Mary McFarland in 1950. In July of that year my father boldly invested thousands of dollars. He found a spacious building in the East Yard of the former South Portland Shipbuilding Corporation at 148 Pickett Street. He put up a big sign on the side saying: "Luigi's." He put money into the newest canning, cooking and sterilizing equipment. My brother, Angelo, worked beside him, helping with the sauces. I did the bookkeeping.

We had troubles at first. With the outbreak of the Korean War there were shortages of tomatoes and tin. As the shortages ended, my father began travelling up and down the east coast, demonstrating Luigi's products. He was especially successful at Gimbel's in New York. Pizza sauce poured over English muffins aroused plenty of favorable comment in the big city. Orders grew, reaching a new peak when Jordan Marsh of Boston became a regular customer.

Gimbel's Department Store, New York City, 1950.
Giovanni Polito selling English muffin pizza's with his beloved sauce.

In October 1953 my father became ill and died. In the summer of 1954 we all ran the Napoli Restaurant, but it was not the same without my father. He was the one that brought life to the place. Finally we realized that we all had our own lives with young children to consider. We decided to sell. It was a difficult decision.

Angelo took over producing Luigi's Sauces and I continued the bookkeeping until we had to relocate to another place on Preble Street. In the 1980s Angelo made a contract with a canning company named Snow's in Scarborough to produce the sauces. He continued to monitor production for a few years, but in 1983 he grew ill and died. After that his wife, Helen Mary continued to watch over the production of the Luigi's Sauces. By this time there were many sauces on the market. They were sold in large jars at low profit. We knew we could not keep up quality while producing large quantities at a competitive cost, so eventually we were forced to stop production.

This was the end of my father's particular American dream. His broader dream had been realized. He'd wanted to make a good life for his family and he knew that dream would come true here in the United States. He was gracious, proud, and had a big heart. As sad as it was to see the end of his business legacy, I knew his spirit lived on, bigger than life itself. He was a remarkable man.

As my father has noted, as one chapter closed, another had already started on October 25, 1947, when I, Nancy Jo Polito was born to Armando Arnaldo Polito and Isabel DiMatteo Profenno Polito.

A Father's Daughter
By Nancy Jo Polito

Somewhere along the way my father's name Armando was shortened to just Armand. I think this happened when he started teaching at Deering High School. I do know that as far back as I can remember he went by Armand, not Armando.

I knew Armand Polito as a daughter knows a father. The father I knew had a bright smile of beautiful straight white teeth. He had black wavy hair, a dark olive complexion, stood approximately 5'8", and had deep dark brown eyes. Put it all together, and he was extremely handsome. He was also the most amazing, brilliant, talented, likable and interesting person I knew.

Yeah, that was my Dad.

He looked like Desi Arnaz, so much so that my brother, John, would sometimes call him "Babalu." It helped that my mom, with her tall willowy frame and reddish brown hair, looked a little like Lucille Ball. She was always telling jokes, pulling pranks, and her choice of clothes was sometimes dramatic.

Laughter seemed like a member of the family, bursting out at any moment. We never knew when Dad would start yelling: "Mannaggia il diavalo." That's Italian for "Damn the devil." Whenever we heard him shout that phrase we came running. When we got there Dad would be flailing his arms, yelling in Italian, and generally showing his exasperation with whatever spark had started it all. Often as not, the woman he loved was at the heart of the matter, which meant that whatever had happened could probably be cured with laughter.

Though this might sound bizarre, it wasn't. These eruptions weren't hopelessly out of control. They were the healthy reactions of a man who knew that humor is the most natural thing in the world. Dad was compassionate, but he was no pushover. Throughout our lives he always expected great things from us. He and Mom raised us to respect and honor elders and to always think about how our actions would affect others. When we were less than perfect, Dad would tell us what he thought with a sincere animation that forced us to take him seriously—this despite the fact that it was hard to keep a straight face when he was in the midst of a rant. At such moments his brow would furrow, his arms and hands would wave, and Italian swear words would shoot from his mouth rapid-fire. He was the kind of man who couldn't stop moving, pacing, and expressing himself.

It happened so often that even Mom would walk away rather than try to withstand the emotional torrents emitting from this human dynamo. As for me, I couldn't help it. Whenever I heard him I always had to run to see what was going on. If I could calm the waters, I did, but more often his explosions were justified, so what could I do? I would talk, listen and then offer sympathy. After awhile he simmered down and felt better.

The Polito/Lacivita Family

My Grandfather Giovanni "Papa" and Grandmother Gioconda "Grammy" Lacivita Polito

Dad's older sister, Aunt Josephine (Guiseppina) Polito and Uncle Joseph Urbano, and their son, Tony (Anthony)

Dad's other older sister, Aunt Angie (Angiolina) Polito and Uncle Dinny (Donato) Profenno, and their two sons Cammie (Camillo) and Donnie (Donato)

My parents, Armand Polito and Isabel Profenno Polito and their son, Johnnie (John), daughter, Nancy Jo (me), and son, Armand Jr.

Dad's younger brother, Uncle Angelo Polito and Aunt Helen Mary McFarland Polito, and their daughters Joan, Cynthia, Susan, Mary Frances, Judith, and son, Tony (Anthony)

Dad's older step-sister, Antonietta Lacivita Negri Polito and her husband, Joseph Faietta, and their children, John, Theresa, Domenic, Julia and Marie

The Profenno/DiMatteo Family

My Grandmother, Sabia "Grammy" DiMatteo Profenno (My Grandfather Camillo Profenno died in 1929)

Mom's eldest brother, Uncle Dinny (Donato) and Aunt Angie (Angiolina) Polito Profenno, and their two sons Cammie and Donnie

Mom's older sister, Aunt Filomena Profenno Donatello and Uncle Tony (Anthony) Donatello, and their two daughters Barbara Jean and Patty (Patricia)

Mom's older brother Uncle Dom (Domenic) Profenno, never married

Older brother, Uncle Sam (Samuel) Profenno and Aunt Glenys Wing Profenno, and their two sons Sammy (Samuel) and Tommy (Thomas)

Though we are listed above in my father's family, we also belong here: My parents, Isabel Profenno Polito and Armando Polito, and their sons Johnnie, Armand Jr. and daughter, Nancy Jo

Mom's younger sister, Aunt Rose Profenno True and Uncle Maurice True, and their sons Mike (Michael), Jimmy (James), and two daughters, Jani (Janice) and Betsy (Elizabeth)

Mom's baby sister Aunt Angie (Angelina) Profenno and Uncle George Hutchins and sons Georgie (George) and Kevin

My Grandmother's brother, Uncle Rosario DiMatteo and Aunt Josephine Proietta DiMatteo, and their children, Bart, George, John, Angela and Mary

Polito Family Tree

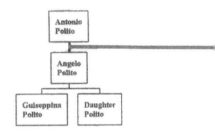

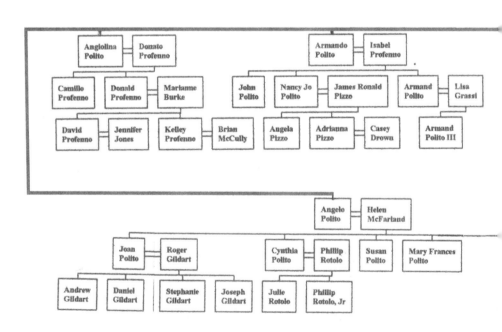

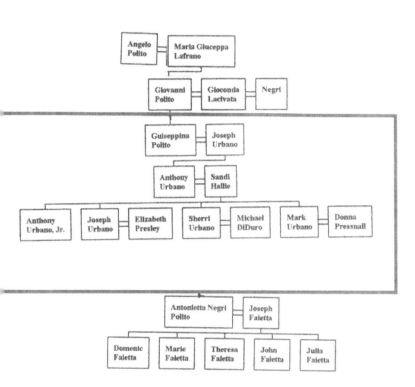

Angelo Polito — Maria Giuceppa Lafrano

Giovanni Polito — Gioconda Lacivata — Negri

Guiseppina Polito — Joseph Urbano

Anthony Urbano — Sandi Hallie

Anthony Urbano, Jr. — Joseph Urbano — Elizabeth Presley — Sherri Urbano — Michael DiDuro — Mark Urbano — Donna Pressnall

Antonietta Negri Polito — Joseph Faietta

Domenic Faietta — Marie Faietta — Theresa Faietta — John Faietta — Julia Faietta

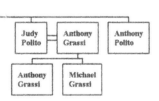

Judy Polito — Anthony Grassi — Anthony Polito

Anthony Grassi — Michael Grassi

Profenno Family Tree

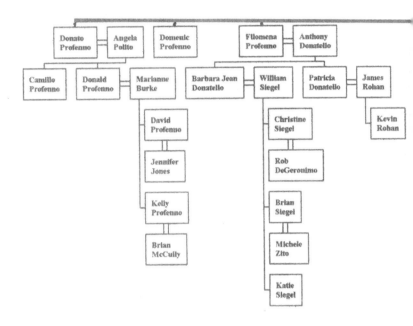

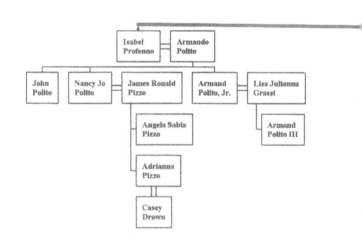

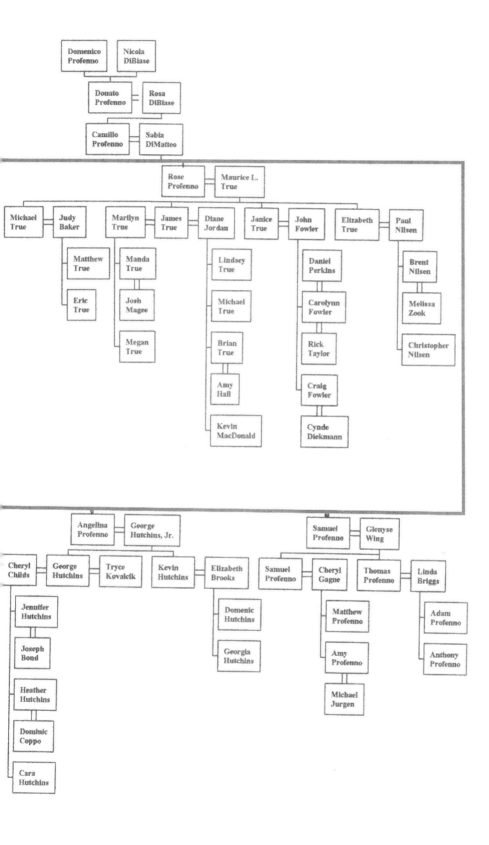

DiMatteo Family Tree

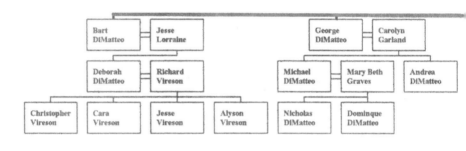

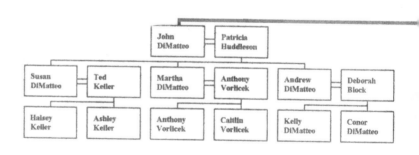

Lettomanoppello

Filomena, Sabia (1881-1959) and Rosario DiMatteo (1888 – 1975) were born in Lettomanoppello, Italy (known in the local dialect as "Lu Lette") to Bartolomeo and Angela Celsi DiMatteo. Lettomanoppello is not far from the Adriatic coast, approximately 21 miles west of the city of Pescara. The first records of Lettomanoppello date back to the 11th century. The town was renowned in Roman times for its asphalt mines.

Their mother Angela Celsi DiMatteo died when Sabia was seven years old and Rosario was only nine months, leaving their father, Bartolmeo to take care of these children. When Sabia was fourteen and Rosario was seven their father died and their grandparents took them both in. Filomena was already married and living elsewhere. The grandparents could not afford the tuition and books which Sabia and Rosario would've needed to continue at school, so their education ended.

Rosario was twelve when his last grandparent passed away. The village people offered him an apprenticeship as a shoemaker or a tailor. He chose to become a shoemaker, working twelve hours a day. At 19, Sabia was working and living in an orphanage. By that time she was dating Camillo Profenna, son of Donato and Rosa DiBiase Profenna from Lettomanoppello. Rosario worked hard at his apprenticeship. In the evenings he and his friends would walk to a nearby town to serenade girls their age. On one of these walks, he met the two Proietti sisters. He got to know them well.

Move to America

Camillo Profenna and Sabia DiMatteo married and moved to America in 1906. Camillo Profenna had worked as a mason in Italy so when he arrived in Portland, Maine he went to speak to the head caretaker of Fort Williams.

"I am a mason," Camillo said. "I can fix walls and any stonework. If you do not like the work, you don't have to pay me. Just give me a chance." That became his first job in the States.

Back in Lettomanoppello, Rosario was now 18. That meant he had to spend a year in the Italian Army. Once he'd done that his sister, Sabia, hoped to have him join her in America. Rosario's year was almost up when Italy went to war with Ethiopia. This more than doubled the length of his service. Finally Rosario returned to Lettomanoppello to work as a shoemaker. He wanted to earn enough money to go to America, but Italy went to war with North Africa and he was called back to the military for two more years.

While Rosario was serving his country, Camillo and Sabia had three children: Donato, Dominic and Filomena. About this time Camillo got sick. His doctors said that if he didn't have his kidney removed he would die. Not trusting American doctors, Camillo went back to Italy. Sabia and the three children went with him. He was so sick they had to carry him onboard on a stretcher. The Italian doctors confirmed what the American doctors had said: the kidney had to go. Even after it was out his doctors told Camillo that he wouldn't live much longer.

Rosario arrived in America in 1913. He came to help in the store Camillo had built at Nason's Corner in Portland. The building's first floor served as a grocery store with the family's living area on the second. They rented the third floor.

Camillo Profenno was quite the entrepreneur. He formed Camillo's Construction Company, which built houses and commercial buildings in Portland. (The last name was changed from Profenna to Profenno at Ellis Island. This happened with many family names, and most Italians did not correct the spelling, thinking that this was the American way to spell their name.)

Rosario started a shoemaker's shop in Portland's Munjoy Hill section. As a shoemaker he earned enough money to go back to Italy. He intended to marry one of the Proietti girls. He arrived there thinking he would marry the younger one, but their parents said that their older daughter must marry first. Though Rosario had felt more attracted to the younger Proietti, he wound up marrying the older one, Josephine Proietti from Pescara.

Back in the U.S. Rosario and Josephine lived on Munjoy Hill. For the next ten years Rosario ran his shop there. At the end of that time he moved his shop to Pleasant Avenue in Deering Center in Woodford's Corner. Sabia and Camillo lived nearby on Stevens Avenue.

Knowing that his time on this earth was limited, Camillo kept buying land, building houses, and starting businesses all over the Portland area. He became a respected businessman. New immigrants sought him out for jobs, loans or any other help they needed. He was a very generous man. With the addition of Samuel, Isabel, Rose and Angela, Camillo's family had grown, increasing his personal responsibilities. He made sure his wife and children would be well taken care of when he was no longer there.

He showered his children with gifts and surprises, even buying the first automobile in the area. After he passed away their mother continued to give her family everything they could ever want.

Everything was in Sabia's name, but when Donato "Dinny" graduated from college, he, along with Samuel and Domenic, took over Profenno Construction Company. Rose and Filomena worked in the office doing payroll and paperwork. Sabia signed the checks.

Evenings at the Profenno's were taken up with family and friends. Sabia started where her husband had left off. She performed charitable works, buying food for those less fortunate, donating used clothing, and often giving money directly to those who were in need. She earned a place as one of Portland's most respected citizens.

Rosario and Josephine had seven children, Bartolomeo (named after his father) died at childbirth; Angela (named after his mother) lived to be nine months old and died of pneumonia. Again they named the third child Bartolomeo and their fourth child Angela, followed by George, Mary and John.

Rosario finished his working life at Fort Williams where he made shoes for disabled Veterans. In 1958 he retired, and he and Josephine moved to High Street. Josephine died in 1962 and Rosario eventually went to live with his daughter and son-in-law, Angela and Jean Wilson. Rosario died 1974.

As you can see, my mother and her brother married another brother and sister. As a child I never really thought about the fact that when I spent time with the Profenno side of the family, my cousins Cammie and Donnie would be in attendance and then when I spent time with the Polito side Cammie and Donnie were there as well. It was a unique situation.

Two Opposites

My mother and father were opposites. Mom loved people, loved to talk with them, and was never at a loss for words. I remember being embarrassed sometimes when we were shopping downtown. Outgoing, hilarious, and compassionate to a fault, she would talk to anyone about anything. Dad would tell people that she had sympathy for everyone but him. Always ready to make a fashion statement, she chose bold colors and constantly changed her hairstyle. When shopping, she always loved a bargain.

Mom wasn't always well. She worried about everything and everyone to the point of falling ill. This concern certainly played a part in her endless list of surgeries. These included three ulcer operations, a hysterectomy, a vagautomy, operation on her gallbladder and an intestinal re-routing. Later in life she suffered from severe depression, had a hip replacement, and fell victim to a stroke.

Mom missed out on a lot because of illness, but she always kept her sense of humor. Along with Dad, she was the center of a loving family, full of fun, and as normal as any other intelligent, funny woman. On an evening when she and Dad were going out she would come down the stairs, all "dolled up" as he would say, and his face would break out in a smile that lit the room. With the contrast of his dark complexion and with her fair skin, they always made a striking couple.

Dad was more private. He seldom stopped to talk beyond a quick "hello"or "Che se dice? [What do you say?]" He minded his own business and preferred that others mind theirs. He was critical of "half-assed" work, and adamant about doing things the right way. Most people thought him rather quiet and reserved, and this was usually the case.

The great exception came when he was home. Around us Dad was completely different. Though he was strict, he also had a mischievous side, which came out in his quick wit and love of a good joke. Jokes were always part of our birthday celebrations. Dad would spend hours down in his private cellar office coming up with a grandiose presentation for the birthday gift. His best ones were always for my mother.

Napoli Restaurant

My first memories of the Napoli Restaurant in Old Orchard Beach date back to when I was no more than five. I recall my grandfather, "Papa" Giovanni Polito, as a short man, but robust. He smiled constantly, and despite my youth, he seemed to think I was ready for the kitchen. He often called: "Nunziatta, andiamo." [Nancy, lets go.] I would hurry back to the kitchen where he would show me how he prepared the orders. I would get an orange soda from the machine under the stairs that led up to the apartment and bedrooms, then I would go in, sit on a stool, and watch him making pasta dishes.

There wasn't much for Jovnnie (what I called my brother, John, when I was young) and my cousins Cammie and Donnie to do at the restaurant. Mostly they played on the gravel driveway alongside the building, or talked to Cousin Tony, the oldest cousin, who worked there.

Old Orchard Beach was one of the biggest tourist spots in Maine. Every Memorial Day the first wave of Canadian tourists arrived.

The waves kept coming until Labor Day. Businesses on the road to the causeway counted on those Canadians for their livelihood. The Napoli Restaurant was one of those businesses. To a child it seemed that the town never changed. Every summer it was the same hotels, the same businesses, and many of the same people. Old Orchard Beach Amusement Park, the Pier, the Palace Playland, and one of the most beautiful beaches on the east coast were all barely 500 feet away. We weren't allowed anywhere near the Amusement Park by ourselves, but we could often hear its sounds. Dance bands played nightly at the ballroom at the end of the Pier, and the rides were open day and night. In the summer months Old Orchard Beach was filled to capacity. There was seldom a motel within three miles that had a vacancy.

After a few summers my cousin, Donnie, was allowed to work through the summer at the Napoli, along with his mother, my Aunt Angie. Donnie would bus tables, wash dishes and help my Grandmother strip the beds and clean the apartment upstairs.

One day as my Grandfather was tending to a big pot of pasta he yelled for me to get his rifle from behind the kitchen door. As soon as I offered it, he grabbed it from my hands, pushed the screen door open, raised the rifle, and shot a pigeon perched on the railroad tracks. He crossed the tracks, grabbed the pigeon by the feet, and ran back into the kitchen. There he lifted a lid from one of the pots of boiling water that was always ready for an order of pasta, and dropped the bird in. I watched, stunned and excited. He went back to his other cooking, but after a few minutes he pulled the pigeon out and plunged it into pot of cold water. After leaving it in the cold water for a few minutes, he pulled it out and tossed it onto the prep table where he proceeded to pluck it. All through this my Grandfather kept telling me how good it would taste cooked cacciatore style, with a little fresh tomato and garlic.

Watching my Grandfather, Aunt Angie, Aunt Josephine and my father cook at the restaurant was the beginning of my love affair with cooking, especially Italian cooking. That love has lasted to this day.

On the day after Labor Day I always felt sad watching the businesses board up their windows. Suddenly the motel parking lots were empty. The amusement park sat in silence and the beach lay, completely void of sunbathers. With its wax-smeared windows, upturned chairs on the tables, and "CLOSED" sign, even the Napoli looked stark. We'd stripped the beds, emptied the bathrooms, and now we too would return home. Another summer at the Napoli was over.

Sunday Nights

My Polito grandparents lived with my Aunt Josephine, Uncle Joe and their son, Tony. Whenever there was a holiday or celebration my Grandfather, "Papa," took great pleasure in presenting his family with the best menu one could imagine. He even put a second stove and refrigerator in the cellar so that he could cook all the dishes necessary for a complete holiday feast. When we would arrive we would stop for a moment, and read the menu he'd posted on the outside front door—a preview of the wonderful feast he was about to serve us. One Christmas he grouped us by family, sat us down at the table, and presented each family its own roasted, stuffed chicken, with vegetables to go with it. Each father was in charge of carving and serving his family. Seeing the excitement of my father and uncles was a culinary learning experience. Soon roars of laughter erupted as some had a difficult time with the carving.

My cousins and I were thrilled by the anticipation of holiday meals. We toasted the blessings of our good fortune, as everyone, including children, drank a glass of my Grandfather's homemade deep burgundy wine from the glass gallon jug in the middle of the table.

My Grandmother Gioconda, "Grammy," left the cooking to my Grandfather. Her one duty was to be in charge of the antipasto. It was the only part of the meal that I ever saw her actually make. It was always an artistic masterpiece, with rows of celery, olives, cheeses, salami, roasted red peppers, mozzarella, and any other Italian condiment that she felt like serving. She labored to bring symmetry to these ingredients, finally presenting it before the main meal started. With a good piece of hard crusty bread it was really all one needed. I thought it was the best part of the meal.

We really didn't need to wait for a holiday. It was a Sunday night tradition to gather at my Grandparents' house for Italian food and talk. As the family grew, and the table couldn't fit everyone, we, the young cousins, would eat from TV trays in the living room. Shortly after we'd dined on the world's best food, the priest from St. Peter's, Father Romani, would arrive with his housekeeper, Maria Speara. St. Peter's was the only Catholic Church that had a mass in Italian. Every Sunday the Italians gathered there at noon for a high mass that lasted it seemed as a child for hours.

Maria Speara lived near the church. She worked in the rectory and often chauffeured Father Romani around town. My aunts and my mom always remarked on her impeccable taste in clothes. With her mink stole and beehive hairdo Maria was always well dressed. Father and Maria were inseparable. This raised some whispers among my aunts and uncles—could there be something else.....hmm?

To me when Father Romani entered a room it was like a visit from God. When he and Maria came into the hallway word would pass: "Father Romani and Maria are here." At that moment we kids had to be on our best behavior or risk the evil eye stare of the adults. Someone would take their coats, then the two of them would enter the living room. Each of us had to stand up and greet them. Father Romani would then bless us, one-by-one, in his accented English, handing out prayer cards each with a picture of a Saint. Once this was done, he disappeared into the dining room with our parents and grandparents.

Once Father Romani left we would pull our prayer card collections from our pockets, add the new one, then play the card game

"Go Fish" with them. It was the best way to keep track of our doubles and triples of Saint Christopher, Our Lady of Assumption, John The Baptist, Immaculate Mary, Michael The Archangel, Francis of Assisi, Vincent de Paul and all the others. That kept us out of trouble while the grownups talked in the other room.

Aunt Josephine gave us ginger ale in the tiniest drinking glasses, to wash down our Cheetos. This was our standard treat. Between that and the card game we were set for the evening. After awhile someone would call out, "Father and Maria are leaving. Come say goodbye." As soon as the priest entered the room, we had to leap up, say our goodbyes, then remain on our feet until he was gone. We had to show our respect for him, though I never knew why.

Camp Sabia

In 1952 my Grandmother, Sabia DiMatteo Profenno bought a small family camp on Little Sebago Lake in Windham, Maine. My Profenno uncles were in construction, and they added on to the camp, making room for the entire Profenno clan. Each couple had their own bedroom, a double bed with metal bunk beds for us children. Those old bunk beds were probably army surplus.

The kitchen was huge, big enough for seven assigned family tables, as well as three refrigerators, and two stoves. Besides the first floor kitchen and pantry, the living room was big enough to accommodate a huge stone fireplace. A sign over it read, "Camp Sabia." The first floor also had three bedrooms, a sun porch, a card room, bathroom and an attached garage with two more bedrooms. The second floor contained another bathroom and two large bedrooms. The place fit all 29 of us.

At the end of each school year we packed up the car and drove up to Camp Sabia. We spent those summers with my Grandmother, and the rest of our Profenno relatives. Uncle Tony, Aunt Phil "Filomena," and our cousins Barbara and Patty lived on Long Island, but they spent their summers with us in Maine. Sometimes Patty's motion sickness led them to take the train because it was faster. They were the only ones who didn't live in Portland.

We knew other children whose families summered at Little Sebago Lake, and our parents became friendly with theirs. We already knew some of them. Our family doctor, Francis Dooley, had a camp down the end of the road. He and his wife, Frances, would stop by on Saturday nights to play beano with the grownups.

Our family's bedroom was upstairs, across from Uncle Maurice, Aunt Rose and my cousins, Michael, Jimmy, Janice and Betsy. The bedrooms up there had sharply slanted dormers. My father was forever whacking his head on the low rafters. Many a night I awoke to hear him swearing in Italian and English, "Mannaggia il diavolo! [Damn the devil!] Those God damn things!" It always seemed inevitable that he'd whack his noggin and swear out loud.

Those beams, and Uncle Sam and Aunt Glenys's cat, Scattergood, never failed to send my father into a swearing frenzy. The cat would jump on the beds in the night. My father hated that cat so much, he would sit up in bed, wave his arms and swear, "Va fanculo, you little stronzo! [Go f.... yourself you little asshole!] Get the hell outta here you little bastard!" The cat would run away. This seemed to happen every night because there were no doors to the upstairs bedrooms, just curtains strung across for privacy and the cat would wander about all night.

LABELING

At Camp Sabia all of our food had to be labeled especially the milk. When the poor milkman arrived with his weekly delivery, he couldn't help but be confused. In this huge household of many families, who wanted what? How much did they want? And, most important for him, who owed what? Our parents devised a system using colored elastic bands. Each family was assigned a particular color. The band of that color went around the necks of their milk bottles. That way everyone would know whose milk was whose.

As children we were taught that we had to obey rules, and respect each other's property. To avoid mistakes we labeled the shelves in the pantry with family names. Each family cooked its own food. Of course, there were those times when kids from another family were eating something that looked a helluva lot better than the food on your plate and there would be tears. But, despite such culinary envy, we made it work. All in all such difficulties never got in the way of having fun. I don't recall a single fight with my cousins.

Sometimes my Grandmother Sabia's brother, Uncle Rosario DiMatteo would visit the camp for a day. His family and grandchildren came with him, adding twelve cousins to our ranks. It was Uncle Rosario's tradition to show up on the Fourth of July with a huge watermelon. He would then sit all day, puffing on his black Perodi cigar, and spitting. The Perodi is the classic Italian stogie, hard and black, with a strong, earthy aroma. It makes a man look as if he's smoking a black twig. Uncle Rosario would smoke it down to a tiny stub, then crush that up, place it in his pipe and smoke the rest. He was forever spitting out dark brown liquid.

MOTEL?

Sometimes people would get lost and drive down the road to our camp. Inevitably they would ask for directions, and often they would ask, "Is this a motel?" With all the cars and people it certainly looked like one. The back yard was large enough for wiffle ball (which we played against our parents nightly), badminton, volleyball, and bocce. The place was big enough that Uncle Dom let us take turns driving his pick-up truck up the driveway, around the oak tree, and back. Of course the boys got to do that more often than the girls.

There was plenty of room, which might be a reason why so much junk collected from one summer to the next. It seemed as if people brought whatever they'd been planning to discard, thinking some cousin, aunt, or uncle at Camp Sabia certainly could find a use for it. So the collection would grow, almost to the point of creating a fire hazard. Because of this we began each summer by cleaning out the garage and making a dump run. Despite those efforts, summer always ended with a garage that was overflowing again.

Jail Break

Almost every evening at nine o'clock my cousins and I played Jail Break. We would've played it all night, but at some point our parents would notice how late it was getting, and tell us to stop; usually it was almost midnight. It was a game you had to play in the dark. One person was "it," and the goal was for that person to capture and jail as many other people as possible. You captured them by shining a flashlight on them, then you jailed them by putting them in a roughly 8'x8' area recessed between the garage and one of the first floor bedrooms. There the "caught" people waited. Their only hope was that someone who was still free could sneak up, unobserved, and tag them. When you tagged someone in jail you ran off into the shadows and shouted: "Jail Break!"

Running around in the woods in the dark made contact with poison ivy or poison oak almost inevitable. Such contact made for a miserable few weeks of healing, which was certainly no way for a kid to spend his or her summer. We never went looking for it. It was just a part of being at camp.

Sunday Nights

On Sunday nights at eight we all gathered in the living room to watch the Ed Sullivan Show, one of the most popular TV programs of the era. It was a variety show with singers, dancers, comedians, acrobats, and almost anything else that fit on a stage. Watching it prompted us to put on our own talent shows. The act we loved to imitate was that of Señor Wences. Wences was a ventriloquist whose specialties were a puppet face made from his hand, and a box with a head in it. When Señor Wences opened the lid of the box, the head would say: "It's Alrrrright!" with a Spanish accent. Then Wences slammed the lid shut stating: "It's Alrrrright!"

In a different act, an Italian puppet mouse named Topo Gigio would come on stage and sing to Ed. At the end of the song Ed would go over to the puppet's elevated stage where Topo Gigio would say: "Hello Eddddieeee." The two would banter, then the mouse might sing a little song. He would finish by saying, "Eddddieeee, Kissa me goooodnight."

We watched other shows, including the infamous "The Honeymooners." That starred Jackie Gleason as Ralph Kramden, along with fellow Honeymooners, Alice Kramden, Ed Norton and Trixie Norton. These shows provided us with hours of material to make into skits of our own. We would spend all day planning the entertainment we would perform that night.

Cousin Cammie acted as commentator for these weekly shows. We even made up our own versions of commercials, including ones for Maxwell House, Camels, and Wonder Bread. Sometimes Uncle Dinny accompanied us on his violin. We always ended with a round of our family's applause.

AUCTIONS AND TRIPS TO BOOTY'S CORNER

On Saturdays they often held auctions on a nearby farm. We would pile into several cars, feeling as if we were going to a carnival. My cousins and I ate hotdogs, and played hide n' seek among the rows of antiques. I'm sure we irritated buyers and sellers equally. Sometimes the buyers were among our own family. Most of Camp Sabia's kitchenware came from these auctions.

Grandmother Sabia loved auctions. She always sat in the front row, not wanting to miss any item. My mother and aunts would stand in the back row so they could keep a close watch on us.

One Saturday my mother was bidding on something, but a woman in the front row kept raising the bid. In frustration, my mother muttered out loud, "Who the hell is that person that keeps bidding against me?" My brother, Johnnie answered, "It's Grammy!" We all burst out laughing. Mom shook her head. Grammy won the bid. It wasn't until the auction was over that we all went up to the front row. There was Grammy telling one of our aunts: "Someone back there kept bidding against me. I don't know who it was but I was getting very irritated!" We never told her who it was.

Of course we had swimming, fishing, marshmallow toasting, and riding in the back of the milk truck to the beginning of the camp road to pick blueberries. And then later that afternoon we would keep a close watch on all the pies my mother and aunts were making. Sometimes we dressed up like cowboys and Indians. We built forts, or played softball with our parents. Once in awhile someone would get hurt, and we would go see Dr. Dooley.

A trip up to the intersection of Booty's General Store was always fun. It was a huge building with squeaky wooden floors. The store was like a five-and-dime, selling everything from candy to hardware to beach towels. An old farmhouse at the end of the camp road sold fresh eggs. A weekly trip kept us supplied with fresh baked cakes, cupcakes, and cookies.

Sunday and Church

On Sunday morning we piled into cars again, and attended Mass at St. Joseph's College Chapel. It was usually so crowded we had to stand outside. There we stood, waiting for someone to say it was time to go. After Mass we might have breakfast at Cole Farms Restaurant in nearby Gray. People stared at us, intimidated by our sheer numbers. We could fill most places to capacity.

Duke, Time Out Bench, Fishing

Our wide lakefront had the best sandy beach on our little cove. On one side we had a long dock for *Duke*, the rowboat my Uncle Dom built. On the other was a small wooded area where the dogs pooped and where we threw any dead fish we found floating in the water. Uncle Dom built a huge, heavy, long bench for that fishy, smelly, dog pooping area. This was where we had to sit if we misbehaved. We never went near the "Time Out Bench" unless we had to. We kids even tried to move the bench from that dreaded corner of the property, but it was too heavy. There's still a bench in that dreaded area, and the young cousins know its history. They loathe it as much as we did.

As the sun went down after supper anyone who wanted to fish lined up on the dock, and piled into *Duke*. We had to wear those lifejackets that looked like two orange loaves of bread. They had little neck pillows, and straps than went around the waist, then up from the back to the front via your crotch, then clipped and tied all together at the waist. They were uncomfortable enough when dry, but when our younger cousins used them for swimming out to the raft, they got waterlogged and heavy. Lord knows how they saved anyone! To this day I believe that rather than helping you float, they would have held you underwater!

Onboard *Duke*, an uncle or aunt would man the oars. Mom and Aunt Glenys loved to fish. They would take a few of us out at a time so we could try our hand at it. We all wanted to bring back the largest bass and break the record. We would fish for bass, pickerel, white perch, and yellow perch. We were always on the lookout for turtles on the rocks near the small islands, about 300 feet from the shoreline.

Mom didn't have a fishing license but that didn't stop her from casting a line. Once I sat next to her as she showed Armand Jr., my brother, some angling basics when Aunt Glenys noticed a boat approaching. The two men onboard had binoculars and appeared to be watching us.

"Isabel," Aunt Glenys said, "those men are getting closer and they seem to be watching us. Do you suppose they could be game wardens?" Mom turned, saw them, and waved, saying: "Oh, Glenys, they're fishing too. See the rods in the boat? They're just being friendly."

But a few minutes later Aunt Glenys said, "I hate to tell you this, Isabel, but those men are heading straight for us! And, they have badges on their shirts!"

Mom turned just in time to see them coming within ten feet of us. She pushed her pole into my hands, saying, "Shut up! Don't say anything. You are the one fishing. Not me!"

As they pulled up, one warden grabbed the side of our boat. "Hi ladies. How's the fishing tonight?"

"Not very good," said Mom.

"Do either of you have a license to fish?"

"I do," Aunt Glenys said, pulling her license from her pocket.

The warden glanced at it, then turned to Mom, "And you?"

Mom said, "Well, warden… ahhh, I don't have a fishing license, but I wasn't fishing. I was showing my daughter and son how to fish."

"That's not what I saw," the warden said. "I've watched you casting and fishing for the last twenty minutes." As he talked he reached in and grabbed my mother's fishing rod. The worm was still on the hook. He set the rod in his boat, grabbed a clipboard with a form, and asked, "What's your name?"

She gave it to him, and he proceeded to fill out the form. When he handed my mother the bottom copy, he said, "See you in court."

As they motored away Mom yelled, "Hey, he took my rod and worm. Now these kids can't fish! What a bastard!"

The following week Mom went to court, paid the $50 fine, and got her fishing rod back. The dead worm was still on it.

When we weren't out on *Duke* we often took our poles to the end of the dock to see if we could catch the big ones. One day Cousin Sammy was fishing there, and our cousin, Georgie, was standing behind him. Suddenly Georgie screamed. He was jumping up and down, holding his ear, obviously in pain. Sammy had accidentally caught the back of Georgie's ear with one of his casts. We all came running. Georgie stood there, frozen, his mouth wide with fright, pointing at his ear. His mom, my Aunt Angie, was a nurse. There at Camp Sabia she was always on call, rescuing us from danger and pain, and calming the worst situations. When drama was involved she was at her best, so, of course, she saved Georgie's ear.

DINNERTIME

The adults planned everything with an eye toward all of our needs. The rule then was no swimming for an hour after a meal. We ate our meals all together, so we could all go back in the water at the same time. If one family ate earlier they got back in the water long before the rest of us. That got the other cousins pissed off. Our parents knew the consequences would be listening to the rest of us that had to wait always yelling and tattling, "How much longer do I have to wait? How many minutes left? Michael put his foot in the water!! Johnnie is on the pier!!" We saw it as a kind of penance. Our parents saw this, and tried to keep to the structured schedule. Once the hour was up we ran to the water so fast you would think that we had never had a chance to swim before. The phrase "I'm bored" wasn't in our vocabulary.

Our Beloved Uncle Dom

Uncle Dom never married, but he devoted his life to making sure we all had the best toys and best times at camp. Though he said little, and often had a stern look, he was a big kid at heart. We were all a little afraid of disappointing him, for he was like a god. When Uncle Dom spoke you listened and you listened good! Once in a while he would laugh at something we'd done, but that was rare.

He drove a big pickup truck and we all fought to ride with him, yet whoever got to ride would sit in silence the whole way. He also had an old 1956 Thunderbird. The boys fought to ride in that. In the T-Bird he drove fast enough to impress, and even scare them a little. They thought he was the coolest.

He built a kayak in his garage and brought it up to camp to surprise us. It tipped so easily it was too dangerous for the younger cousins to use. He built the best raft on the lake out of big oil barrels. Every summer he made us paint them bright orange "Profenno Orange", because that was the only color available at the construction company's shop. The raft had a construction staging with a platform so that we could dive off, doing summersaults into the water. He covered the platform with canvas so that we wouldn't get splinters. Every kid around wanted to swim and dive off the raft with us. He built our first pontoon boat, *The Barge*, from a picture in a magazine. Measuring about 12' by 9' with silver painted pontoon barrels, and metal cones attached to the front, it had a railing, a steering wheel at the helm, and a 10-horsepower motor on the back. We would set folding chairs on the deck, along with a table and umbrella in the center, and take a ride around the lake. Other boaters would point and stare. It looked like someone's porch floating down the lake.

The first homemade pontoon boat on Little Sebago Lake, 1965.
Looked like someone's porch had broken away and floated down
the lake with chairs and a table with an umbrella.

Every weekday morning, Uncles Dinny, Sam, George, and Maurice would leave early to go to work. They would return just in time for dinner. Though Uncle Dom had his own room out in the garage, he never stayed at camp. He would always eat dinner and drive back to Portland. On the weekends he would rise early, arrive at camp by 6am, then bang on the back door, and ring the cowbell to wake us all up. Did he even realize how late we'd stayed up? When you stumbled to the door to let him in, he'd smirk and say, "What the hell's the matter with you?" This would be followed by an agenda of chores for all us. He'd have us do yard work, paint picnic tables, or clean out the garage. Though he put us to work, he also surprised us with things we considered as awesome and fun.

All of this went on until Labor Day when we would close camp and head back to our homes to start another school year. Labor Day was always a very sad weekend.

CLEANING/LAUNDRY

My mother and my aunts had an organized method for keeping Camp Sabia clean. We were never allowed to run through the camp with wet, sandy feet. We kept life preservers, oars, fishing rods, inner tubes, beach toys and whatever else in the large garage attached to the back side of the camp. Inside of the garage, along one wall, Uncle Dom built five wooden stalls for changing into swimwear. Aunt Angie and Aunt Rose sewed curtains over the front of these stalls for privacy. This didn't always work, especially for us girls. The boys would always run by and pull open the curtains or steal our underwear. I vividly remember my Uncle Sam and Aunt Glenys' dog, Gingerpeach, stealing my underwear from the stall. I was afraid of dogs, and when she ran out to the lawn, ears flapping, and my underwear in her mouth, it sent me into a screaming frenzy. The laughter of everyone within earshot didn't help at all. We all hated using those stalls.

Saturday was washday, and that morning the kitchen would look like a laundromat. We had an old-style wringer washer hooked up to the kitchen sink with a hose. On the top of this washer was a wringer with a set of huge rollers with a handle that my mother and aunts took turns turning and pushing the clean clothes through. These huge double rollers rotated as they threaded the clothes through and turned the crank. Squeezing and pressing each item, extracting most of the water. Then they took the clean wet clothes outside and hung them on the clotheslines. On a sunny day the clothes were dry by early afternoon. That's when they would set up the ironing board in the kitchen. They needed every table to hold each family's pile of clean clothes. Folding, ironing, sorting, and putting away clothes took most of the afternoon.

THE CUSHMAN TRUCK

Sweets were the key to getting any of us kids to work at Camp Sabia, so once in a while my mother, or one of my aunts would bake, usually making a huge sheet cake or three or four pies. The next best thing to these homemade treats was the Cushman Bakery station wagon. It stopped by Camp Sabia every other week. When that black-and-white station wagon pulled into our driveway we would all run to greet it. All the mothers came out looking for a sweet treat to go with that evening's meal.

Cushman Bakery was famous for oatmeal cookies, scotch cookies and cupcakes. My father loved their plain doughnuts with his morning coffee. The Cushman deliveryman loved our camp. He knew he had a guaranteed big sale every time he pulled into the driveway.

DAD AND CAMP

My father never really enjoyed Camp Sabia. He was not a sun worshipper, and he'd never learned to swim. Once, when he'd first come to the United States he'd almost drowned at Deering Oaks Park. He'd been walking around the park's duck pond when he fell in. Though the pond wasn't deep, his inability to swim made it a frightening experience that he never forgot. In addition he never liked the summer heat, and the idleness that came with it. He wanted to accomplish something every day. Instead of coming to camp he often helped out at the restaurant in Old Orchard Beach. Other times he'd go to Scarborough Downs Racetrack where he would meet up with his brother Angelo.

It was a funny sight whenever Dad went into the lake to take a bath. Wearing swim trunks, he would go in up to his waist, crouch down, and splash the water over his shoulders and neck. Then he'd stand up and start washing with a bar of soap. As soon as he was finished washing he would crouch back down a little, rinsing off. Finally he would come back in to shore. For Dad that was it.

Mom and Dad, 1984, at Camp Sabia, Little Sebago Lake, Maine

A NEW COUSIN

Our little cousin, Elizabeth "Betsy" True was born on July 17, 1953. The day my Aunt Rose and Uncle Maurice brought her from the hospital to Camp Sabia we had a big celebration. My uncles, aunts, and cousins lined the sides of the driveway with homemade signs as if they were part of a parade. We all shouted, "Hurrah!" as my Aunt Rose stepped out of the car, a bundle of pink there in her arms. All we could see was a little face surrounded by mounds of dark brown hair. We ecstatically welcomed our new cousin.

Little Sebago Lake, Camp Sabia, 1981, a hot summer's day gathering

TEENAGE YEARS

As we grew up, some of us got summer jobs, and only went to Camp Sabia for weekends. Once my brother Johnnie and cousin Donny had their driver's licenses, on Saturday nights we would pile into one of our parents' cars and take off for the Windham Drive-in for a double feature. When we reached the end of the camp road we pulled over to decide who would hide in the trunk and behind the front seats. We would pay for four tickets, the driver, Donnie; the front passenger, Johnnie; and the two back passengers, Michael and Cammie. We would then proceed to the very back row—the darkest part of the drive-in theater yard. Once the car was parked, Johnnie would get out and open up the trunk and let out Georgie, Sammy, and Jimmy. Under Michael and Cammie's legs in the back seat Janice and I were hidden by pillows. Three of us would lie on pillows on the car roof while six squeezed into the car. We stayed until both features were over, then crammed ourselves in for the short ride home.

Once we reached our teens, on Saturday nights, we were allowed to stay at Camp Sabia by ourselves. We would drag the mattresses from all the bedrooms into the huge living room, and lay them on the floor by the stone fireplace. Our parents trusted us to be good, and for the most part we were. We all watched out for each other and we never disagreed or fought about anything.

By his senior year Donnie had a car of his own and we would sometimes drive to downtown Portland and cruise around looking for funny things to do. One evening we found a wig, bright red lipstick and an old dress up in one of the bedrooms. With these we dressed Donnie up as a woman, stuffing his chest so that he looked well en-dowed. We drove to a Middle Street strip club called The Scarecrow where a female impersonator, Stanley the Stripper, danced every Saturday night.

We thought it would be funny to have Donnie stand outside of the club trying to pick up guys. From a packed car across the street eight of us watched as men approached him. Donnie waved his cigarette around, talking in a weird falsetto. We were all laughing hysterically. When a policeman came along and started grilling Donnie, Donnie nervously told the policeman that his ride had arrived. He ran across the street, jumped in, and said, "Let's get out of here! Quick! Those guys really thought I was a woman!"

Camp Sabia, 2001

THE PROFENNO COUSINS

We loved spending all summer together, and when winter came we still got together for movies, ice skating or tobogganing. Uncle Dom had a toboggan so big it could fit us all. It was wooden, and had plaid stuffed padding. It was so huge and heavy that Uncle Dom needed the back of his pickup truck to transport it. He would pull into the parking lot at Riverside Golf Course where the boys would help him get it off the back of the truck. They lugged it to the top of the hill where we piled on, smallest first. The bigger boys boarded at the end. Janice and I were somewhere in the middle where we were protected.

Going down the hill was a feat. There was really no way to control the thing. Once that toboggan started gaining momentum there was no stopping. Whenever we veered off course people scattered. It was so heavy that it only took a couple of trips to wipe us out. Dragging it back up the hill was what did it. Donnie, Johnnie, Michael and Jimmy usually did the towing. Aunt Angie and Aunt Glenys would show up with hot cocoa and we would take a break. We would convince our aunts to ride along on a run, then laugh when they took a spill at the bottom.

Sometimes, when it was very cold but snowless, we ice skated at Camp Sabia. Once the snow came there was no way we could shovel off a big enough section for skating. Arriving there in winter always felt so strange. The camp looked stark, gray, empty and void of neighbors. Inside we would light a fire to take the chill off, but the cold dampness remained, a stark contrast to the smells and sounds of summertime.

Italian American Community Center

In 1955, my mother's brother, Donato C. Profenno became one of the original founders and the first President of the Italian American Community Center. Along with many other members, my uncle wanted to create an organization dedicated to the promotion of Italian culture and heritage. Another uncle, Joseph Urbano, became the second President. For two or three years members met at each other's homes, and held functions at different Grange Halls. Some of their activities included annual banquet dinner/dances at the Eastland Hotel Ballroom, and the Columbus Day Dinner/Dance at the Presumpscot Grange Hall in October of 1956.

In 1957 they finally bought a building on Pearl Street. It became a lively gathering place for all Italians. Every month they held fundraisers to provide for those in need. These events included fashion shows, Christmas fairs, rummage sales, dinner/dances, and casino nights.

My father, mother and their siblings took part in many of these events. Dad helped cook charity dinners. Aunt Rose and Aunt Angie Hutchins put on fashion shows. Mardi Gras was a big hit, with everyone dressed in costumes.

As a young girl I loved watching my mother get all "dolled up." One time she wore a fringed roaring twenties dress, while Dad had on a bright striped jacket. Mom had spent hours sewing it, and Dad topped it off with a straw fedora. Another event was a formal ball. The men dressed in tuxedos and the women wore evening gowns. My dad wore tails and a top hat, and Mom looked like a queen, with a big hooped petticoat under the skirt of her dress.

Italian American Community Center Roaring Twenties Night - 1955.
Angie (Angiolina) Polito Profenno & Dinny (Donato) Profenno.

Halloween was another event my parents dressed up for. They tried to win the first place prize for Best Costume, but Uncle Sam and Aunt Glenys won it, as a prizefighter with his coach. With a bald wig, pail, white towel, and a cigar in her mouth, Aunt Glenys was the coach. Uncle Sam wore boxing trunks and boxing gloves.

They played their roles hilariously.

These functions were open to the public and most of them sold out.

Our telephone would ring all the next day, as everyone compared notes on the great time they'd had.

Mom and Dad at one of the many functions held at the Italian American Community Center. Dad especially liked being with Mom when she was, "All dolled up."

*1956 - Mom and Dad goiing to a grand affair with rented tux and
ball gown at the Italian American Community Center.*

Arbor Street

Our first home was a little duplex owned by my Grandmother Sabia, on the corner of Arbor Street and Stevens Avenue. Mom had a small beauty salon in one of the front rooms of the house. It seemed like someone was always there, under the dryer or waiting to get their hair done. I can hardly recall a time when we were alone as a family. I spent many days watching my mother work. Hairdressing fascinated me. While Mom cut hair I would sit on the floor picking up the fallen tresses and re-cut it, and I also tried to practice on my dolls. I would wash, cut and set their hair until finally there was none left on their heads. When Dad bought me a huge stuffed horse, I washed, curled and styled the mane and tail until the same thing happened.

My father wasn't thrilled with my interest in hairdressing. He saw how hard my mother worked and how little money she made. Nevertheless I was fascinated. Every day I asked my mother who was on her schedule. Once I learned to read then I would get this information from her appointment book. I recall schoolteacher, Margaret Welch. My mother finger-waved this woman's long gray hair into a horseshoe framing her face. Mom then braided the back, twisting it into a bun at the base of her neck. This hairdo was held in place by long hairpins matching the hair color perfectly. Some of Mom's other regular customers were Mildred Ackley, Edith Woodman, Mary Gross, and Grace Morris.

Mom had a huge machine for permanents. With its heated plates and wires clipped onto every roll of hair, it looked like an octopus. As these women sat for hours getting their hair curled, Mom made them tea and snacks.

On Call

Mom was "on call" for Hutchins Funeral Home. There she fixed deceased women's hair. George and Lena Hutchins, with their three children, Rosemary, George Jr., and Allie, lived up the street from the Profenno home, and they were friends. There were times when Mom would be called to do someone's hair on a Saturday or Sunday morning. We would be left waiting for her to come home so we could go to camp or do something else that was fun.

DEEP WAVES

In our living room whenever Dad sat back in his favorite chair, I would grab a comb, cape, hairpins and wave clips and start combing and styling his hair. Dad had the most beautiful hair. It was black, thick, and fairly long on the top. It fell in deep waves that intrigued me. I combed and placed clips for hours while Dad fell asleep. Whenever he dozed off I took the opportunity to pin curl his hair all over.

When he finally woke up he would feel the clips all over his head, and say, "What the hell are you doing? Get those God damn things out of my hair! Isabel?" Then he would reach up, touch his head, and feel all the clips, and start laughing and shaking his head.

NO PRIVACY

As we grew older my father, brother and I would sleep in on Saturdays, while Mom hosted a room full of yakking women downstairs. Still in our pajamas, we would creep down to the kitchen trying not to be seen. But inevitably, as we got breakfast, a keen-eared customer would always yell out: "Hi, Johnnie" or "Is that you, Nancy?"

Privacy wasn't an option. The only bathroom was off the kitchen on the first floor. My father hated having to walk through the kitchen to get there. Some customer would always cry out: "Hi Armand." He politely put up with the chitchat and laughter. He endured many, many years of the scent of hairspray and permanents. Every once in awhile, he would shake his head and say, "What the hell! Puzza! [Stink!] That shit smells the whole God damn house up! God it stinks in here!"

UNCLE ANGELO

Once a year at the start of school my Aunt Helen Mary Polito and her daughters, Joannie, Cindy and Susan would come in on a Saturday for perms and cuts. It was an all-day job. Uncle Angelo would drop them off first thing in the morning, then head to the race track. Late that afternoon he would pick them up on the way home. Between the haircuts my mother would make everyone lunch. When they weren't busy with their hair, I played with the girls. Having no sisters, I enjoyed playing with my Polito cousins.

I was especially fond of my Godfather, Uncle Angelo. With his jet black hair, infectious smile, and perfectly straight white teeth (a Polito trait), he looked a lot like Dad. He was always funny and at get-togethers at my grandparent's home he kept everyone laughing. Aunt Helen Mary seemed to always be pregnant. She had six girls: Joannie, Cindy, Susan, Mary Frances, Laureen Elizabeth (who died shortly after birth), and Judy. Finally she had a boy, Tony.

HELPING OUT

Mom was always sickly. It was hard to say what was wrong with her, but she was always popping pills and "lying down" to rest. She would come home from seeing Dr. Dooley carrying bags full of samples. These samples lined the shelf in the bathroom. She would try one drug, complain, then try something else. Dad would say that she never stuck with anything long enough to see if it worked.

I realized at a young age how much my father needed someone to help him. I also knew how much my mother needed me to help her. Between the two of them I was busy, and had little time to play. My cousin, Janice and I were two years apart, and, not having sisters', we would spend time together. Other than that I was usually doing chores, or watching my mother do hair. Whenever I could I would help my father with projects, and I was learning how to cook by watching him.

One afternoon, as I was helping Dad paint the kitchen ceiling by holding the ladder steady, Uncle Sam and Aunt Glenys stopped by. Aunt Glenys was comical, and we loved being around her. That day Aunt Glenys was talking to my Dad when Mom came into the kitchen.

Mom looked up at my father standing on top of the ladder. "Gee, Armand, it looks like you missed a few spots. Isn't that section a little cloudy? Do you have enough paint on your brush? It's definitely going to need two coats!"

My mother left. Aunt Glenys looked up at my father and said, "Armand there will be a place in heaven for you."

Without missing a beat Dad said: "It can't happen soon enough!" We all laughed, but I wasn't sure what was so funny. I'd seen it before though. Poor Dad! Whenever he was doing a project Mom put her two cents in. She never helped, she only criticized. "I don't want it to look tutto stutto!" she'd say, meaning discolored or messed-up.

"I'll tutto stutto you! Get outta here!" he'd reply and shoo her away.

TELEVISION

One day in the mid-1950s, my father surprised us by bringing home a huge piece of furniture displaying a tiny octagon screen. Just below the screen were a lot of knobs. Underneath the knobs were areas covered with gold mesh-like material. These were speakers, and the whole thing was our first TV. Pretty soon Mom and I were sitting down every afternoon to watch "Queen for a Day" and "Liberace".

"Queen for a Day" was hosted by a man named Jack Bailey. He would bring four women on stage, one-at-a-time, to tell why they wanted to be "Queen for a Day". They had hard luck stories, always of hitting rock bottom. Members of the audience would start crying. When the women were done the audience was invited to clap for each one, as an applause meter measured the decibel levels. The one who drew the loudest applause won. The woman who won received her wish. It was a real tearjerker!

It seemed a little bizarre to me. I remember watching one woman tell about her six children, and how her husband's back problems kept him from working. She couldn't work because that would mean her children would be home alone. Her washing machine had broken down, and she listed many other woes. When Jack Bailey asked, "What would you want if you were Queen for the Day?" she replied, "A set of golf clubs for my husband."

How strange, I thought. With everything falling apart around her this woman wanted golf clubs for her ailing husband.

The winner would be draped in a red velvet robe, crowned, presented with a dozen red roses and maybe a free vacation. Despite my reservations about golf clubs, I would get wrapped up in it, just like Mom. We cried our eyes out.

One day, when a snowstorm forced schools to close, Dad stayed home and watched us watching the women. "Tu sei pazzo!," [You're crazy!] he would say. "You crazy fools. What a bunch of suckers!" He walked away shaking his head.

Every afternoon Liberace's show came on, showcasing him on piano, with his brother, George, accompanying on violin. Liberace intrigued me with his amazing hair. It looked like Dad's. I also liked his piano with its candelabra. Sometimes he had a guest singer. At the end he always made an affectionate mention of his mother, Frances. I found this to be really sweet.

On Saturday mornings Jovnnie and I would sit close to the screen and watch Happy Trials with Roy Rogers and Dale Evans. Other Saturday morning regulars were Rin Tin Tin, The Lone Ranger, Abbott and Costello, and Laurel and Hardy.

Soon Dad was having fits because every Saturday we sat down in front of the television, and we didn't move for hours. Dad would take the on/off knob with him when he left the house to go grocery shopping, but Jovnnie solved this with a pair of needle-nosed pliers. Dad would pull into the driveway and Jovnnie would turn it off and run up to his bedroom and pretend to read. My father was big on reading books, but he didn't like comic books. Jovnnie hid his collection of Dick Tracy, Sky King and Flash Gordon comics, pulling them out at night to read by flashlight under the covers. When Dad found them he threw them out. Jovnnie protested, yelling that he would just read his friend's, Skipper or Buddy's comic books instead.

PRETENDING

When I wasn't helping Mom, I liked to dress up in her clothes. I would put on a dress with high-heel shoes, a big hat, and a necklace of beads, then I would paint my lips with her bright red Tabu lipstick. I pretended I was Mom, taking my doll carriage outside and walking around the yard, making believe that I was shopping downtown.

One day Dad pulled into the driveway, got out of the car and said, "If I see you with that red lipstick on your face again, I will wash your mouth out with soap! Don't ever wear that again!" Then he went inside and told my mother, "I don't want Nancy wearing your red lipstick, she looks like a little puttana [whore]!" He despised my dressing up to look older than I was.

He didn't mind me dressing up like a nun, with a black dress, rosary beads, and black shawl. He even made me a cardboard cutout for my face, stapling the shawl around the cut out so that I looked like I had on a real habit. It was okay to bless everyone or line up my dolls while pretending I was teaching Sunday School. Sometimes I pretended that the dolls misbehaved and I whacked them with a ruler. I wanted everyone to call me Sister Perpetua, which was the name of my Sunday school teacher. I loved how she walked around with her arms folded in under her long black dress. I was fascinated by the idea of dedicating myself to God. Though they never met Him, the nuns thought of themselves as being married to Him. My cousin Janice was the only one who would play "nun" with me. We were like-minded on this, and would spend hours pretending to be nuns, teachers, or mothers with babies.

COFFEE, ROYAL LUNCH AND DONUTS

Jovnnie and I both attended Morrill's Elementary School just around the corner from where we lived. Dad would get my brother and me up before he left to teach at Deering High School. Sitting at the kitchen table Dad would pour us cups of coffee and then give each of us a Cushman's donut or a couple of Royal Lunch crackers for breakfast. It wasn't long before Jovnnie discovered cereal, hounding Dad to buy some. Dad gave in, but would only buy Cheerios, Rice Krispies or Corn Flakes. He deemed the others to be, "Too sweet. Like eating candy." Jovnnie drove Dad nuts by eating whole boxes of cereal. Cereal was more expensive than donuts or crackers and when my brother would sit down for breakfast and eat the whole box, my father would go nuts! He said it was a waste of money if Jovnnie had to eat the whole damn box to be full! Through high school I stuck to drinking my coffee with Dad every morning.

Every day at noon Jovnnie and I came home for lunch, usually leftovers from the night before.

FOUR EYES

Morrill's only went up to the fourth grade and then we had to transfer to Longfellow School down the street. Jovnnie was responsible for keeping me safe, but he didn't like doing it. Preferring to walk with his friends he would call me names like "fatso" and "fancy pants." When I had to get glasses, he had a field day with calling me "four-eyes." Though I could see much better I cried the day I came home with those ugly cat-eyed glasses.

I'd gotten them after Dad saw me watching television with one eye closed. One day, in his endearing way of addressing a problem, he asked Mom, "What the hell is wrong with her eye?" That led to those thick ugly glasses. Dad was the only one who said I looked beautiful in them.

I was already chubby, and very shy. When I had to add those ugly glasses I lost any self-confidence I might've had. I seldom played outside with the other kids, feeling more comfortable indoors.

On days when Mom wasn't sick or working in her beauty shop, she would teach me how to do laundry, wash the floor, iron my father's handkerchiefs while standing on a soap box, and vacuum and dust the house. Her illnesses made these chores difficult for her. She also taught me how to knit, crochet, embroider, and sew. Despite her poor health, she devoted many hours to teaching me how to be a "little domestic princess." When my father came home from school he would be amazed at what I learned to do at such a young age. He always praised my work.

COOKING

Dad did the grocery shopping and cooking, and my mother mostly baked cakes, cupcakes and Italian cookies. When they'd first married he'd bought her "The Settlement Cookbook" for Christmas. Inside he'd written, "To 'Wife' With hopes that you will take over some day, (soon I hope). Love, Hubby, 'the cook' December 23, 1944." His hopes were never fulfilled.

Instead after each long day of teaching, Dad would come home and start supper. He was meticulous, disliking anything that was, as he would say, "handled too much." It was his thought that cooks who had to handle food a lot didn't know "what the hell they're doing" and he would shake his head stating, "schifo" [disgusting]. He always started by placing a dishtowel over his shoulder, then he would take an aluminum dish from the cupboard and place it on the stove. The dish held his utensils so he wouldn't make a mess on the stove and counter.

Late afternoon was the most exciting time of the day for me because I got to spend it learning cooking from my father. His recipes were all in his head. If Dad wanted chicken he always bought a whole one, cutting it into serving pieces himself. One day, as I watched him wielding a meat cleaver and filet knife as he separated meat from bone, I leaned in too close. The countertop was at my eye level, and as I leaned my head in to see better, his knifepoint hit me right between the eyes. He slammed down his knife and yelled, "Mannaggia il diavolo![Damn the devil!] What the hell are you doing standing so close? Are you all right? You're always up my culo! [Ass]"

He grabbed my face, and moved my head back and forth, checking to see if I was all right. I was lucky. I wasn't cut, just a little scared.

Dad held my face firmly, kissed my forehead, and apologized. "I am sorry dear. Are you okay?" Even his kiss had a forceful authority. Though his sternness was a little frightening, I loved his mannerisms. I knew his soft side, which few others ever saw.

THE CALORIC STOVE

I remember the day in 1954 when the new Caloric gas stove was delivered to our house. It was so heavy that it took two big strong deliverymen to get it to the kitchen. Dad was so excited. Here was a stove with a big cooking surface that could hold large pots. It had an oven for baking on one side, a broiler on the other, and under the oven side was a warming bin. Under the broiler was another, smaller broiler, and a large back splash with a timer, light and a clock.

Mom made sure everyone knew how expensive it was. She would tell customers, "I know it was expensive. It was over $300.00. But, he likes to cook, so I guess it is worth it."

When a meal was over, and we were clearing the dishes, Dad would be bent over the stove wiping it down and taking the grates off the gas burners to clean them. He was particular about keeping it clean. For over 40 years Dad cooked every meal on that Caloric stove. I only remember him having one problem with it. In the late '90s Dad had to bring in the gas company repairman to lower the flame on the right front pilot. The high flame was heating the covering, and burning under the plate that held the individual grates, causing a build up of black soot underneath. This also caused the top of the stove to get very hot. The repairman told him, "That stove is not safe. The buildup of the soot underneath could cause a fire, Mr. Polito. You can't get parts for these stoves anymore. Maybe you should think about getting a new one." After the repairman left, Dad spent all afternoon looking for the stove's warranty on the stove. He knew it was down in his workshop somewhere.

Once he found it he called the Caloric Company only to be told by a representative that they did not make that style of stove anymore. The rep offered to give him a more modern stove in its place. Dad hung up, muttering, "That will be the day! Yeah, right! They take mine and give me crap! They don't make stoves like this one anymore. They're nuts! I'll keep this one and fix it myself!" Dad spent a full day running up and down the cellar stairs between workshop and kitchen, working on that stove.

I came in to find the stove disassembled, and I asked, "Hey Dad? What are you trying to do?"

"I am trying to cut this piece of metal so that I can somehow place it above the flame to prevent the top of the stove from getting hot!"

I looked, and said, "Dad, that's not reducing the amount of flame. The gasman said the flame was way too high and couldn't be controlled. What you're doing is stopping the flame from heating up the metal plate above it, right?"

He stopped what he was doing. His glasses had slipped down to the tip of his nose, and he had a disgusted look on his face. "Yeah! What's your problem? It will be fine! I will keep an eye on it so nothing will happen! Never you mind!"

I left him alone. He finished what he was doing, and started cooking dinner. I never heard him complain about the stovetop getting too hot again. Every night after dinner as he wiped off his beloved stove, I would see him check under the stovetop plate to see how the pilot was burning and if any soot had formed underneath. I don't know how safe it was, but he made it work and never burned the house down. Dad's Caloric Stove still sits in my garage, along with the life-time warranty.

THE ICEMAN

Our refrigerator wasn't a modern one; it was the kind that needed ice. It was the size of a narrow bureau, standing approximately four feet high. It had two doors on the front. The larger of these doors opened the top section. This was for food storage, holding milk, eggs, meats and other perishables. The smaller bottom door opened to where you put the ice to keep the upper level cold. Underneath was a small drip pan to catch the water as the ice melted.

Every few days the iceman came. As soon as Jovnnie or I saw his big truck we ran to tell Mom. He drove up in front of the house, jumped from the cab, and ran around to the back. There he opened the hatch, and put a big piece of leather over his shoulder. At this point he grabbed the ice tongs, and in one smooth motion he pulled out a huge chunk of ice, and flung it up over his shoulder onto the leather. From there he carried it into the house where my mother would be waiting.

He'd been delivering ice to our house for years, so he knew exactly where to go. In the kitchen he would carry the ice to the icebox, open the bottom door, and push the huge block into the metal-lined cubicle. When he had it in place he shut the door, then turned to my mother and said, "See you in a few days Mrs. Polito." Outside he would stop, take out his ice pick, and chip off chunks of ice for Jovnnie and me to suck on.

JOVNNIE AND HIS FRIENDS

Jovnnie and his friends Skipper Basso, Buddy Basso, Ernie "Billy" Vandermast, and cousin, Georgie, were always busy building go-carts or dismantling old radios. They got the radios from the radio repair shop down at Morrill's Corner. Jovnnie had tubes, wires, and knobs strewn all over my father's cellar. Their goal was to make radios of their own, or, better yet, to rebuild the radios and sell them. That never happened.

Jovnnie dismantled just about everything he ever got, but putting things back together was another matter. When he was ten he got his first new bicycle, a red English-style Schwinn with brakes up on the handlebars. In those days this was the bike to have. As soon as Jovnnie got it he started taking it apart, hoping to make adjustments to make it faster. He never put it back together. Three years later, when we moved out of our house on Arbor Street, my father swore about all the parts from "that damn Schwinn." He packed them up, and took them to our new home on Washington Avenue. Years later he threw them out in disgust.

Westbrook College was just up the street from us, and behind the college was Gulliver's Field. On Saturdays all of us neighborhood kids rode our bikes there. A dirt path led from the side street behind the college to the huge field. There we would play ball, collect tadpoles and ride our go carts down the dirt hill. It was a secluded place where our parents could not see us, hear us, or yell to us. We listened for the sound of the noon alarm at the firehouse. That meant we had to head back home for lunch.

My father spent hours helping the boys build a go-cart. He devoted so much time and attention to it that soon he'd taken over the whole project. He attended to every detail, even salvaging the wheels from the carriage my mother had used for Jovnnie and me when we were babies. Dad did the work while the boys stood around, watching. It was the best and fastest go-cart in the neighborhood. Racing it down the dirt hill at Gulliver's Field was always exciting. One day my father came to the field to see how fast they could make it go. He stood there laughing at the boys. They had so much fun.

In the summer the Stevens Avenue Congregational Church held auctions across the street in the church's back yard. Buddy, Skipper, Georgie, Billy, my brother and I would sit in the back row, watching the bidding. One day my brother decided to bid two cents on a brass twin bed and to our surprise he got it. Laughing, we all grabbed pieces of bed frame, and headed across the street to our house. My father took one look at the huge brass headboard and footboard and said, "What the hell am I going to do with that damn thing?"

Jovnnie always had a nose for a bargain, something that's stayed with him to this day. The problem was, once he had something, he couldn't let it go. If he saw the slightest chance that an item might be of some future use he had to hang on to it. In this he was like Dad, but it may have come from both sides. The Profennos were known for collecting everything, but not parting with anything.

Morrill's Corner was a busy intersection, with a five-and-dime, Walkin's Dry Cleaners, and a candy store all on different corners. This produced so much traffic that the city selected that spot to install the first set of traffic lights equipped with pedestrian walk buttons. My brother got the bright idea to test the buttons to see if he could stop the traffic all four ways. Skipper, Buddy, Billy, and my brother each took a corner, then pushed all the buttons at the same time. The lights turned red, traffic stopped, then the boys rolled marbles into the intersection. The drivers started honking, yelling, and getting out of their cars. We all took off in different directions. Someone we knew must've seen us, and told on us. My mother found out, and threatened to call the police if we tried it again.

Aunt Rose's

In our house we didn't have casseroles, bologna, peanut butter and jelly, orange juice or chocolate milk. Our diet was almost all traditional Italian. While Dad loved fish, my mother didn't want him cooking seafood in her kitchen. She'd grown up without seafood, and had never gotten acclimated to its smell. I followed Mom's lead on most things, so if she didn't like seafood, neither did I.

When my mother was hospitalized for gallbladder surgery, Jovnnie and I had to stay at our Aunt Rose's. We weren't accustomed to eating in other peoples' homes, and when Aunt Rose served me creamed tuna on toast I thought I was going die! What was this molten mass of white lumpy stuff on my plate?

This problem repeated itself in a different form every night. Soon I got so nervous about dinnertime that I nearly threw up. I took to reaching under the table for Jovnnie's hand to steady me. He would pull his hand away in disgust. My problem went deeper than food. To be away from my parents and home put me in a state of despair. Though I was still with family, including my cousin Janice, it didn't feel right. Some nights I cried myself to sleep.

There were a few bright spots. Every afternoon Uncle Maurice came home from work and asked, "What's for dessert?" Aunt Rose pointed to the kitchen table where there were always dozens of fresh-baked cookies. Uncle Maurice would smile from ear to ear for he loved his sweets. Uncle Maurice cooked too, making the best chocolate fudge without the benefit of a written recipe. The True family had always been known for the best desserts at Camp Sabia. At dinner everyone jostled for a seat at their table for that very reason.

SAINT NICHOLAS

Dad had difficulties with the American celebration of Christmas. He felt that it spoiled us. He would tell us how he had nothing as a child and how his siblings and he were lucky if Saint Nicholas put a few pennies under their plates on Christmas Eve. We'd hear this story every year, along with admonitions about Christmas being a time of reflection, and appreciation for what we had. He would go along with whatever my mother wanted to do, but with great reluctance. As Christmas closed in his attitude always softened. As our excitement increased his opposition bent, then broke, and he gave in to the commercial holiday spirit. Finally, he was ready to have a ball with us.

On Christmas Eve Jovnnie and I would go to bed, only to hear jingling bells and lots of commotion. We would sneak out of bed and from the top of the staircase we could hear Dad saying to Santa: "I don't know if they've been that good!" A moment later we might hear: "They don't need all that!"

Somehow we would fall asleep.

On Christmas morning we would slowly descend the winding staircase, then peek around the corner. When we saw all the presents we would scream with joy. Dad would come in and yell, "Aspetta!" meaning to wait for him. Lacking a fireplace we'd put one of my father's dark blue dress socks on the floor near the Christmas tree the night before. Now it was full of hard unwrapped candy, melted into the shape of a foot, because the house got really warm in the night when the heat came on, with blue fuzz and lint all over it. We ate it anyway.

Dad would take us to the front door, then point outside where fragments of carrot lay in the snow—hard evidence that Santa had been here with his reindeer. Dad would always bring in a knife or two so that he could cut open the wrapped presents at the taped sides and carefully fold and smooth the paper into a neat pile. He took forever to open all the gifts. Wrapping paper, tags, and ribbon were expensive, so we saved them for the following year. "Why not use these tags again?" he would say.

We would moan in disgust.

Waving his knife, and smirking deviously, he would reply: "Unless you are going somewhere and you won't be around next year? Let me know, I will throw your name tags away. Capisce? [Understand?]"

"NO!" we would cry, giving in.

A Baby Brother

On June 26, 1957 my brother, Armand Jr., was born. It was an event that none of us would ever forget. Uncle George and Aunt Angie (Profenno) lived five houses down from us, and when my mother experienced labor pains in her eighth month, my father called Aunt Angie for advice. She told him to call the doctor, who said Dad should bring my mother into the hospital right away.

Aunt Angie sent my Uncle George up the street to stay with my brother and me while my parents were gone, but in the confusion Uncle George went outside got in my father's car with my mother, and drove her himself. My father turned to leave only to see Uncle George and my mother driving away. There was nothing that my father could do but wait by the telephone.

Jovnnie and I watched as my father paced back and forth muttering, "Dio mio [My God]. Mamma Mia. I hope she is gonna to be all right." Finally, hours later, the doctor called. I heard my father tell him, "Doctor, I have two children at home, and they need their mother, if it comes to that decision." I was scared. I thought I was never going to see my mother again. I began to cry. I told my father that I did not want a brother or sister. I wanted Mom to come home. My father tried to comfort me by telling me, "Go to bed!"

The next morning my father told us that we had a new brother. Jovnnie and I looked at each other and said, "So?" We just wanted to know when Mom was coming home. My brother, Armand Jr., was born a month early and weighed eight pounds. The doctors said if he had gone to term he would have weighed over ten pounds.

My mother had been hemorrhaging severely when she arrived at the hospital. The doctors thought they were going to lose mother or baby or both. To this day I don't know what happened at his birth, but he was born with a blue left foot. That was the main topic of our conversation. It took months for the color to go away.

At this point Jovnnie was twelve, and I was ten. With the addition of Armand Jr. our Arbor Street home was too small, so we moved.

Just around this time my brother ordered me to stop calling him "Jovnnie." He wanted me to call him Johnnie, so I did. Dad called him "Giuan." I believe this was an endearing way of saying, "John," and Johnnie never complained about it.

Washington Avenue

On my 11th birthday, October 25, 1958, we moved to 1188 Washington Avenue. Armand Jr. was one year old. Our new house was a large Dutch Colonial with three bedrooms, one for me, one for my parents and one for my brothers. The only drawback was its lone bathroom up on the second floor. When all three of us were trying to get ready for school in the morning, this was a real problem.

My father had a small bathroom built in the basement along with a beauty shop for my mother. By law the beauty shop had to have a bathroom for customers. This worked out great for my father. Avoiding the competition for the upstairs bathroom, he would climb out of bed, go downstairs in his boxer shorts, then wash and get ready in the basement. Along one basement wall he hung a bar holding several garment bags. Using these, he moved all his belongings down there, next to the bathroom. This was his space. No one touched or moved anything. The bathroom was very small, just a toilet and a small sink. For forty-four years my father used it to shave, wash and get dressed for the day.

My mother's beauty shop customers adapted easily to the new house. Soon they found their way up to the kitchen, where they might make a cup of tea. Soon we were bumping into them early in the morning when we were still half asleep. The horrible smell of permanent solution found its way up, waking us with a reeking odor like rotten eggs. My mother would bring Armand Jr. down to the salon where she would set him up with toys, keeping him busy while she worked. As he got older he started climbing the stairs, searching for toys on his own. Mom always kept a watchful eye on him.

Mommy? Fire!

One day while my mother was down in the shop doing someone's hair, three-year-old Armand Jr. was upstairs alone. He'd seen my father grip a nail with pliers, hold it over a gas burner, then push the hot nail point through his leather belt to make a new hole. Armand Jr. thought he might use a similar method to fix the wheel of his toy truck. He dragged a kitchen chair over to the stove, climbed onto it, turned on the gas burner, and held the truck over the flame. When the truck caught fire he dropped it on the floor, and ran to get a towel to put it out. The towel caught fire too. Armand Jr. ran down the basement stairs yelling, "Mommy fire, fire!"

My mother ran upstairs and saw the flames on the kitchen floor and poured water over it. This was a new floor, installed just a few months earlier. As my mother stared at the black, scorched patch she started to cry.

The man who had laid the new floor returned and fixed the burned section. He had the hairiest back I'd ever seen, reminding me of a gorilla. It took him all day to cut out the scorched part then replace it with a new piece. The piece was cut like a huge triangle. My father convinced my mother that it did not show. Yeah, right. It showed for more than ten years, remaining a topic of conversation. Armand Jr. became known as "Destructo" and "Tanker" because everything he touched seemed to fall apart or break.

DID YOU FIND YOUR BABY?

My mother's friend, Grace Morris, had her own car. Some days Grace took my mother and Armand Jr. out shopping. They would drive to Westbrook to Main Street. There they visited Nutter's Dress Shop, McLellans 5 &10, and the Men's Shop where my Dad bought all his suits for school. They often had ice cream at Vallee's Drug Store. My mother use to let three or four-year-old Armand Jr. go by himself to check out the 45 records. This was an era when you could let a child do that alone without worry. Armand Jr. was quite big and looked older than his age. Though he couldn't read yet, he could identify songs and their artists from looking at colors and markings on the labels. He amazed us this way. At the age of three, Armand Jr. was already a 45 collector and listener. He couldn't get enough of them, even taking them to bed where he would study the labels. He toted them around with him in a little carrying case, and on Christmas morning the tree had 45s stuck on all its branches.

On one particular winter day Armand Jr. was off looking at records when my mother noticed that a door to the back of the store was open, probably for a delivery. Knowing that Armand Jr. would think nothing of walking through an open door she got nervous. She ran to the records section but did not see Armand Jr. Calling to him, she ran to the back of the store and out the open door. Looking beyond the driveway just past a steep embankment she saw the Presumpscott River. Picturing my brother falling into the water, she lost it. In an attempt to calm her, Grace took my mother out front to find a policeman. As they hurried up Main Street Mom saw a woman trying to console Armand Jr. He was sobbing uncontrollably. My mother ran to him, thanked the woman, and scolded my brother for walking out the door. On the way home my mother told Armand Jr. not to say anything to my father.

At our house my father was cooking dinner when they arrived. My father stood Armand Jr. on a kitchen chair to remove his snowsuit and boots. As my father undressed him, my brother bent his head down to look at my father in the face, and said, "Daddy, did you find your baby?" "What?" my father asked.

"Daddy, did you find your baby?" Armand Jr. repeated.

As my mother came into the kitchen my father asked, "What the hell is he talking about? Did I find my baby?"

My mother's face grew pale. She sank down onto a kitchen chair and told him what had happened.

My father yelled, "For Christ's sake! What the hell is wrong with you? You know better than to leave him all by himself. He's perpetual motion! That's bad business!"

PIANO LESSONS

Because Dad always loved music we had a beautiful Steinway upright piano in the den. Johnnie and I took classical piano lessons from John Fay once a week. Every spring Mr. Fay would have a recital. I hated to perform, and Johnnie hated it more than me. In the middle of his last performance he stopped, looked around, smiled and then got up and walked away. That was it for Johnnie's piano lessons.

Every once and a while when I was practicing, Dad would get out his piccolo and surprise me by entering the den playing the tune I was playing. Armand Jr. would get his toy guitar and Mom would grab a comb with a piece of wax paper wrapped around it like a kazoo. They would both join in. Dad would look at Mom, shake his head, roll his eyes and burst out laughing. He would laugh so hard he could not purse his lips to play. Then Mom would march around like a tin soldier and Armand Jr. would fall in behind her.

I continued my lessons with Mr. Fay through my freshman year of high school. Finally I begged my father to let me change to a teacher who would teach me more modern music like jazz. They hired Mr. Phillips. With him I continued for a couple more years. Eventually I got too busy with friends and working part-time at Porteous Mitchell & Braun department store. I know Dad was disappointed, but he never said anything to me when I decided to stop taking piano lessons.

INTRODUCTION TO BOWLING AND OTHER GAMES

As Armand Jr. grew he developed an interest in bowling. One Christmas Mom bought him a plastic bowling set. He would set up the pins at one end of my mother's beauty shop, using that as his lane. The women under the dryer had to tuck their feet under the chairs so as not to trip Armand Jr. or get hit by the ball. My chalkboard hung on the basement wall in the back, past the beauty shop door. Armand Jr. would keep score of everyone that he was bowling for, and whoever was under the dryer would help him calculate the score. Many ladies got into it, screaming whenever he got a strike or spare. We nicknamed one lady "Goonie" because she was a little strange and loud. Goonie loved to cheer him on. Upstairs in the kitchen, when my father would hear the screams and yelling, he would shake his head and say, "What the hell are they doing down there? Sounds like Goonie is enjoying herself!"

When Armand Jr. wasn't bowling in the basement, he used the hallway from the kitchen to the living room. One Sunday morning while we were still in bed, we all heard a thud from downstairs. We all came running. We found Armand Jr. with the stem of a pumpkin in his hand. Pins were strewn all around in front of the front entry door. The pumpkin had broken into three sections. Johnnie and I could not stop laughing; Mom was upset. This perfectly round pumpkin had been a gift from a customer the day before. Dad just shook his head and said, "For Christ's sake, does he ever stop?"

Armand Jr. could entertain himself for hours. He had imaginary friends that he incorporated into games he'd invented. One was a bowling game using the various colored marbles from Chinese Checkers. I was always vacuuming up those damn marbles from under his bed. His socks were there too. It was my job to do the impossible: keep his room clean and neat.

Armand Jr. spent hours with his friend Kevin Foley, hiding baseball cards in the cellar. Dad had the cellar packed with empty boxes, parts to washing machines, refrigerators, old hair dryers from my mother's salons, every nut, bolt or screw from every item he ever owned, and

Luigi and Napoli Restaurant business papers covering decades of business. It was a great place to hide something.

Squirt, Squirt

When you came in the side door to our home you climbed three steps to the kitchen. Once when Dad came in from grocery shopping he put the groceries on the kitchen table. As he put them away, Armand Jr. came up from the cellar, squirt gun in hand. He leaned across the top step into the kitchen, waited until my father was bent down to a low cabinet, then very slowly squeezed the trigger and shot several squirts right at Dad's face. Dad stayed bent over, slowly turning to face Armand Jr.

"Hey, let me see that thing," Dad said.

"Sure Dad. Here!" Armand Jr. said, jumping up.

Dad took the squirt gun, holding it in his hand he turned it back and forth as if to check it out, then he laid it on the floor, and stomped it as hard as he could. Plastic flew everywhere. Armand Jr. stood there with his mouth hanging open. Dad said, "There. That outta do it!" Armand Jr. shrugged his shoulders and walked away saying, "I guess it does."

Ring, Ring

Our telephone rang all day long. My mother's friends and customers called to chat with her about everything. She was a wonderful listener, friend and confidante, spending hours at a time on the phone. Just as she would hang up from one call, another would come in. Dad used to say, "They call your mother before calling the police or ambulance. She has to be involved in everyone's God damn business." Or he would mutter, "Ah, for Christ sake, they have to tell Isabel everything." Sometimes he would roll his eyes and make a face at her. Dad was too private a person to understand why people told my mother their "sob stories."

Mom had all the sympathy in the world for anyone but Dad. She knew she didn't need to feel sorry for him. Dad did everything: cooking, washing floors, grocery shopping, emptying the trash, changing the beds, mowing the lawn, snow blowing, and gardening. It was not uncommon to see him, balanced like a monkey, painting the house, or cleaning the gutters.

Mom was at her best in her beauty shop or talking on the telephone with family and friends. This was true despite her ailments. The minute her last customer left, or she hung up the phone, she needed to lie down or take a pill. I never understood why she could do hair and help her friends, but the moment she was alone with her family she was always tired and needed to lay down. I use to think that possibly, we made her sick?

Dad was always there to help her through whatever was bothering her. He would analyze what she'd eaten, or whatever upsetting events had transpired. It drove everyone crazy.

He would talk out loud to himself, wondering: "What the hell did she eat today that bothered her stomach? Maybe she should stay away from tomato sauce. It's just too much acid! I'll put her on a bland diet that will fix her stomach problems. She doesn't know how to take care of herself, she is completely helpless! She likes those God damn pills too much! Ah, for Christ's' sake, I give up! Va Fanculo!"

Asbestos

In our Washington Avenue house asbestos covered most of the basement heating pipes. When asbestos removal became an issue Dad got a quote for the job. When he heard the high price, he decided against having it done. What we didn't know was that he still planned to get it all off the pipes. Every night after we'd gone to bed, Dad went down in the basement and removed a little asbestos, pipe by pipe. Once we realized it was gone, I asked him how he did it without harming himself.

"Ah, it was nothing," he said. "I wrapped a wet hanky around my nose and mouth and put on safety glasses."

"And, how did you get rid of it?"

"I hid it in the trash, a little at a time. There was nothing to it. It came off pretty damn easy and it didn't cost me a damn thing!"

BABYSITTING

I was my parents' built-in babysitter. Johnnie was busy with his friends or he would hide in his room, closing the door. There was never any question whether I wanted to do it. It was taken for granted. I would babysit Armand Jr. while Mom and Dad went to the racetrack with Uncle Joe and Aunt Josephine, or attended an event at the Italian American Community Center. Wherever they were going, I was left in charge.

Armand Jr. would not go to sleep unless I lay down on the bed with him. This was a real pain. My girlfriend, Karen, would come over, but I would be stuck waiting for Armand Jr. to drift off. Sometimes it took a half hour or more. If I moved an inch, he would call out, "Nancing, I not sleep!" I would moan, groan and throw my head back on the bed, glancing at the clock as I grunted a loud "Ugh!"

An eternity passed before he finally shut his eyes and fell asleep. With me he pulled this every night, but he didn't do it with our parents. My mother would get him into bed and then putter around. As long as he could hear her doing things, he would drift off.

Mom and Dad let Armand Jr. stay up to all hours of the night, putting him more or less on their schedule. Maybe because they had him late in life (Mom was 40 and Dad was 45, old for having children back then) they got lax with him. My mother told me how hospitals had once kept all the newborns in a separate nursery. Even the mothers had to go there to see them. The day after my mother delivered Armand Jr., she walked to the nursery to take a look at her new son. Another mother stood at the window admiring her own newborn. This new mother turned to my mother and said, "Are you the Grandmother?" My mother was mortified. "Do I look that old?" she wondered. She politely told this woman, "No. I am the mother."

When watching Armand Jr. I sometimes lost patience. When my mother was trying to toilet train him she would yell to me to take him to the bathroom. "Take him up quick before he has an accident!" she would say. Grabbing him by the arm, I would run him up to the second floor, yelling, "Don't you pee your pants!"

One time, as we reached the bathroom, I pulled down his pants, set him on the toilet, and said, "Don't move. Hang on! Just pee! I will be right back!" I went to do something in my bedroom, but a moment later I heard, "Nancing, I'm done!" Back in the bathroom I pulled him straight off the toilet, forgetting his anatomy. He cried, hanging on to his penis, as he jumped up and down, and screamed, "I got a booboo!" I looked down and saw that I had scraped his penis on the inside of the toilet, tearing the skin. I felt so bad for the little guy.

My mother ran to the stairs yelling, "What's going on?" When she entered the bathroom, Armand Jr. said, "Nancing hurted me!" My mother yelled at me, "You need to pay attention to what you are doing! Honest to God! You could ruin him for life!"

MOM BAKES

Johnnie liked to bring cupcakes to school for all of his classmates and teachers. Just before bed he would tell my mother that they were having a party the next day and he needed cupcakes for school. Poor Mom would stay up baking, frosting, and packing the cupcakes so that Johnnie would be able to carry them safely to school.

At a PTA meeting Mom said to his teacher, "I hope your students are enjoying all the birthday cupcakes."

The surprised teacher said, "Thank you. It is so nice of you to bake cupcakes for the whole class."

Mom said, "Aren't they for birthday parties?"

"No. Johnnie just brings them in every once in a while on his own."

Mom could not believe what she was hearing. When she got home she questioned Johnnie about the cupcakes, "Why would you say that you needed cupcakes for a classmate's birthday when there was no birthday?" Johnnie said very nonchalantly, "Because they like them and they all tell me to tell you to make more."

Mom baked her favorite desserts for every bake sale. We would watch Mom create beautiful treats, smell them bake, watch them get frosted and then see her package them up and leave with them. Dad would come down in the kitchen and say, "What are we, peasants? We don't even get a crumb!" She'd return, and tell us how hers were the first ones bought. All the other workers knew how good her baked goods were, and they would buy them all before they even went on sale.

Mom had a few good recipes that she became known for. She baked a yellow sponge cake that was light as a feather, filling the angel tin pan right up to the top. When we were little, Johnnie, Armand Jr. and I all took turns helping, standing on a chair beating eggs. This took from ten to fifteen minutes. We tired of standing there, beating, and waiting for the eggs to turn just the right color before Mom could continue. It seemed to take forever! When it finally went into the oven, Mom would tell us, "No running or jumping or the cake will fall." When the cake came out Mom would turn it upside down onto a shot glass to hold it up off the counter to cool. Amazingly light and airy, the finished cake stood over six inches high. She served it sprinkled with confectionary sugar. I have never been able to duplicate the airiness and height of Mom's cake to this day. My brother, Armand Jr., tried several times and it always comes out like a pound cake. Still, it tastes like hers. It was my father's favorite cake.

Quick Cocoa Cake and Quick Cocoa Cupcakes was another of Mom's best recipes. This recipe is easy. You mix everything in one bowl all at once. What comes out of the oven is the most wonderful, dark chocolate cake. Mom would frost the cake and cupcakes with old fashioned white frosting, topped with chocolate sprinkles.

Mom's macaroni-and-cheese was the best, a great favorite at any family gathering. She would labor over the roux, adding several types of cheeses. Growing up my Dad didn't like casseroles, unless you call lasagna a casserole. Macaroni and Cheese was it. To this day "Auntie Bell's Macaroni and Cheese" is still in demand at our family gatherings.

My mom perfected her Italian Cookie recipe after watching her own mother, who never measured anything. Grandmother Sabia, spoke little English, so when she tried to show my mother how to make Italian Cookies, she poured oil into a wooden spoon. As she poured, she would empty the spoon and count, "Uno, due..." Holding the spoon upside down, she kept pouring oil into the bowl, defying exact measurements. None of the old timers measured anything; they would just use their eye to know how much they needed.

Mom would whip up a pan of the moistest, chewiest Butterscotch brownies ever. Placing them in between her Italian cookies, she made a magnificent display of Christmastime sweets.

And Then There Were Pets

PETE

My father never liked pets of any kind. He would say, "Wild animals, that's what they are!" It took persistence, but over the years we managed to try a few different pets. When my mother came home from Kreskie's Five and Dime with a parakeet Dad was not happy. We named the bird "Pete." This bird was really smart. Johnnie spent hours teaching him all sorts of tricks. He trained Pete to come when he called. He taught him to retrieve. My brother would put a bell on top of a metal cabinet, then get Pete to throw it off. Finally he taught him to talk.

We had Pete for a few years until one day my mother noticed that he had this lump growing on his neck. Mom and I took him to the veterinarian. The vet said Pete had what they call a "crop" on his neck. It was collecting all his food preventing it from entering his stomach. He would eventually starve to death. The vet said that he could try to operate and take all the collected food, but it would eventually fill up again.

We knew my father wouldn't pay for an operation on a bird, so we had to put him to sleep. My mother and I cried all the way home and when we told my father about it he shook his head and said, "Come on, ah, for Christ's sake, it's just a bird! You should have brought him home; I would have cut the damn thing open! I have seen it done in Bovino with the hens. They would get that crop growing on their neck and it would be loaded. The men would just slice it open and let the stuff fall out and put a few stitches in it and the bird would be fine!"

The ordeal was hardest on my mother. She got emotional when pets got sick and died. After Pete she swore never to have another pet again, but that didn't stop us from trying.

Tom and Jerry

One Easter Uncle Dom rang our doorbell, then ran away. There on the doorstep he'd left two colored ducklings. We named them Tom and Jerry. These two soon grew into huge ducks, pooping everywhere, nipping, and being very unruly. Finally our parents said we had to give them away. The ducks went to some farmer who had plenty of land for them… or so we were told. For all I know we might have eaten them for supper that night!

Chico

During my freshman year at Portland High School I had a parakeet named Chico who talked and did tricks. Chico would go in my bedroom, perch on two glass figurines on top of my bureau, and examine himself in the mirror. For hours he would sit kissing his image and talking to himself. I would come in the house, yell out to Chico, and he would fly down the stairway into the kitchen where he would land on my shoulder. He would stay there, giving me kisses, as I walked around the house. One day I came home, yelled, but he did not come. I yelled again and still no Chico. I ran up to my room and saw he was not on the glass figurines, but I also noticed feathers and dust everywhere. I turned and ran back down to the kitchen, screaming for my mother. She was coming up from the beauty shop, yelling to me at the same time.

"Nancy," she said, "I have to talk to you." I knew something was wrong and I ran over to Chico's cage in the dining room. He was not on his perch. When I looked down into the cage I saw him lying on his side, dead! I screamed, "What the hell happened to him?" My mother came running over to meet me at the cage and said, "There was an accident! Little Armand, wanted to show Chico to one of my customers and he ran up into your room to get Chico and Chico took off flying around." Mom took a deep breath then continued, "When he couldn't catch him he shut the door to your bedroom and took the dust mop and started swinging until he hit him. Then he came down the stairs into the beauty shop with the bird in his hand, shaking him and yelling to me, "Mommy, I got him."

My mother was upset, but still she kept watch on me to make sure I didn't hurt her "Little" Armand. As Armand Jr. came up from the cellar I screamed at him, "I'm gonna kill you!" He cried, "Nancing, I didn't mean to do it. He wouldn't come." I shouted, "Never come into my bedroom again and stay away from me!" As I ran up the stairs I heard him sobbing, as he told my mother how sorry he was.

When Dad and Johnnie got home and saw what had happened they could not stop laughing. I asked Dad to help me bury Chico in the back yard and he said, "Ah… Just flush him down the toilet. That will be good enough!" Chico was buried in the backyard by the fence and Dad helped me bury him.

I wouldn't talk to "Little" Armand for days. My refusal to speak to him upset him so that my mother told me to stop treating him so badly. After all, she said, he was really sorry. Yeah, he was sorry. Little Destructo strikes again!

ROCKY

Rocky the hyper beagle seemed impossible to train, but maybe it was because we were all so busy we really didn't have the time. Rocky's ass was always up in the air as he dug holes all over the back yard. Dad poured black pepper into the holes to make him stop digging but it didn't work. Every evening, when Dad tried to bring Rocky in for the night, the dog would get loose and run in circles around the yard. We would watch from the sun porch window as Dad chased Rocky yelling, "Look you little, gepetost [hardhead]! Come here you, stronzo [asshole]! Get the hell over here you little son of a bitch! You little puzzolenti! [little stinker]" Dad hated that dog for he was nothing but a lot of work for him.

At night Dad would tie Rocky to the kitchen table to keep him from roaming the house, but Rocky would bark and yelp, dragging the table across the floor. He was relentless. Night after night my Dad would go downstairs, put back the furniture, and get Rocky back on his bed. "Hey, yio [boy]. Stop it! Now you go to sleep! Stata zitto" [be quiet]! After a few months of trying to train the little bastard, Dad gave him away to "someone on a farm, with a lot of land for him to run around on." We never questioned Dad about Rocky.

MITTENS

After hearing from a customer about a lady giving away kittens my mother brought home Mittens. Mittens was a beautiful grey cat with double paws and zero personality. She loved only my mother, and would not let anyone else come near. We stayed away from her.

One day, when Mittens was about three, we were sitting in the living room watching TV when the cat came up and started rubbing her face against my mother's shoes. She loved doing that. Mom was wearing that early '70s style of shoe, big and clunky, with thick heels and large hard toes. Mom had her legs stretched out straight in front of her. The cat pushed hard against the toe of the hard shoes rubbing back and forth really hard. At that moment we heard a crack. We looked over and saw the cat lying motionless. Mom screamed, "Oh… something is wrong with the cat! Oh my God!"

Dad ran in. "What the hell happened?"

We all stared at the cat. When she started to get up and move she collapsed. Then she tried again and this time she could not walk frontwards only backwards. She kept falling to the side like a drunk.

Mom yelled, "She must have a concussion from hitting her head on my hard shoe."

The next day we took Mittens to our veterinarian, Dr. Ernest "Ernie" Vandermast. Ernie said that we would have to wait and see if she got any better after the swelling on her brain went down. We got home and told my father. He said, "Poor bastard. She's not gonna make it."

A few days later my father and I went to see Ernie. Mom was so upset she would not come with us. Ernie confirmed that Mittens had not improved much. He advised us to put her down. Dad agreed and we left without her. When we walked into the house without Mittens, my mother walked away and cried. Dad just shook his head and said, "Why does she do this to herself? She gets too attached to every God damn animal we ever had! When is she gonna learn? That God damn cat gets more sympathy than me!"

PETE THE PARROT

Pete the parrot came to us through friends of my mother's. They were travel-minded people who did not have time to take care of him. When we he tried to pet him and talk to him we learned that Pete wasn't friendly. He would flip out whenever we came near. After several months we gave up on him.

He just existed there in his cage in a corner of the kitchen. He was well fed, his cage was cleaned, he was covered with a blanket at night, but other than that we didn't pay attention to him. We had him for about a year before my mother found a little old lady who wanted to take him in.

Mom packed up his food, toys, and blanket and drove him to the woman's house. A couple of weeks later my mother called to see how Pete was doing. As the women talked we heard Mom laugh. Soon we heard her explaining how things had been when Pete was with us: how Dad always sat at the kitchen table correcting papers and chain smoking sometimes until three in the morning. During these sessions Dad talked to himself, swearing at his students' errors in both English and Italian. Now Pete's new owner was describing Pete's foul mouth. At first she'd thought she'd misunderstood him, but now she could clearly hear him say, "Son of bitch! God damn bastard! For Christ's sakes!"

The woman could not make out some of the words—most likely the ones in Italian. Also, Pete coughed excessively leading her to think he had a bad cold. My mother explained that Dad had a smoker's cough, and Pete was probably imitating him. We were all amazed. In over a year we'd never heard a peep out of him.

TOOTSIE

Another nut case was Tootsie. She too preferred my mother over everyone else. Tootsie was a beautiful black, white and yellow marbled cat. The only time she wanted to be held was when my mother was on the telephone. When the telephone rang, Tootsie would run into the kitchen. There she would find my mother, sitting with the phone to her ear. While Mom talked Tootsie would jump into her lap, nesting there as she purred. No one else got this treatment.

Tootsie loved to climb the artificial Christmas tree. Though we tried to stop her, we often came home to a lopsided tree with bent or broken branches. Dad spent one Saturday figuring out how to keep the tree upright by pounding nails over the archways and windows and stretching wire from the tree to the nails. With all this wire the tree looked like a permanent fixture. It resembled one of those string-wrapped pictures of a ship. When my mother saw all the wire, she yelled at Dad, "Do you have to go overboard with everything you do? It looks tutto stutto [all messed up]!" Dad replied, "Let that bastard try knocking it over now!"

Every night Dad sent Tootsie to the basement and every morning he went down to the basement to wash and let Tootsie upstairs. A couple of times a week Dad would find Tootsie had gotten into my mother's coiled cotton in the beauty salon. Tootsie liked to chew on the long strands of cotton hanging out of the large box on the floor. This was cotton Mom put over her customers' ears to keep the hairdryers from burning them. We tried to make sure no cotton was left out, but Tootsie always found some. It made her sick. For a few days she would be lethargic, then Dad would find a big piece of puked-up food crusted with long strands of cotton on the basement floor in the morning. This went on for years.

One morning my father found Tootsie dead on the cellar floor. Dad came up the cellar stairs to the kitchen door and yelled to me, "Nancy! Nancy! Come here! Make sure your mother stays upstairs for a few minutes. Don't let her come down in the basement. The God damn cat ate her last piece of cotton! Fungool! [slang for f..k" Dad went back down, scooped Tootsie up in a blanket and took her out to the garage. When he came back in he said to my mother, "Have you had enough? Jesus Christ! Basta! [Enough!]" Dad buried Tootsie in the corner of the backyard.

SADIE

Sadie was a marbled black, yellow and white cat that Mom brought home. When Dad saw her he said, "This is it!"

Sadie was another strange cat. No one could hold her and she ran from the fast-moving grandchildren. In the living room Sadie took Grandmother Gioconda's favorite stuffed chair for her own. This had always been my chair. Mom placed an old blanket over it and Sadie would lie there all day, leaving it covered with white cat hair. One day the priest from St. Joseph's Church came in, and sat down in Sadie's chair. Mom and I looked at each other, both thinking: *This guy's black clothes are going to be covered in white cat hair!* After a while he got up to leave. He gave us a blessing, then turned to walk to the door, his whole backside white with cat hair. As Mom shut the door behind him we both broke out laughing. "Poor bastard!" Mom said. "Wait until he takes his clothes off and sees that mess of hair all over the back of them."

Sadie lived for quite a few years before she developed some type of kidney and bladder problems and she had to be put to sleep. Another traumatic animal event and another burial in the backyard.

Helping Others

ORPHANAGE

Mom was always willing to help the less fortunate. One Christmas she and her sister, Angie, each decided to take in a child from a local orphanage. She convinced my father about how great it would be to give this little girl a wonderful Christmas.

Johnnie, Armand Jr. and I didn't really care, until Mom walked in with this thin, pale, unhappy-looking little girl. Mom said, "Kids, say hello to Kathy." We all said, "Hello. Can we open up our gifts now?"

There in the living room we all looked at her blankly as she sat very still with her head down.

Dad looked at Mom and said, "Hey? Isabel? Got any other ideas?" We all became quiet as we passed her gifts. As Kathy opened each gift, Mom asked, "Do you like your gift?"

Each time Kathy nodded, then stared at the floor.

Johnnie, Armand Jr. and I started comparing and playing with our new gifts. Kathy was left to sit, watching us, until Mom accused us of ignoring her. I left to help set the table for Christmas dinner, Johnnie retreated to his room and Armand Jr. went to the sunroom to play records. Kathy stood outside the sunroom doorway watching the four-year-old Armand Jr.

Suddenly she started screaming and crying. As Mom and I ran towards the sunroom, Armand Jr. was running out. Mom grabbed the back of his shirt and yelled, "Did you hit her?" Armand Jr. turned and said, "She touched my record player! She's going to break it!" Mom looked at Kathy who was holding her face.

"Did he bite you?" Mom asked.

Kathy lowered her hand. A huge welt surrounded by tooth marks had swollen up on her cheekbone. Mom's face went pale and she hurried Kathy into the kitchen to put ice on her swollen face.

Dad took one look at Kathy, and said, "Now, what are you going to tell them when you take her back with that God damn welt on her face? For Christ's sake! I don't know why you bother, Isabel. Why can't you just let things be instead of worrying about the whole God damn world?"

All through the Christmas dinner, Kathy sat with her head bent down, not saying a word. Later we said our goodbyes, and she left. Mom had to explain the welt to the nuns. We were all glad to see her to go. When Mom came home Dad said, "I hope you're happy. That was a complete disaster!" When Armand Jr. walked into the kitchen, Dad added, "And you! For Christ's sake, what the hell did you bite that little kid for?"

HATS AND MITTENS

Aunt Rose, Aunt Angie and Mom would knit hats and mittens for the poor. They would hold huge rummage sales where they would collect clothes and furniture and contributions. The money went to different organizations serving the needy. The Italian American Community Center would hear about a family that was struggling to make ends meet. Mom and her sisters volunteered their time and efforts alongside other members, making sure the family's needs were met. Dad always had a comment about Mom's volunteering efforts, "Hell…If I was dying, your mother would step over me to help someone else!"

FREE HAIRCUTS

A few streets over from where we lived, Mom knew of a family with four young boys, a father who could never keep a job, and a mother who took care of her bedridden grandmother. Of course, Mom's heart of gold went out to them. She would give the four boys free haircuts, pick up clothes for them at rummage sales and give them clothes my brothers outgrew. Mom loved seeing them in the clothes and shoes she found for them.

Whenever Dad answered the back door and found one of the boys looking up at him saying, "Can Aunt Isabel cut my hair today?" Dad would roll his eyes and reply, "Let me see what 'Aunt Isabel' is doing. Go downstairs and wait." The kid would run downstairs, jump up into the chair, and wait for my mother. The whole way upstairs, Dad would mumble, "'Aunt Isabel' huh! Since when?" When he found Mom he would say, "Hey! One of those damn kids is here to get his cucuzza [squash/head] cut! Why don't they call first? For Christ's sake! How many of them are there? They all look the same!" Mom would go down, happy to see whichever boy it was, leaving Dad to stew. "Everyone loves Aunt Isabel!" he would say. "She's a sucker! When is she ever going to learn to not get involved? Stupido! [stupid one]"

Halloween

Dad never understood Halloween. Why would we want to go around dressed up in weird costumes, taking food from people we didn't even know? But Mom got into it. She helped us find the right clothes then watched us leave, each with a pillowcase, to meet up with our friends. We would be gone for hours.

When we came back home my father would empty our pillowcases onto the kitchen table. Johnnie and I would yell, "Don't touch our stuff! What are you going to do with it?" Dad would put to one side all the candy that was wrapped, then he would dump the unwrapped items in a paper bag. Johnnie and I would watch wondering what Dad was going to do with the bag of candy.

The moment a late trick-or-treater rang the doorbell, Dad turned to us, saying, "You stay here! I will get the door." With that he took the bag of unwrapped candy and dumped it into this last trick-or-treater's bag. When he came back into the kitchen he would smile and say, "That little bastard hit the jackpot!" And we all started laughing.

Dad never bought candy that any of us liked. He would always buy hard candy like Squirrels, MaryJanes, lollipops, and Sugar Daddys—ones that didn't go bad. It drove us crazy. Mom would yell at him, "You cheap bastard! If you had your way, you wouldn't give them anything!" "Ah, non rompere I coglioni! [Don't bust my balls]" Dad would sputter as he walked away ignoring Mom.

No matter how many times we requested chocolate candy bars or any other type of candy that we liked, Dad ignored us. When October came around, Dad would pull out his bag of old candy left over from the previous Halloween. We would all moan in disgust and he would say, "Hey, there is nothing wrong with this candy. It's a little harder, but if they suck on it long enough it will soften! It will keep those little bastards busy for a while."

Our next door neighbors on one side were George and Shirley Russo, and on the other was Margaret Dow, who lived all alone after her father died. Every Halloween Shirley Russo made candied apples but Johnnie and I never got one. It wasn't that we didn't try, but she only made a few. We ate at six, so other kids always beat us to them.

Margaret Dow would only turn her porch light on for an hour for the trick-or-treaters. Mom was so bothered by this that she decided to dress up and go over to Margaret's house and ring the doorbell in the dark. Mom raided Dad's closet area for clothing that was way too big for her. With Dad's oversized boots, gloves, sunglasses and a ski hat she went as a bum. With so much clothing you could not tell who she was. With an empty brown grocery bag she started down the driveway towards Margaret's house. Dad, Johnnie, Armand Jr. and I watched from the living room window as Mom made her way up the unlit porch stairs. She rang the doorbell, waited a few seconds, then rang it again. No answer, Mom rang again. Finally the porch light came on. Margaret opened the door. Mom opened her brown bag, paused as Margaret threw something in, then Mom turned to come back down the stairs. As Mom put her foot on the first step, Margaret turned the porch light off. Mom missed the next step and tumbled down the rest.

Dad, Johnnie, Armand, Jr. and I started laughing hysterically. Mom pulled herself up, grabbed her bag, and stumbled back across the sidewalk to our house. As she came in we ran over to make sure she was all right. Dad shouted, "You could have broken your neck!

Are you all right?" Mom could not stop laughing. As she sat down in the chair, she said, "Look, I peed my pants!"

"I kept ringing the doorbell," Mom told us, "and finally Margaret came to the door. When she opened the door and saw me, she said, 'My, what a big goblin! And you are so persistent! Wait here!' Margaret turned around, walked into her kitchen, grabbed her pocketbook, came back to the door, reached into her pocketbook and threw one lifesaver into my big brown bag."

A few days later when Mom was hanging clothes out on the line she saw Margaret drive up. Mom went over to the fence and asked, "Did you have many trick-or-treaters the other night?"

"No, not really," she said, "but I did have this one big kid come to my house after I had turned the light off. This kid would not stop ringing my doorbell. I finally answered it to make him stop."

Mom never said a word.

Halloween 1972 - Dad surprised me when I threw a Halloween Party at my house and he showed up in my brother's old Army clothes with a Groucho nose, eyebrows and mustache. I opened the front door and he just stood there saying nothing.

Profenno Construction Company

My Grandmother Sabia died, March 23, 1959, I was 12 years old and it became increasingly harder to have us all together for the summer because of our many outside activities and commitments.

Baseball leagues and summer jobs took their toll on the summer months and trips to Camp Sabia. My cousins Donnie and Michael, and my brother, Johnnie, started working summers at the Profenno Construction Company when they were in there early teens. From then on most of our visits to Camp Sabia were only on weekends.

My grandfather, Camillo Profenno, had started the company in 1905. The company earned a great reputation, building King Junior High School, Catherine McAuley High School and high schools in Gardiner, Rumford, Jay, Waterboro and York. They also built Bangor State Hospital, the New England Rehabilitation Center in Portland, and National Guard armories in Sanford, Auburn and Gardiner. Its major projects were not limited to public buildings, but also included the Northeast Bank in Lewiston, the Pepsi Cola Bottling Plant in Portland, the research laboratory at S. D. Warren Company and the Westbrook-Warren Congregational Church, both in Westbrook.

Uncles Dom, Sam, and Dinny (Donato) would put the boys to work digging in the ditches with all the other construction laborers. Johnnie would come home so dirty that my mother would make him strip in the kitchen so that she could put his clothes through the washing machine right away.

Dad would pack my brother a lunch of four sandwiches, two quarts of milk, fruit and some cookies. These weren't thin, white-bread sandwiches. We're talking huge Italian sandwich rolls, filled with salami, provolone and some special ham, or pepper and egg, sausage and peppers, meatballs or meatloaf. Each sandwich was individually wrapped as tight as a drum! My father was always afraid that someone would steal them, so he wrapped in wax paper so tightly that it was hard to get the damn thing out. Sometimes for extra security, he would place them inside of a paper bag and staple all along the top. Then you would hear him say, "There, tutta bene. [All good] That's not falling apart!"

Johnnie managed to get them out. When he got home his lunch pail was always empty.

Dinnertime

Dinner was the only time we all came together as a family. It was usually a fiasco. Whenever one of us kids would reach for something, knocking over a glass of milk, my father would jump up and start yelling, "Mannaggia il diavolo [Damn the devil]. Ah…for Christ's sake! Get the dish towel! What a mess!" He would clear off the table while muttering: "What the hell is wrong with you?" Milk would seep down between the leafs, dripping all over the floor. That sent him into another tantrum. After cleaning up and settling back in his chair, he would place his fist in the middle of his chest, tap fast and say, "Now I have agita! [Heartburn/indigestion]"

What's for dinner?

Nothing irritated Dad more than when one of us came in the kitchen and said, "Dad, what's for dinner?" He would stop, get a disgusted look, and say, "Cazza e cucchiai [shit and spoons]."

One night Johnnie got into it with him. "Dad, I am just asking! God!"

"You don't know what it is like to go without!" Dad yelled back. "For Christ's sake, you would think that I was feeding you garbage! You should be grateful you have a meal to eat every night. All I ever got was a piece of dry, stale bread, if I was lucky!"

"Dad, we are not living in Italy! And besides, that was way back then, you are in America now, remember?"

"Yeah, hmmm, I remember….that's just it."

Waiting for Petite

Whenever one of us refused to eat supper, Dad would get up, grab the plate take it to the refrigerator, put it in, slam the door shut, then come back to the table and sit down. "We will wait for Petite, for he will come," he'd say, while shaking a pointed finger at us. We would say, "Good he can have it… whoever he is." Dad would eat without saying another word to us. Later on, when Johnnie and I would get hungry and we would go to the kitchen. Dad would sneak in from the dining room table where he was always perched correcting his students homework and ask, "What's the matter?" If we said we were hungry he would say, "Hm, I see that Petite has arrived?" And we would say, "Petite who?" Dad would stand there laughing at us for what he really was saying was that our "appetito" [appetite] had arrived. Dad would then take the plate of food from the refrigerator, put it on the kitchen table and say, "Hey Yio! There you go!" As he went back to correcting papers he could hardly keep from laughing.

Johnnie would yell, "I'm not eating that! You eat it! You know Dad, not everyone likes the same food as you. What about more variety… like what my friends eat?"

"You want variety? Then go live with them! For Christ's sake!"

He knew we wouldn't eat what we'd refused at supper, but he got a big kick out of torturing us. It would just "fry my ass" (as he would say) that we refused good food when the less fortunate had none. He would just mutter under his breath, "You're all nuts! Something is wrong with your cucuzza[One's head or squash]. You don't know what it is like to be hungry!"

My favorite picture of Dad.

TATER TOTS

As my brothers and I got older we constantly begged my father to buy the kinds of food that all other kids ate, but if he hadn't grown up eating it, or hadn't acquired a taste for it, he seldom did. He didn't like ketchup, relish, bananas, pickles and mayonnaise, refusing to eat anything "loaded with that stuff!" We begged for Tater Tots. One day he brought some home, baked them up and served them, but we were sorely disappointed that we didn't have ketchup. We folded our arms across our chests and complained. Dad's answer was to heat up a bowl of Luigi's Spaghetti Sauce so we could dunk the Tots in that. When we groaned he said, "What's the matter with you? Now, this is good sauce! Taste it for Christ's sake! Mangia!"(Eat!)

The next time Dad cooked up Tater Tots he called us to supper and when he pulled the Tater Tots out from the oven we all moaned because we knew that there was no ketchup to dip them in. Dad slowly got up from the table and said, "Uno momento [wait a minute]." He opened the door to the pantry, went in and closed the door, came out with something behind his back, sat down at the table, pulled out a bottle of no name brand ketchup and said, "Here you go!" Johnnie and Armand Jr. jumped and screamed for joy for we finally had ketchup and they did not care that it was not Heinz! My father sat there laughing at them and then he said, "Go ahead, load it on, ruin the meal!" as his hands waved up into the air in disgust.

SODA, BOLOGNA, PEANUT BUTTER & HOT DOGS

We also begged for soda, bologna, hot dogs and peanut-butter-and-jelly sandwiches. Our pleas were relentless, but Dad gave in only a little at a time. "Can you buy us some stuff that we like to eat?" we would ask whenever he went to the grocery store. "Why don't you take 'your' money and go get what you want?" he'd say.

But gradually he came around. He even tried some things himself, such as the soft drink, Fresca (when he said the name he pronounced it: "Frrrrrrrresca," exaggerating the "r" and rolling it for a long time.) Sometimes he ate a hotdog with a touch of mustard. He came to chew gum occasionally, and even ate potato chips. He never got used to ketchup, mayonnaise, pickles, or bananas, and he rarely ate away from home unless it was a family event. Even then he usually waited until he returned home, then made himself something to eat.

FLAT AS HELL

Whenever I spent time around Dad in the kitchen he would add his favorite spices, saying how good the meal would taste. He hated anything cooked without plenty of salt, stating that it was, "flat." He would taste his pot of pasta e fagioli [pasta and beans] [slang: pasta fasul] and say, "Flat as hell!" then reach for the salt. He'd never gotten over his memory of his first crossing from Italy to New York. That's when the passengers never got anything cooked with salt because water was rationed. He despised almost any food that was not seasoned with enough salt.

6PM SHARP!

We always ate supper at 6pm. Each spring as the days grew longer we tried to get Dad to serve supper earlier so we could go out and play after dinner. He didn't budge. "We always eat at six," he would say, "and that's the way it is!" When we were called into supper we would tell our friends that we would be back out shortly. "Shortly" often got longer, and when our friends became tired of waiting for us they would come sit on our back steps until we were finished. Hearing them out there, Dad knew that we were itching to join them, but he would go to the door and ask, "What are you doing?" "We're just waiting for Johnnie and Nancy to come out," they would answer. Dad would then say: "You are, are you? Well, they're not coming out! We're in the middle of eating dinner! They will see you tomorrow! Ciao!"

Johnnie and I would ask him, "What did you tell our friends?" He would reply, "I told them that you were eating dinner and you would see them tomorrow." As he said it he always smirked, waving his right hand with a smart-aleck "good-bye" gesture. Johnnie and I would cringe and moan, but Dad just kept eating.

House Rules

These were some of the rules:

1. Lunch and dinner were to be eaten at home, not at a friend's. (If we ever called to ask if we could eat at a friend's house, Dad would immediately say, "No! Hey, you eat here not there! Come home! Capisce? [Understand?]"

2. No surprise guests for lunch or dinner. (Whenever we asked Dad if a friend could stay and eat he gave the same response: "Don't they have a house to eat in?")

3. If you don't like what is cooked for supper, then forget about it! "You can starve!"

4. There will be no sleepovers at our house. (This was not debatable!)

5. You will not be sleeping over anyone else's house. (Out of the question!)

6. Playing is to be done outside not inside (Whenever my brothers and I horsed around inside, Mom would yell, "I just dusted! You're making dust! Stop it!" Dad would come running, the infamous towel slung over his shoulder. "Your mother just dusted! Hey, Basta! Enough!"

7. No borrowing anything at all. "If we don't own it, you don't have one!"

8. No lending of toys or games (Dad brought us up to appreciate our belongings and to take care of them. He always reminded us of how he had nothing as a child and how he worked so hard to get what he had in life).

9. Supper at 6pm sharp! (Dinnertime never changed in the 55 years that Dad cooked supper).

10. When playing outside and Dad whistled for us to come, you better come fast!

11. When it was time to leave IT WAS TIME TO LEAVE! (When Dad got restless or he'd "had enough!" we all moved quickly, except Mom. Dad would get so impatient waiting for her that he would start muttering, "What the hell is she doing in there? Come on, andiamo! Let's go! Basta! She always has to be the last one to leave! Ah, for Christ's sake!" Then he would walk away waving one hand high in the air as if to slap some tall person's face).

12. You don't salt the food Dad cooked. He considered it to be an insult if one got up from the dinner table to get the salt shaker in the cupboard to add more salt to the food he prepared. Johnnie was notorious for getting up and grabbing the salt before he even tasted the food and started shaking the salt shaker rapidly over the whole plate. Dad would sit there and shake his head in disgust.

The Couch/Sofa

Mom's love of antiques had her stopping at every garage sale, rummage sale, and estate auction she could find. Antique furniture filled our house. She squeezed each purchase into whatever space she could find. Dad and I did most of the housework together, and I often heard him mumble, "She's got way too much crap in here! One can't even move around, for Christ's sake!"

Most of the furniture was mahogany. Though it was beautiful it was impossible to keep dust free. I knew this because I was the one that had to dust it. The item that got the most use was her beloved Victorian Sofa. She'd picked it up when she and Dad first got married. With its beautiful tapestry covering it looked stunning. The only problem was that it was far too small to lie down on. Its armrests alone took up space, spiraling under it. A strip of ornate wood ran along the back so you could not rest your head there. If three people sat on it that was a crowd. For a family with children it was basically useless.

When one of us was sick Mom would cover it with a sheet so we could lie there, with a puke bowl under our chin, watching television. For some reason the sofa became the place to recoup. When we were little it seemed huge; as kids we could even stretch out fully. Then we got older and bigger, and soon it became difficult to put our feet up. You had to lie on your side or have your feet stuck up in the air over the rolled arms. Mom would lay on it in a fetal position, her neck all twisted, and her legs tucked under her.

One time when Dad called us for dinner, we heard Mom yelling from the living room, "Hey, I can't move. Somebody help me!" We found her stuck, twisted like a pretzel and unable to move. Apparently she had been in this position for some time so Dad moved her slowly, a little at a time. As she finally sat up, Dad muttered, "What the hell is wrong with you? You know you can't recline on this damn thing! Hey, it sure looks good though! And we all know how important that is!"

Homework and School Projects

Homework was always a challenge because my Dad would take over the minute we sat down to do it. He would stand over you, reading everything you wrote, correcting you as you went along. Whenever we didn't understand something he got upset. When we made mistakes he would say, "You are not using your cucuzza [one's head/squash]." If we did our homework without him he would correct it after we went to bed. He would wake us up early the next morning, saying, "Come on, you got some work to do. Let's go. Andiamo! [go]" Then we would crawl downstairs half awake to do it over correctly. No other kid we knew had to do homework twice.

Johnnie and Dad would argue about this. "So what if it has mistakes!" Johnnie would yell. But my father was too much of a perfectionist to allow us to hand in homework with errors. He might shake his head, but he would not give up on us.

I would labor for hours over a book report, but just when I thought I was done, Dad would come by. As he would read it I would cringe. I knew I would have to do it over. After spending all evening writing it over he would finally say "we" were finished. Only then could I go to bed.

The next morning as I would come down to the dining room table I would find that I had a report cover, drawn and colored to look like the cover of the book. Dad would spend most of the night drawing this on construction paper, then he used that to replace my scribbled cover. I would run down the cellar stairs screaming to him that he was the best Dad in the world. He would smile and say, "You're going to get an 'A' for sure."

Optical Illusion

Dad took over Armand Jr.'s fifth grade science project. Armand Jr. had seen optical illusions in the National Geographic Magazine and decided to put on a demonstration. Dad got right into it, explaining how to take a pencil, poke it through a paper plate that was half one color, and half another. When the plate spun fast enough the colors would appear to merge into a single shade.

Dad disappeared into the basement and a few minutes later he emerged with a motor salvaged from my mother's old clothes dryer.

Dad started gathering pieces of wood to make a stabilizing mount for the motor. When he plugged it in it sounded like an engine for a small plane, but that didn't stop him. He cut circular pieces of cardboard and, under his direction, Armand Jr. attached the different color combinations, punching a hole in each center, and pushing the circles onto a pin sticking out from the motor. Dad turned the motor on, spinning the circle, and merging the colors.

It was simply mind-blowing to see the effort Dad put into these projects.

The optical illusion project proved to be a bit heavy. The motor weighed over ten pounds, cumbersome for a young boy who had to carry it to school. Using an old leather strap, Dad rigged up a strong handle so the motor could be carried easily. Just to be sure nothing happened to the project, Dad drove Armand Jr. to school that day.

Armand Jr.'s presentation mesmerized his whole class. The kids were amazed at the motor, the spinning, and the colors changing right there in front of them. Kids in the front row had wind blowing on them as if they were sitting in front of a fan. Classmates shouted out different color combinations to try. Needless to say, Armand Jr. got an "A." That made Dad happy.

*Dad stored the optical illusion project in his basement and he presented it to his grandchildren some 20 years later when they needed a project for school. It sits in my basement to this day waiting for another "A".

Deering High School, Portland High School & Wentworth

BRODIES

Johnnie's time at Deering High School often seemed like a disaster for him and my father. Johnnie was a bit of a daredevil who loved to entertain his friends. One November day, while Dad was in a classroom teaching Spanish, Johnnie was out on the football field doing "brodies" with my father's car. (brodie: a severe vehicular skid) The Principal came into my father's classroom and told him what Johnnie was doing. Johnnie had his friends draped onto the hood of the car as he drove in circles to make them fall off.

How had Johnnie started Dad's car? He'd forced another Ford sedan key into the ignition. They finally stopped him, but that wasn't enough for Dad. When he and Johnnie got home Dad couldn't stop yelling. It was so embarrassing; he could have ruined the car, or even killed one of his friends! Johnnie wasn't upset. He got Dad worked up to the point where Dad took off his belt like he was going to hit Johnnie. Johnnie ran around the dining room table yelling, "Catch me if you can, Dad. Come on Babalu." This got Dad laughing and yelling at the same time. "Look you bastard!" he shouted. "If I get a hold of you....Va Fagool!" Laughter defused Dad's anger.

Johnnie took my father's Spanish class—another big mistake! Dad failed him. As Dad sat correcting homework papers at the kitchen table he would come to Johnnie's work, and, as he corrected it, he would get so upset. The following year he begged Johnnie not to take Spanish II. I think the day Johnnie graduated was better for Dad than it was for Johnnie.

PORTLAND HIGH

By 1962, when I was starting high school, the City of Portland tried to solve an overcrowding problem by drawing district lines for each of the two high schools, Deering High School and Portland High School. In this new plan, I would go to Portland High School. After my brother's experience at Deering High School, I felt this was for the best. This was true even though I now had to wait for the bus, even on mornings of snow, sleet, or rain. Portland High School was no easier. My teachers still knew my father. But, I was the "good child" and people knew I would never do anything to disgrace my family— especially my father.

JOSE

In 1962, Johnnie started at Wentworth Technical Institute in Boston. It was wonderful to have him and his teasing gone. His first year at Wentworth proved to be a big fat social event. When my parents drove down to meet with the Dean they were greeted by students saying how much fun they had with their son "Jose." My father was completely bewildered. He soon caught on that "Jose" was Johnnie. Johnnie had won election as class president, largely because he instigated so many fun activities. His classmates praised his social ability, saying he was always there to help them out. When, after a year, it became clear that "Jose" was having too much fun, he left Wentworth Institute and moved back home. That fall he attended Southern Maine Vocational Technical College for a two-year course in Building Construction Technology. After graduating in 1966 he got a job working for the State of Maine in their Highway Engineering Department and married his high school sweetheart, Jane Baade. They lived in an apartment in Yarmouth, Maine. Dad said, "One down, two to go."

St. Joseph's Church

We always attended Saint Joseph's Church. That's where we all made our first communions, and that was where we went for Sunday Mass. My parents preferred the 11:30am High Mass with the Latin and choir. We found this long Mass to be sheer torture.

During the school year, through six grade, we had to attend the 8am Mass. We sat with the other children in the first few pews, monitored by a nun who always pursed her lips and regarded us with distain. When Mass was over, we marched from church to St. Joseph's School on the other side of the parking lot. There we had another hour in Catechism classes. In those days Catholics couldn't eat anything in the two hours prior to receiving communion. My family was always running late on Sunday morning so we would forego breakfast.

Knowing we would be hungry after Mass, Dad would secretly meet Johnnie and me outside of the church. We would run to Dad's car by the school where he would have a thermos of coffee, a donut or a couple of Royal Lunch crackers waiting for us. He would feed us quickly and then pack up and say he would be back to pick us up in an hour.

THE CONFESSIONAL

Twice a year, usually at Christmastime and Easter, we had to go to confession. Johnnie and I dreamed up things that would shock the priest. Confession took two hours, most of it spent waiting in one of two long lines that formed on each side of the church.

Finally Johnnie just plain refused to go to confession. After that Dad would drop Armand Jr. and me off at St. Joseph's, usually on the Saturday before the holiday. One Saturday, before Christmas, when Armand Jr. was eight or nine, Dad dropped us off for confession. I stood behind Armand Jr. in a line of about 50 people. The line moved ever so slowly. One by one, the people went in, confessed, then emerged. From there they went to the front pews to say their penance, usually a few prayers. Two hours passed. Armand Jr. got restless.

Finally, as our turns approached, Armand Jr. turned to me and whispered, "Nancing? I have to pee!" In a stern whisper I said, "You gotta be kidding me? We're not going anywhere now!"

Again looking up at me, he said, "Nancing? I have to go pee. I can't hold it!" Determined to ignore his emergency I whispered, "You'll have to hold it! You're up next! I told you, we're not going anywhere!" He turned and leaned against the wall, his head bowed, half crying. Finally, it was his turn to enter the confessional booth. I pushed him forward towards the door, "Get in there!" He opened the door and slowly went inside. I stood leaning against the wall waiting for him to confess his sins and emerge. As I looked around, bored to death, my eyes widened. A stream of fluid was seeping from under the confessional door. Staring at the growing puddle, my mind raced.

After an eternity the door opened. Armand Jr. came out, a look of horror on his face. He walked like a stickman, his pants soaked with pee. I grabbed him, and pointed to the pew next to the confessional booth.

"Sit!" I said, "I mean, stand there! And don't move until I come out!" He put his head down and cried.

Stepping over the stream of pee, I carefully got into the confessional and closed the door behind me. I reached down and touched the cloth on the kneeler. It was soaked with pee. I panicked! I crouched over, trying not to collapse into the pool of urine. I got my face near the little window so that the priest could tell someone was there. I was held up by stretching my hands from the closed door to the inside wall. It was the fastest confession in history. Finishing, I ran out, grabbed Armand Jr. and left the church.

Outside Dad was waiting in the car. I opened the door to the car and shouted to Dad, "He pissed all over the floor in the confessional! It was so embarrassing! I didn't know what to do!" Grabbing Armand Jr. by the back of his jacket, I opened the back door to the car and yelled, "Get in!" Dad shouted, "Hey! For Christ's sake don't sit on the seat! You kneel on the floor of the car until we get home!" I climbed into the front seat and Dad started the car. Halfway home Dad turned to me smirking. "I pity those poor bastards that have to use that confessional. Boy are they in for a big surprise!"

The Piano

One afternoon I walked into the den to ask Armand Jr. a question and noticed my beautiful Steinway piano was missing. I started screaming for Dad who was down in the basement in his little office/work shop room, "Dad? Dad?" I yelled running down the stairs, "What happened to my piano? Where is it?" Dad looked up. "Ah, for Christ's sake, you never played it anymore! So, I took it all apart! We need the space." I yelled back, "Where is it?" With a sheepish grin he said, "Look in the garage."

There I found several large boxes each with pieces of my piano. Dad had taken the whole piano apart, piece-by-piece. He was going to put it out a little at a time each trash day. He wasn't about to pay to have it hauled away. I was crying, and as I turned around I saw him looking at me through the basement window. He had one raised eyebrow, half a smile and his eyes were partially closed. He was holding back a satisfied laugh. It was the look that always made my brothers and me shiver in frustration. I went back inside to ask Mom how she could let him destroy my beautiful Steinway piano.

Mom shrugged, "Go ask your father why he did it. You know how stubborn he is especially when he gets his mind made up to do something." I couldn't bring myself to even talk to Dad, so I went up to my room and threw myself on the bed and cried.

I later learned that Armand Jr. had helped Dad take the piano apart. Armand Jr. had his nose right up Dad's butt the whole time. He was intrigued by all the strings. "Wow, look at all those strings! What are you going to do with them?" Armand Jr. asked Dad.

Dad waved his arms in the air and said, "Get out of the way! I'll show you what I am going to do with them!" Then Dad took a huge wire cutter and started cutting the strings one by one. With each cut a string would snap apart, fly up, and make a "boinging" sound.

For the next several weeks each night before trash pickup Dad would go out to the garage and hide pieces of the piano among our household trash. He dragged the heavy boxes of parts down to the curb. The next morning he always got up early to watch from the window, laughing as the trash men struggled with those boxes. Then he would turn and say, "Now that's the way to get rid of it. Let those poor bastards lug it away." He would chuckle and walk away, beaming with great satisfaction.

Never You Mind

Dad had everything he needed in his basement room. It was his getaway. His big mahogany desk was stacked with notes he'd written to himself. He had a stapler, and an old Russell Stover Candy Box filled with pens, pencils, erasers, paper clips and elastics. On the left side of the desk sat the big black Underwood typewriter that weighed about fifty pounds. He'd used it to type many things, including all of the invoices for the Napoli Restaurant. No one was allowed to touch that typewriter.

Along one side was a workbench. A peg board hung over it holding every type of hammer, pliers, screwdriver, wrench, wire cutter, extension cords, and all sizes of bungee cords imaginable. On the bench were glass jars filled with nails, nuts, bolts and washers. Tacks and small brads were stored in plastic Herb-Ox bouillon jars, their covers marked appropriately. Whenever he dismantled anything he kept the parts, "just in case".

Dad never liked to be questioned about what he was doing, especially if he knew it would upset Mom or one of us kids. If he was in the midst of a project and one of us asked, "Hey, Dad? What are you doing?" He always would say, "Never you mind." He would continue to work, while ignoring you. Eventually we tired of watching him and left. Mom would ask us, "What is your father doing down there?" One of us would reply, "I don't know." Finally she would go down to the basement, only to come up and hear us ask, "What is Dad doing?" Mom would shrug her shoulders and say, "I don't know."

Pizziola

One fall weekend Johnnie decided that he was going hunting with some of his senior high school friends. Dad went ballistic. "It's bad business! For Christ's sake, you have never gone hunting before let alone handled a gun! You know people mistake other people for a deer and get shot to death?"

Johnnie insisted, "Dad, I know what I am doing! I will be careful!"

Dad paced around the kitchen table, shaking his head, "Yeah! You will be careful! It's bad business to go out in the woods and not know what the hell you are doing! There are a lot of dead people that knew what they were doing too!"

Johnnie borrowed some hunting gear and a shotgun, and left. All day Dad paced, mumbling, "I am so worried about that kid!" When Johnnie came back he was excited that he'd shot a rabbit. Johnnie placed the rabbit in the driveway by the garage door and ran in to tell Dad what he had shot. Dad's response was, "What the hell are you going to do with a rabbit? I'll tell you one thing, you can't leave it in the driveway. It will start to stink and rot."

"I know Dad. I already gutted it out in the woods, its okay." said Johnnie.

"Yeah, well, let me tell you something. You need to skin it and cut it up. What the hell were you thinking when you shot the damn thing anyway, it was going to clean itself?"

Johnnie stared back, with a serious look on his face, and said, "I was thinking pizziola!" (Pizziola is a style of cooking meat or chicken with fresh tomato and spices.)

Dad couldn't stop laughing, "I'll pizziola you!" Dad knew the rabbit would sit there until he did something with it. As Dad went out to get the rabbit he swore under his breath, "Mannaggia il diavolo! [Damn the devil!] That kid is going to drive me crazy!"

As he grabbed the rabbit our next door neighbor, George Russo, called, "Armand, what are you going to do with that rabbit?"

Dad replied, "I'm going to clean it and cut it up. Why? Do you want the meat?"

George did not hesitate, "Yeah, if you are not going to eat it Shirley and I will."

Dad was happy to give it away, "I'll be over when I'm finished George." Dad headed back down to his basement workroom. After lining the floor with newspapers, he hung the rabbit up on a hook from the ceiling. He laid out an assortment of knives, tools and saws and began to butcher the rabbit. When he was done he walked across the yard and gave all the meat to George Russo.

Bad Business

"Bad business" was a phrase that Dad always used if something was not quite ethical, realistic, feasible, or if someone just wasn't thinking. For instance:

It was "bad business" to "take a dump" and not flush before using the toilet paper. That could plug up the toilet. That meant Dad had to come in the bathroom, yelling, "How many times do I have to tell you to flush first? What the hell is wrong with you? Get out of the way! I'll do it! For Christ's sake!" The rule was, "Always double flush, once without paper, then with paper." Dad made sure we all knew the rule about fixing this: Break it up with a hanger. The hanger was kept in the corner of the downstairs bathroom. When referring to these rules Dad would always announce, "I am not snaking out anything!"

It was "bad business" to fill up with liquids before and/or during supper.

It was "bad business" to let your gas tank go below ½ a tank in the wintertime because it just might freeze the gas line overnight and, "You won't be going anywhere!"

It was "bad business" not to have a spare car key tucked away in your wallet in case you locked yourself out of your car. Dad thought whoever had invented the little black magnetized car key box for the underside of the car, was a genius.

It was "bad business" to not have a shovel, oil, windshield solvent, bungie cords, rope, blanket, rags, an empty gas can, antifreeze and a small pail of sand stored in the trunk of one's car. You never know when you might need one of these items.

It was "bad business" not to have your car tuned up every fall in preparation for the long, cold winter. Faithfully Dad would take his car to the mechanic to have it "winterized." This meant having the oil and filter changed, antifreeze checked, studded snow tires, and the front tires rotated.

It was "bad business" not to close and lock all your first floor windows before bed or before leaving the house. Criminals could easily climb through an unlocked window. He made no exceptions, even if it was summer and 90 degrees. Sweat it out or get robbed!

It was "bad business" to have too much to drink or to follow the crowd. "Are you stupid?"

It was "bad business" not to be prepared for a storm. Always have a flashlight, batteries, canned food and candles easily accessible.

It was "bad business" not to have some cash on you when you left the house. You never knew when you might need to call home or take a cab. "Remember! You can't do anything without some money in your pocket!"

It was "bad business" not to have extra food in case company came for dinner.

It was "bad business" to try to take a left, without a light, on to Washington Avenue from Shaw's unless you drove around to the entrance that had a traffic light.

It was "bad business" to put your trash out the night before because the "hawks" (it was really the crows) and other animals would get into it and strew it all over the neighborhood.

It was "bad business" to mix different alcoholic drinks. If you start with one drink you have to stay with it. Never change from hard liquor to beer or wine or vise versa. You will get deathly sick.

It was "bad business" if you did not clear your windshield and car windows properly after a snowstorm. You should be able to see through every window clearly. Whenever he saw someone who'd cleared a little hole to peek through, he would say, "Look at that moron! Yeah, peek-a-boo to you!"

It was "bad business" to fail to take the time to brush the snow off the roof of the car. When the inside of the car heated up, the rooftop got warm, causing melting snow to slide forward over the windshield in one large mass when you applied your breaks. This was deemed to be, "Very, very, bad business!"

It was "bad business" if you didn't break down the trash. In other words, "Tear it up for Christ's sake!" Instead of using ten bags Dad would sit down on a kitchen chair and go through all the week's trash and re-tear it into minuscule pieces. He'd shove it into one bag saying, "I'll fix them bastards! Those damn bags are too expensive. I will make it all fit in one!"

It was "bad business" to not dry your hair completely, especially if you were leaving the house. Dad insisted that you would get a "calpo d'aire" meaning a punch of cold air would give you a sore throat or cold.

It was "bad business" to take back a gift given in good faith because of ill feelings. If you give someone a gift and they get pissed off at you and return it in anger, that gift can never be brought back into your house, or any relative's house. It holds bad karma.

It was "bad business" to give someone the sign for the evil eye (malocchio) unless you really meant it. This is a hand sign where one extends the pinkie and index finger, while keeping the other fingers folded back, then gestures in a downward motion. It is supposed to bring misfortune. It also can be used to ward off evil spirits others have cast upon you. If you hold your hand up in front of you, with the fingers pointed up, it means that your spouse is having an affair. There is also a charm in the shape of a horn (il corno) to wear around your neck to help eliminate evil curses.

It was "bad business" to hang a horseshoe upside down for your luck would run out. The same principle applied to elephant figurines that had their trunks in a downward position. This was deemed to be bad luck.

Pierre's School of Cosmetology

When I graduated high school in 1966, my dream was to go to Pierre's School of Cosmetology and be a hairstylist like my mother. My Dad was not happy about this. He wanted me to go to work in the telephone company or become a schoolteacher. Those were secure jobs with great benefits. When I didn't want to take either of his suggestions he finally made a deal with me. He said, "Do me a favor and I will do you a favor. Attend Plus Grey's Business College for one year, and at the end of that year, if you are still interested in going to

Pierre's, I will pay your tuition." It sounded like a good deal to me. I had no money so I figured that I would give it a try and see what would happen. Grey's Business College was uptown so I could still live at home and attend classes during the day.

That September, when I started business classes at Plus Grey's, I met several wonderful girls from the Jay-Farmington area of Maine. I studied hard, got good grades, and my Dad was proud that I was giving it my all. But as soon as the year was over I went to Dad and said, "Dad, remember what you said to me about going to Plus Grey's?"

He gave me a worried look and said, "Yes?"

"Well, I think I would like to go to Pierre's in the fall."

Looking over his glasses, which were down to the tip of his nose, he said, "Well, you kept your end of the deal so I guess I will have to keep mine."

Dad didn't like my decision, but what could he do? He had made a promise and he had to come through for me. In the fall of 1967 he reluctantly registered me and I started Pierre's School of Cosmetology. It was run by a wonderful married couple, Pierre (Nicholas) and Dot Koutsivitis.

On my first day at Pierre's each student was given a large case with a handle. It contained a set of rollers, a hundred metal clips to hold the rollers in place and to make pin curls, cutting and styling scissors, a styling razor, thinning shears, a straight comb and a rat-tail comb. When I brought this case home to show my Mom and Dad, Dad immediately took it downstairs to his work shop to put my name on the inside of the case, "Gimme that damn thing! I'll make sure no one steals anything from you!"

After two hours, I started to wonder just what the hell Dad was doing down in his workshop. As I entered his "little haven" I noticed that every roller, hair clip, and all the cutting instruments and combs were laid out in a line on his work bench, "Dad? What are you doing with all my stuff?"

"I am making sure no one steals any of it."

He grabbed a pair of the scissors and said, "Look! I made three notches with this file on the inside of the handle. Everything has three small notches scratched into it so that you can tell that they are yours. And I did every one of the hundred clips too!" I could not believe my eyes. He actually took each individual clip, and ran a steel file across one end to make three small lines so that I could identify my hair equipment.

A little while later Dad came upstairs. "There you go! No one can lie to you about not taking your stuff. You can prove that it is yours if anything is missing."

Mom was sitting at the kitchen table reading the newspaper. She looked up, "All you need to do is use red nail polish to mark all of that stuff. That is what we used to do when I was in hairdressing school."

Dad's head spun around so fast, "Yeah, nail polish, my ass! That stuff will come off over time when it comes in contact with all the solutions and wet hair. You don't know what you're talking about!" He proceeded to open the case to show Mom what he had done.

Mom looked up from the paper, took a glance at his masterful work. "Hmmm," she said, then continued to read the paper.

The next day I went off to school with my equipment case. All my tools were marked with three lines, giving me the satisfaction of knowing that, if something was mysteriously missing, I could prove what equipment were mine. It was always comforting knowing that Dad was so protective of us and all our belongings.

In Training

Without me knowing, Mom taught me her job at the funeral home. When the elder Hutchins died, the Funeral Home was taken over by Allie Hutchins and his wife Joanne. They moved the family business to Williams Street and with the help of their three boys, Matthew, Michael and Mark they kept it going. Mom was "on call" for them. We had only one car, so there were times that I would drop her off and go back to pick her up. Most times there were viewings, visits, or other funeral business going on, so Mom would not allow me to beep the horn to let her know I was there. Instead I would park and go inside to see if she was ready. She would take me downstairs to show me the work she had done and explain what she had to do to make the people look "nice." Sometimes she would have me help her fix the hair or ask my opinion about the way the person looked. It didn't bother me. I grew up knowing that my mother loved doing this job and she was damn good at it.

MEETING DELORES (MULLY)

I was never so happy as I was that first day when I walked into Pierre's. I saw all the equipment and chemicals lined up on the shelves, and watched the students cutting, drying, shampooing hair. Customers were coming and going through the front door. I was in my glory! This was exactly what I wanted. I passionately loved every minute of it.

On the very first day of class I met Delores Pizzo, aka "Mully" (the nickname I gave to her), and we became inseparable. Not many of the new students were good enough to be placed on the floor working on customers, but we were ready, and, between learning and thinking up pranks to play on the other students, we had one helluva good time.

Dad wasn't interested in what I was learning, but Mom was enthralled with it all. On weekends Mully would come over to my house. Mom, Mully and I would go down into the beauty shop and spend all day bleaching our hair different colors. Every week we would have a new style and color. Dad would roll his eyes and say, "That's different." He really left us alone to do what we wanted. He would only comment on my hair if I cut it too short; he loved my hair long. He would say, "Well, well, girlie!" and shake his head, looking at Mom for her reaction. If Mom was okay with it, Dad was too.

It was customary at that time to wear sterile-looking white uniforms and white nursing shoes. I started Pierre's in September wearing a size 16 uniform; by January, I was in a size 4. Dad gave me money to buy new uniforms and Mully and I went to the Uniform Shop uptown. I stayed in the dressing room while Mully handed me uniforms over the top of the stall. She started with a size 14—too big; size 12 followed—too big. Size 10 was too big, as were sizes 8 and 6.

Finally Mully exclaimed, "What the hell, you're as small as me!" With that she threw me a size 4. It fit perfectly. When I stared at myself in the mirror I could not believe my eyes. I finally realized how much weight I had lost.

Dad would get upset when I would come home from school at 6pm night after night and fall asleep on the couch. Several times during the evening he would come into the living room and say, "Hey? Come and eat something. You have to eat, girlie." He would check on me again at 8, then at 9, then 10, and finally at 11. That's when Dad would finally help me up off the couch, saying, "Come on, let's go. It's time for bed!" I would drag myself off the couch, climb the stairs and throw myself into bed, then start all over again the next morning. After doing this for four straight months, I'd lost so much weight that Dad insisted that Mom take me to the doctors to make sure I was still healthy. I was.

Riding the Laundry Truck

Hair was my life. I could not wait to get back to school and start learning again. Mully and I were naturals. We knew we were good, and we started building a regular clientele. We were also the class clowns, always getting into trouble.

One day when the delivery man left the linen truck running, while he loaded up the stock room with towels, Mully dared me to drive the truck around the block. All it took was her egging me on. The next thing I knew I was behind the wheel, with Mully hanging out the door yelling, "Hey Munga, [a nickname she gave me] you have plenty of room on this side!" I drove that damn truck down an alley that was barely wide enough for it. I had a hard time maneuvering, but managed to get through and turned onto State Street. We went up State Street to Congress Street, then stopped at the school's back door. The driver stood on the back steps, staring in disbelief. Laughing hysterically, we jumped out of the truck and ran back into the school.

There we came face-to-face with the head instructor, Hilda Brooks. She took one look at us and said, "You are both expelled for a week! Go home!" Mully and I looked at each other and smugly said, "Okay. See ya!" And we left.

When Mully and I arrived at my house my mother asked, "What are you girls doing home so early?" We told her and she laughed, but added, "I know this was a joke, but make sure you are not rude to people, or do anything hurtful."

We hadn't been home long when the telephone rang. It was Hilda calling to speak to my mother. "I want Nancy and Delores back first thing in the morning. And make sure they are not late! They have customers booked early. Pierre and Dot will be back from California and they will handle how the two of them will be punished." My mother promised to make sure we were back bright and early. She said she would talk to us about our prank. She assured Hilda it wouldn't happen again.

Smug as ever, Mully and I walked into Pierre's the next morning. Most of our classmates—and even Hilda—said that they had actually enjoyed our escapade. They were laughing hysterically about it. They couldn't believe that we had stolen the truck. Hilda had already told Pierre and Dot, so Mully and I stood in front of all of them, awaiting our punishment. To our surprise there was none—just a speech from Pierre. "Now girls," he said, "you could have gotten hurt or you could have hurt someone else. I do not want you to do anything like that again. You understand, jelly bean? And when the delivery man comes back next week you need to apologize to him."

Then the overhead loud speaker came on, "Those of you that are in class all morning, please head downstairs. Those of you on the floor this morning, come get your patrons." That was it.

Everyday at Pierre's was the same for Mully and me. Each day we tried to think of some type of joke to pull on someone. It wasn't something we worked at. It came naturally. We thought the same way. Most of it was good pure fun. We never did anything hurtful.

SILVIO

There was a handsome student from Italy named Silvio. Many of the girls swooned over him and his sexy Italian accent. One day Mully and I collected hair off the floor from a patron who'd just had her long locks cut off. We had two bunches of hair over a foot long. Mully laid back in one of the shampoo chairs. She put the two long tresses under her armpits so they looked like massive growths of underarm hair. She yelled, "Silvio, do you think I look beautiful now?" Silvio rolled his eyes, jerked his head up in the air and walked away. Everyone else laughed hysterically, including Dot and Pierre.

SCHLOSBERG FURRIERS

Next door to Pierre's was Schlosberg Furriers where a huge picture window faced Congress Street. It displayed mannequins clothed with real furs. One lunch hour Mully and I went over there to try on some furs. Once we each had a beautiful fur on, we looked at each other and both got the same thought at the same time: *jump up in the picture window and model them.* With Mully on one side and me on the other, we each struck a pose and stood, unmoving.

Congress Street had plenty of foot traffic during lunch hour. As people walked by they would glance at the display. Whenever someone stopped to stare, Mully and I moved ever so slightly. The people watching would jump in disbelief, their startled faces showing their doubts. Had a mannequin moved? Stifling our laughter, we posed for our entire lunch hour. Soon everyone back at school heard what we were doing and came over to see for themselves.

Finally the women at Schlosberg's got mad and told us to stop. "Those furs are too expensive to be fooling around with!" they said. From that point on we were banned from patronizing Schlosberg's.

SOULE'S CANDY KITCHEN

Two doors down from Pierre's was Soule's Candy Kitchen, where Mully and I, and most of the other students, got breakfast every morning. Every day we each got a hot chocolate and a grilled English muffin wrapped in wax paper. We took our orders back to the school lunchroom to eat. They didn't clean their grill properly, and every day my English muffin had a thick piece of blackened grease stuck to it. I picked off this black stuff, leaving the muffin looking as if it hadn't been grilled at all. After putting up with this for months, one morning when Ann, the owner and cook, asked me what she could get me, I blurted out, "Oh! I'll have an English muffin with a side order of grill!"

Ann went ballistic. Mully was pissing herself laughing while Ann screamed at me, "Get out of here! Don't you ever come back in here!" Mully and I walked out laughing.

After that for weeks I would send Mully to get my breakfast. Ann knew, and would ask Mully, "Are you buying this for Nancy?"

"No," Mully would say. "I am very hungry today!"

One morning, weeks after the incident, Mully told me that Ann missed me, and wanted me to come in the next morning. I was stunned! How could this be? So, I went in the next morning like nothing had ever happened. I placed my order as usual (without the snide remarks, of course) and Ann informed me that she had cleaned the grill. She said she was sorry for yelling at me. She even said she missed me. How about that? And for the rest of the school year I never had a piece of blackened grill on my English muffin again.

MANICURE & FACIALS

Every Saturday night I would practice manicures and facials on Armand Jr., Mom, and Dad. After dinner I would have them all sit at the kitchen table, pin back their hair off their foreheads, and mix up all these different facemasks. We would all laugh hysterically as they sat there with green paste all over their faces, waiting for it to dry. After removing the mask I would evaluate their skin and advise them as to what they should be doing to enhance their complexion. Dad would just roll his eyes and say, "Get outta of here! I don't have time to do all that shit!"

DAD'S HAIR

Mom always cut Dad's hair, but once I had learned how to use electric clippers, I wanted to try it. "Hey, what the hell can happen?" he said. "It will grow again."

As I put the cape around his neck and proceeded to grab the comb and clippers, he yelled, "Get your mother down here now! She needs to monitor you." As soon as I started to comb and touch his beautiful wavy hair, he fell asleep. I went to town, cutting and clipping his hair. He didn't wake up until I nudged him. He opened his eyes, looked in the mirror, and smiled, saying, "Pretty good job Nancy. Perfecto! Can you shampoo it for me too?" I was so happy that he liked his haircut, and now he wanted me to shampoo his hair too.

During the shampoo he fell asleep again. I noticed a little grey around his temples, and decided to give him a henna rinse. I'd seen my mother give henna rinses hundreds of times. I grabbed a bottle of black henna dye, mixed it in a bowl of hot water, and combed it into my father's hair. I covered the grey at his temples really well. When I was done I combed his hair back, placed a hair net over his head, and put him under the dryer. Ten minutes later I took off his hair net and told him that he was all done. He thanked me and went up stairs to correct papers.

I didn't say anything about what I had done. It was night, so my mother didn't notice. It really didn't look that different...or so I thought.

The next morning Dad got up for school, and went down to his private basement bathroom to wash. Dad liked to lean over the bathroom sink and throw water onto his hair before he combed it so that his beautiful waves would dry into place. That morning, as water dripped down his face, he noticed it was black.

The next thing I knew I heard him swearing, "Mannaggia il diavolo! [Damn the devil] What the hell did she do? Jesus Christ Almighty! I gotta go to school! Nannnnnnncy?" I ran downstairs. When we met at the bottom, I burst out laughing. The towel around his neck was covered with black henna.

He screamed at me, and made me shampoo his hair again and again, until all the henna was out. I promised to never do that again. At the end of the day, when he got back from school, I thought for sure he was going to bring it up again, but he never did.

For the rest of Dad's life I cut his hair. He trusted me completely with his beautiful waves, and I enjoyed our time together. "Hey, I gotta get a haircut!" he would say, as if he were going out to see a barber. I loved that. He always fell asleep the minute I touched his head.

Scarborough Downs

My father and mother loved the horses. Scarborough Downs was their race track through most of the summer months. Uncle Joe and Auntie Josephine would meet them there, and they would spend the evening with their many friends from there. Among these were Betty Gerard, Coy and Jean Matthews, Gig, and someone we nicknamed Coke because she wore thick, coke-bottle glasses. Uncle Angelo would be there too. Johnnie and I spent our days at the track running around the paddock area, seeing all the horses, and collecting the different colored tickets that everyone threw down in disgust after losing.

When Johnnie and I lost interest, Mom and Dad took Armand Jr. along with them. Dad told Armand Jr., "Once in a blue moon a winning horse will be disqualified for some reason and the horse that finished 2nd, or placed, would be bumped up to 1st place, the 3rd place would be bumped up to 2nd and so forth. When this happens someone might have thrown their ticket to the ground thinking that they lost. Go look for those tickets, you could win some money."

One night it happened. A horse was disqualified and Armand Jr. immediately ran off to find a discarded winning ticket. He kicked over some tickets, and picked up others, looking for the right one. He was like a pooper scooper, going eight feet behind the people who were tossing their tickets down, then scooping them up to check them out.

Low and behold, he found a stack of winning tickets right near a bench. He grabbed them and headed back to find Dad. Dad was looking at his program trying to decide what horse to bet on in the next race. "Hey, Dad!" Armand Jr. yelled.

Without looking up from his program Dad replied, "What is it? You already had French fries!"

"No, Dad. Look!"

"What?"

"Loooooook! Are these worth $3.80 apiece?"

Dad turned his head, his glasses down to the tip of his nose. "I don't know," he said. "Let me look." After examining them, he turned to Armand Jr. and said, "By God they are!"

Within a few seconds Dad and Armand Jr. saw a man storm through the glass doors into the ticket hall like he was a drunk coming out of a saloon. The man looked left and then right, then directly at Dad and Armand Jr. He headed toward them. Dad put the tickets in his shirt pocket. As soon as the muttering, spitting man passed by, Dad said, "Let's go upstairs and cash these in." The minute we got up to the second floor, Dad said, "You wait here and watch for that guy."

Dad went up to the cashier. Armand Jr. watched the cashier pass Dad some money. Dad came to Armand Jr. with this "cat that ate the mouse" smile on his face. "Here's ten dollars!" he said. "Take this!" They went back down to find Mom. Dad gave her money too. Armand Jr. believed that the tickets were worth about $45-to-$50 dollars. When Mom heard what had happened, she sent Armand Jr. on a mission, directing him to stand near the bar entrance, watching. She realized that people who drink don't know what they're doing. They throw away a lot of tickets by accident. From then on, whenever Armand Jr. went to the track with Mom and Dad, this was his job. He loved every minute of it.

John moves in, I move out

After graduating from Pierre's in 1969, my first job was at a Bradlee's Department Store Beauty Shop. I was living at home and I'd started dating Mully's brother, Jim. Jim had just gotten out of the Navy, and Mully, her boyfriend, Roland, Jim and I would hang out together. After several months at Bradlee's I quit and took a job at Ronald's Hair Fashions, a busier beauty shop where I could make more money and build a larger clientele. I worked all day then came home to help Dad prepare the dinner. I was still doing a lot of the housework. Mom was still doing hair in her beauty shop downstairs and she was still on call for Hutchins Funeral Home. She had her good days and her bad days.

PONTIAC LEMANS

In early 1971, my brother, John and Jane divorced, and John moved back home. On weekends John and I would go out to different bars drinking and partying. One Saturday evening John wanted to borrow my new Pontiac LaMans to impress one of his many girlfriends. I let him. At four o'clock Sunday morning the telephone rang. Dad and I came out of our bedrooms at the same time, both of us running down to the kitchen to answer the phone. My father got there first, and I heard him say, "Yeah, she is here. What's the matter? Okay, we will be right in to pick it up." Dad turned to me and said, "Your brother has left your car parked in front of a fire hydrant in front of Mercy Hospital. They want it removed or they will have it towed. Don't tell your brother that I told the police not to tell him that we picked the car up. When John calls to report it stolen don't tell him that we moved it. Let him think that he is in big trouble." Of course, the police thought that it was a great idea and were ready to play along.

Dad gave me a ride in to get it. Back home both of us sat waiting for John to report that the car was stolen. Around 9am he called, and said, "Nancy, you are not going to believe this! I went out to get in your car and it was gone! Someone stole it! But don't worry I'm at the police station reporting it now."

I started screaming at him, "What the hell happened to my car? You better find out what happened! I'll kill you if there is scratch on it!"

John was so upset he could barely talk. Then I heard someone in the background tell him, "It's a big joke. Your sister came and got her car." That's when Dad took the phone and said, "What the hell is wrong with you parking in front of the hospital and a fire hydrant? Do you need a ride?" John told Dad one of the policemen would give him a ride home. When John walked in the house, we were all laughing. He made a face and said, "Real funny!" Then he went to bed.

NIGHTLY HOCKEY GAMES

John was working for General Electric Company at a plant in South Portland. When he arrived home each night he and Armand Jr. would go in the den and set up a huge game of tabletop hockey. One would set the timer and they would start to play. They wouldn't come out until someone won. Dad would go in the den again and again, telling them that supper was ready. "Hey, John, Armand! Let's go!" he would say. "Time to eat! Andiamo!"

John would yell, "Give us a few minutes! The game is almost over! I gotta beat his ass!"

Armand Jr. would shout, "No way! You're dead meat! I'm gonna whip your ass!"

Dad would return to the kitchen, sit down and read the paper. Mom and I would sit at the kitchen table, watching television. All of us were waiting for them. We could hear them scream at each other, then we'd hear the puck hit the window across the room. Dad would run back there, yelling, "That's enough! You're going to break the window! Come on, let's eat! Hey, we're waiting!"

If it wasn't hockey it was tabletop football, and it went on every night for years. All we could do was wait.

FooFoo

John was oblivious to Mom's illnesses. He paid little attention to Dad's triumphant husbandry, or my efforts to help at home. John was too busy with friends, dating, and work.

One day John came home from work with a bad chest cold. He found Dad, Mom, Armand Jr., and I sitting at the kitchen table. He said that he'd told everyone at work that he had to go home and get the "foofoo" out, but none of his co-workers knew what a "foofoo" was. He had tried to explain that a "foofoo" was something you used to help you breathe when you had a cold. He'd described how it provided moisture, helping to open your breathing passages, but, no matter what he told them, they couldn't figure out a "foofoo."

We laughed hysterically. Finally Dad said, "It's a vaporizer you fool! We just call it a 'foofoo' because that is what you called it as a child."

The contraption they were talking about was a huge round heater with a gallon jug full of water, and a nozzle where the steam would come out. You set the jug upside down into a funnel-shaped holder feeding water into the heater. As the water heated, steam came out the spout adding moisture to the room. The first time John heard the steam coming from the nozzle he said it made a "foofoo" sound. Our "foofoo" made steam so hot it could peel off wallpaper.

When John realized his mistake he got mad at Mom and Dad for never correcting him. "Geez! Why didn't you tell me the real name of it? I looked like a fool!"

Dad replied, "So what! Maybe you are!"

Getting Married

June 26, 1971, when I was 24 years old, Jim and I got married at St. Joseph's Church. John had been off with his Army Reserve unit, and almost didn't make it home in time. At the last minute he got permission to come home for the weekend. On the morning of my wedding I came home from some last minute errands, went upstairs, and found him sitting on my bed. We hugged and cried, and he whispered in my ear, "I wish you all the best and I hope that things go better for you."

John wasn't one to show his emotions, so he didn't have to say too much for me to realize he meant it. He wanted only the best for me.

1971 - One of my favorite pictures of Dad and me.

Jim and I moved to a two-family home on Clinton Street. We'd bought it from my Uncle Dinny (Donato) and Aunt Angie (Angiolina). It was hard for my mother because now she felt that she was left to do everything I'd been doing all those years. In the coming months we both came to see that things hadn't changed as much as she'd feared. Jim had a job at S.D. Warren Paper Mill. When he worked nights I would go have dinner with my parents and brothers. I still helped Dad decide what to have for dinner, and I helped him prepare it.

Dad drove himself crazy trying to figure out what to cook for my mother. At one point, when Mom had severe stomach problems, the doctor put her on a gluten-free diet. Dad and I spent hours looking up recipes we could feed her. Although most of the diets she tried did little to help, Dad spent his entire life trying to find dishes that she could digest. To this day I believe that what bothered Mom's stomach wasn't so much the food as it was life itself?

Dealing with all the chores and emotions of keeping a home, raising a family, and working was too much for her. Mom was a fun-loving woman, always ready to play a good prank, or listen to your troubles. Dad was more serious and opinionated, and wasn't always understanding when hurt feelings were involved. He was more likely to say, "Ah, forget about it! Why do you let that bother you! What are you going to do anyway? That shit happens all the time!"

Dad's Favorite Movies/Television Programs

Dad loved war movies and any kind of western, especially those with John Wayne.

In 1965 *Dr. Zhivago* came out. It starred Omar Sharif as a Russian doctor and Julie Christie as a political activist's wife with whom he falls in love. The story shows hardships they suffered through during the Bolshevik Revolution. The movie's theme song, "Somewhere My Love" became Dad and Mom's favorite song. One day I picked up the sheet music, and played it on my piano for them just as they came into visit me at my house. They were so surprised.

In 1972 Jim and I took Mom and Dad to see *The Godfather* at a local drive-in. Though the dialogue had captions whenever it departed from English, whenever the characters spoke Italian, Dad would translate. He had a comment about every scene shot in Sicily. When Michael Corleone courted Apollonia, and her whole family followed the couple on their walk through her village, Dad chimed in, "That's the way they did it back then. Out of respect, the whole damn family had to be in attendance!" During the violent vendettas he would comment, "Yep! That's what they did!" or "That'll teach them!" And he would second guess everything, saying "That guy's gonna get it!

Watch this! They mean business! You don't fool around with those guys! I know! They're mean bastards!" When the movie came to television, he watched as if he'd never seen it before, making the same comments all over again.

When Dad watched television, his favorite shows, stars and characters included Ed Sullivan, Jackie Gleason, *Sanford and Son*, Victor Borge, Carol Burnett, Archie Bunker and anything that had to do with history or news. Dad was a walking encyclopedia. He knew a lot about almost every subject, especially history and the world news.

1972 - John, Armand Jr., Nancy, Mom and Dad.

1974 John moves out again

In 1974 John decided to move in with his girlfriend, Cheryl Watts, and her daughter, Kimberly. He and Cheryl got married.

Though John had always tormented Armand Jr. with wise-ass remarks, head slaps, and walk-by sucker punches, when Armand Jr heard the news he announced, half crying, "I'm gonna miss John!"

For Mom it was a reprieve from her cellar station by the washing machine where she had what seemed like a complete laundering/dry cleaning operation just for John's dress shirts. Mom was damn good at laundry and ironing, and John was damn good at providing Mom with an overabundance of work. God forbid if John did not have a clean, starched shirt to wear to work everyday. Sometimes he would tell Mom he needed a certain color shirt for the following day. Late that night she would be downstairs getting it washed, dried and starched for "Mr. Perfection."

GERMAPHOBIC

With John moving out we thought Dad would finally stop swearing about John's preoccupation with fingerprints on the drinking glasses. When it came to drinking glasses John was obsessed about cleanliness. Whenever he got a glass from the cupboard he put it up to the light, scrunched up his eyes like a jeweler checking a diamond, then turned the glass, checking for fingerprints. If there were prints or smudges John would put it in the sink to be washed. He often went through several before finding one pristine enough for his tastes. He sometimes filled the sink with four or five empty glasses, but he never washed them. This had Dad swearing his head off, "What the hell is wrong with you? Jesus Christ! You're nuts! There's nothing wrong with those God damn glasses! I don't understand how anyone can be so particular about their drinking glasses when you think nothing of taking your supper dish up to the bathroom and sit on the toilet and eat at the same time you're taking a shit!" Dad would wait for John to leave the kitchen, then grab the glasses and put them back in the cupboard. The whole time he'd be muttering, "Who does he think he is? Tutti Pulito [all clean]!"

John has always had a thing about being around anyone with a cough, flu, cold, sore throat, cold sore, or if someone sneezes. "Geeeeez!" he would say, backing away. "Are you sick or something?" As his face would scrunch up he would lean away, saying, "What's a matter with you? Stay away from me!" as if you were highly contagious. John would never think of taking a bite of someone else's food, or sipping someone's drink, or even eating half of someone else's sandwich after they'd cut it in two. That was *not* going to happen!

Guitar Lessons, Bowling Leagues, Race Horses

Armand Jr. loved music and when he became interested in playing the guitar my mother jumped at the chance to have him take lessons. Every Saturday morning Mom drove him to Mr. Landry's home in Yarmouth for guitar lessons. He turned out to be a natural, learning to play many rock-and-roll songs of the era. Armand Jr. played an electric guitar, and he turned up his amplifier, blasting the notes out the speaker. Dad didn't understand all that "loud noise." He didn't see any resemblance between it and the music he'd learned as a kid and loved throughout his life. He would yell, "Turn that damn thing down! For Christ's sake, I can't hear anything!"

When he was 16, Armand Jr. got together with Gino, Chris and Lisa Grassi and Keith Tilton to form their own band, Brook. Dad and Mom were supportive and worried at the same time. They knew these kids would play at weddings and private parties where alcohol was served. To Dad this was one more instance of "bad business."

Armand Jr. was also interested in bowling. He joined a league at the Northgate Bowl-A-Rama up the street from where we lived. All he said to Dad was that he was "bowling with some buddies." It was a little more than that. Soon Armand Jr. had bowled himself into 4th place in his league, then he'd finished 6th in the State tournament. In

1975 he starred on the Greater Portland City team when it won the championship. One article in the Portland newspaper was headlined, "Polito Shatters Lane Records!" To practice more, Armand Jr. got a job at the bowling alley. There he could bowl against league members who were really good.

One evening he talked to Dad about joining the New England Bowling League. Armand Jr.'s doubles partner was a regional pro and member of the Pro Bowlers Tour named Arnold Biondi. Biondi, who came from Cranston, Rhode Island, told Armand Jr. that he had potential. He wanted Armand Jr. to be part of a team of ten men touring New York, Connecticut, Massachusetts and New Hampshire. Armand Jr. asked Dad for enough money to go to the 1976 National Championship. The regionals would be in Virginia, Kentucky, Cincinnati and Akron, Ohio. The finals were scheduled for Oklahoma. It would mean seventeen days on the road.

Armand Jr. talked it up as an honor he should accept.

"What?" Dad yelled. "Jesus Christ! Who the hell is this guy? I don't care who he is… you're nuts! You're crazy!"

Armand Jr. pointed out that he could practice for free at the bowling alley. He tried to convince our father to come watch him bowl, but Dad would not hear of it. *Case closed*, Armand Jr. thought.

A few days went by without a word about bowling, then Dad said to Armand Jr., "Let's go to the credit union and see what you need for hotels and a little extra. Tell me. Do you win anything? What happens next?"

Dad had a talent for listening, yelling, and walking off. He would then absorb what he'd heard, and a few days later he'd suddenly be there, involved, and ready to help. He rarely said no unless he'd decided that what we wanted was "bad business." If he felt there would be trouble, or that we were about to fall flat on our faces, he wouldn't help, but if he concluded that our ideas were good, he was always ready to jump in. Sometimes he got so involved that we would have to tell him, "Dad, let me do it by myself! Geeeez!"

In this case Armand Jr. took off with Arnold Biondi and eight other guys for the Regional Professional Amateur Event in Cranston, Rhode Island. The first day each pro was assigned three amateurs for a four-man event for five strings. Armand Jr.'s assigned professional was Wayne Webb. He'd seen Webb on national television two weeks earlier, and couldn't believe he was going to bowl him. Armand Jr. had never seen this setup before: only three practice balls with no pins. He was up first. "Gulp!"

Armand Jr. bowled a 203 and Webb had 9 in a row, finishing with a 256. Webb turned to Armand Jr. and said, "You have a nice delivery. You throw a nice hook." Armand Jr. thanked Webb and then proceeded to bowl four more games. He was eliminated that afternoon. That night he could not sleep from all the excitement.

Next stop was Oklahoma City where Armand Jr. saw billboards advertising the Tournament. It was a big event for that city, and Armand Jr. could not believe that he was one of the entrants. Even a waitress asked if they were in town for the Nationals.

The American Bowling Congress took over the Oklahoma Myriad Coliseum building 56 lanes with 6,000 seats for the fans. State flags were everywhere. 200 other bowlers were there for the afternoon shift. Armand Jr. got his bowling ball weighed, verifying its legality. He heard the PA announcements: "New York versus Kentucky, lanes 11 and 12… Iowa vs. Maine, lanes 31 and 32." Once again: "Gulp!"

The lights dimmed, floodlights came on, and a high school girl holding Maine's flag told them to line up and follow her.

A bell rang three times, a curtain parted, and next thing Armand Jr. knew he was walking down a carpeted runway, hearing applause and cheers. As the cameras flashed, Armand Jr. could not believe his eyes.

There was his name on the giant scoreboard above the lanes. Scorekeepers prowled the catwalk, listening to their headsets for instructions on what to post on the scoreboard.

By the time Armand Jr. heard the first strains of the National Anthem he was flipping out.

His opponent had been Iowa's State Champion the previous year.

Armand Jr.'s first ball was a strike. In the end Armand's team lost, but he did salvage one win in three games. Maine finished 36th out of 50 that year, managing to beat out thirteen other teams (though thirty-five teams finished ahead of them).

The last event was in Akron, Ohio. They all qualified for day two and it was Armand Jr.'s best night ever, five strings, 1130 for 5 games, for a 226 average. They didn't win a title but the experience was absolutely wonderful and they came home happy.

Armand Jr. wasn't finished with bowling. The next year he qualified for membership in the New England Bowlers Association, and three New England Regional Pro Bowlers. Arnold Biondi of Bangor, Maine, Charlie Parker of Cranston, Rhode Island, and Bill Pascoe of Torrington, Connecticut signed his application for sponsorship. This was the path to take if one was ever going to be anything in this game.

Once a month there were Regional Professional Tournaments in the New England region. They had them in Brockton, Massachusetts, Torrington, Connecticut, Schenectady, New York, Cranston, Rhode Island, Keene, New Hampshire and Paramus, New Jersey. These were the places where the "big boys" bowled.

On these road trips Armand Jr. and Arnold Biondi would compete with some of the biggest names in bowling including Wayne Webb, John Patraglia, Mark Roth and Earl Anthony. These were the guys Armand Jr. watched on television on Saturday afternoons. The only part Armand Jr. did not like about traveling with Arnold was that Arnold liked to listen to opera. On those long drives the AM radio was always set to classical music. At first this irritated Armand Jr. but soon he recognized some of the arrangements and he began humming along.

His highest rank in New England was 28th. He achieved that for about two months with an average of 208. He worked for our family business, Luigi's, during the day, and practiced at the bowling alley at night. Armand Jr. practiced for free for 2-to-3 hours every single night. I do not know if my father ever stopped in to see Armand Jr. bowl, he always listened to his stories and was excited for him.

In 1977 Armand Jr. graduated from Portland High School. He started at the University of Southern Maine that September. He'd always been brilliant at numbers and statistics, so it seemed natural that he would pursue a degree in Business Management. We all thought that's what he would do until Christmas. That's when he announced that he did not want to attend college anymore. Dad was upset, but knew that he couldn't change Armand Jr.'s mind. When Dad finally accepted this John got Armand Jr. a job working at General Electric as a sandblaster.

Yankee Salute N

As the son of my mom and dad, Armand Jr. had grown up seeing all those galloping horses through the fence at Scarborough Downs Racetrack. Over the years he'd rubbed elbows with owners and riders. So it shouldn't have been much of a surprise when he decided to get into the game himself.

Dad was at the kitchen table sipping his coffee, and Mom was eating an English muffin, when Armand Jr. strolled in and, masking his nervousness, made his announcement. "I-I bought something tonight."

"Jesus Christ! What?" Dad asked, his radar going up.

"A race horse." Armand Jr. announces.

Most kids Armand Jr.'s age would have bought a car or a motorcycle, but Armand Jr. had spent almost everything he had on a $500 claimer.

Dad went ballistic. "Jesus Christ!" he yelled. "Where are you going to keep it?" He jumped up and started pacing. "What would make you do such a thing? You're nuts! Jesus Christ! Where the hell are you going to keep the damn thing? In the garage?" Dad pictured a horse stabled right there on the property, stinking up the garage with horse shit.

Armand Jr. tried to explain. "No Dad. I'll pay to have it boarded in a stall at the horse track. It is all taken care of. Don't worry about it."

"Don't worry about it?" Dad yelled. "You are nuts! Do you know how much that costs? Owning a horse is a waste of money! Those damn horses are always lame or sick! You will never make enough money to support the expense of that damn thing!"

Mom listened, watched, but said nothing, until finally she broke into Dad's rant to ask Armand Jr.: "What's his name?" She started paging through Scarborough's program from the previous night. "Who is it?" she asked, sounding almost as excited as he was.

"His name is, Yankee Salute N," said Armand Jr.

Dad's response was, "For Christ's sake don't encourage him!"

Despite Dad's initial objections, Armand Jr. kept Yankee Salute N for several years, then sold the horse to a friend.

Crème de Cacao

Just to the left of the kitchen counters was a pantry the size of a small closet. Four or five wooden shelves ran along one wall. These were filled with pasta, canned goods, cereal, paper products and condiments. The other wall had pots and pans, a box of saved bread wrappers and other plastic remains from packaged foods (God forbid that Dad might throw anything away!). There was flour and, on the bottom shelf, a wastebasket. Alongside the wooden shelves was a long space with a broom and dustpan. This little pantry was chockfull, and couldn't fit anything more.

The pantry, which wasn't built on the house foundation, had a separate entrance into the back of the kitchen. It had three steps and a door that we only opened in the summer when the heat got extreme. In the winter that pantry was so cold that when anyone opened the door Dad would yell, "Hurry up! You're letting in all the cold air for Christ's sake!" When it was cold, no matter how fast you got through the door, it wasn't fast enough for Dad.

Sometimes Dad would disappear through that door, shut it behind him, then reappear a few minutes later with a smirk on his face. One time Armand Jr. asked, "Hey, Dad? What are you doing in there?"

Dad and his beloved Crème de Cacao

"Nothing!" Dad snapped. "Never you mind!"

Armand Jr. decided to investigate. The moment Armand Jr. opened the door, Dad said, "Get the hell outta here! You're going to freeze! It's too cold! You're letting all the cold air in!" But this time Armand Jr. ignored him. Moving aside cereal boxes and jars of Sanka coffee he discovered a big bottle of Crème de Cacao. "Aha! I found it!" Armand Jr. said, holding up the evidence. "Dad, you little sneak! Boozing it up are you?"

The look on Dad's face was priceless. Laughing, he said, "Ah! For Christ's sake, it's just a little kick! Helps to keep me warm!" Just then Mom came in. "What's going on?" she asked.

Armand Jr. laughed hysterically while Dad sat at the table smiling. Armand Jr. showed Mom where Dad hid the Crème de Cacao. She wasn't surprised. "He does it all the time!" she said.

Once in awhile we caught Dad taking a shot glass in there, but usually he just swigged it out of the bottle. He would slip in there, spend a few minutes, then come out smacking his lips. Sometimes, when he had a shot glass, he'd lick the insides, saying, "That hits the spot! Want some?"

He kept doing this until years later, when he got the gout. At that point his doctor advised him to stay away from all alcoholic beverages. And he did.

The Gout

Gout is a type of arthritis that causes sudden burning pain, and stiffness, tenderness, redness and swelling in a joint, usually the big toe. It's brought on by too much uric acid in the blood. The uric acid forms into hard crystals in the joints.

When Dad learned he had gout he changed his diet drastically. He began avoiding beef, pork, lamb, and organ meats such as liver, kidney and brain, as well as some vegetables and seafood. These were supposed to trigger the overproduction of uric acid. Alcohol was also on the list of no-nos, so it was goodbye Crème de Cacao. He never complained about the meats, and managed to be happy with pasta, chicken and vegetables. His doctor put him on Allopurinol to decrease the production of uric acid.

The Gout affected the big toe on his right foot. When it "kicked up" he would hobble about and mumble: "Oh! That damn toe is just throbbing!" He started wearing boat shoes from Zayre's that sold for $2.99. They were two sizes larger than his regular shoes, and were soft with canvas tops. They came in black, tan and navy blue. He preferred blue. The Gout never kept him from running his daily trip "up to Shaw's," and he still prepared a great supper by 6pm.

The gout made it even harder to get Dad to eat anywhere but home. He'd never liked many American foods, and now, with his diet restricted, he had to forego meats and some vegetables, along with the other foods he absolutely despised like mayonnaise, mustard, ketchup, relish, salad dressing out of a bottle, and casseroles, It was a challenge, but he made the best of it. When we got home from an evening out, he would go into the kitchen and make, "A little pepper and egg sandwich, just to fill the hole."

Often we would smell the sandwich cooking, and congregate in the kitchen, joining him in "a little something to make you sleep better." Sitting around the kitchen table, eating together, laughing and talking, was one of our most heart-warming, comforting, endearing rituals. Mom usually went to bed.

Dad Sells Me Down The River

One summer night after work, when I arrived for dinner at Mom and Dad's, the City of Portland was replacing the brick sidewalk in front of the Russo's house next door. The workmen had removed the old bricks, stacking them neatly on the esplanade. I mentioned to Dad that it looked as if the city was going to throw the old bricks away. He agreed, knowing that I was having a hard time finding bricks for a border around my flower garden. We both said that these bricks would work, and a few moments later I positioned my car so we could load them into the trunk.

As I started carefully loading the bricks, Dad stood with his hands on his hips, looking up and down Washington Avenue. To a passerby it would've looked suspicious. I'd loaded ten or so bricks when I noticed a car pull over across the street. The man behind the wheel was staring at me. He slowly drove down to the corner, did a U-turn and pulled up in front of the house. I looked around for Dad, but he was gone!

The man got out of his car, showed me his badge and asked, "What are you doing?" At that moment Dad came out of the house, waving his arms in the air, as he yelled, "I told her not to touch those damn bricks!" My mouth dropped open. The policeman told me to put the bricks back. They were city property, he said, and if I failed to comply, he could arrest me. Looking around I noticed that Dad had disappeared again.

The policeman was nice and didn't give me that hard a time. I put the bricks back, and he left. I found Dad standing at the kitchen counter with his back to me, working on dinner.

"You f…..g turned me in! You just sold me down the river!" I yelled.

Dad's shoulders were shaking. As I walked over to look him in the eye, I saw he was laughing. He looked at me and said, "Ahhhh, you're all right, aren't you?"

As he waved me away, I replied, "You should be ashamed of yourself, turning against your own daughter!"

"Ah, nothing happened to you did it? Besides, someone has to stay here to cook dinner! It's better you go to jail than me!" He just kept laughing. Dad was a tough nut to crack.

First Grandchild

My first child, Angela Sabia Pizzo, was born on January 21, 1975. Mom, Dad, John and Armand Jr. were ecstatic. My Grandmother Gioconda Lacivita Polito had just died on January 19th at 89 years of age. I'd felt a tug of conflicting emotions, missing her funeral even while people were congratulating me on my new daughter.

With the birth of Angela and the death of his mother, my Dad reconciled himself to the stages of life by saying, "The Lord took one and also gave us one. And, the cycle of life goes on." Dad became "Papa" which brought a big smile to his face and Mom became "Mammie" because that is how Angela said Grammy. The first time Dad held Angela in his arms he fell in love with her. He kissed her forehead, saying, "My little bambina."

At birth Angela already had a head of bright red hair, prompting everyone to ask: "Where did she get that hair from?" That was easy. My Dad's Mom, Gioconda, had the most beautiful shade of light auburn hair with a touch of golden brown in it. Jim's mother had auburn hair too, so that's where it must've come from. As she got older the color deepened a little.

Whenever I walked into the house Dad would grab Angela away from me and start dancing her around, singing to her in Italian, "C'e la luna mezz'o mare Mamma mia me maritari". Angela put him in a totally different frame of mind. Whenever Mom and I went shopping Dad insisted on babysitting. He would change her diaper, feed her, burp her, and take her in the kitchen. There he would prop her up in her jumper then talk to her and dance around as he made supper. Once she started walking he would take her outside where they would water the flowers, or she would watch and listen as he talked to her while he fixed something. She was always there, interested in everything her Papa did. Angela was very precocious. Dad took advantage of this telling her all about his life in Italy, his journey to America, and his recipes.

Pork Chops

One afternoon after a shopping trip with my mother, I arrived at the house to hear two-and-a-half-year-old Angela tell how Papa taught her to cook pork chops. "Mommy," she said, "first you put them in the frying pan, then you add salt and pepper, oregano, two cloves of sliced garlic, one bay leaf, a little olive oil and just a touch of water. You put a cover over the pan and put them on the stove on low heat. Then you take a nap. And when you get up they are all done!" And with that last statement she put her hands in the air, looking at me in wonderment.

I looked at Dad and said, "What the hell are you doing? Are you trying to burn the house down? Take a nap?"

While trying not to laugh, he said, "Ah for Christ's sakes nothing happened! I knew when I needed to wake up."

Stunned I said, "You knew when you needed to wake up? You gotta be kidding me?"

Mom piped in "What a guy..." as she walked away shaking her head. Between Angela's innocence and Dad's crazy napping recipe, I could not help laughing. There was my Dad relying on a two-and-a-half- year-old to wake him up before the pork chops burned.

"Don't worry about it! I know what I am doing!" he said. He pointed to his ear shaking his finger back and forth. "A good cook cooks with his ears. I was listening to make sure the pork chops did not dry up because they would start sizzling if they did."

"And you could hear that happening all the way in the living room while you are sleeping?"

He swiped his hand through the air, signaling me to mind my own business. "Nothing happened did it?"

Retirement

In 1975 after 34 years Dad retired from Deering High School. He'd taught Latin, French and English, but he was best known for teaching Spanish. Dad was proud of his profession. Over the years many former students wrote to him to thank him for being such an excellent teacher. I was amazed when people came up to Dad while we were grocery shopping, and said how they loved his Spanish classes.

One time I asked him, "How do you remember all these students?"

"I remember the good students," he said, "and the poor student is not going to say anything to me anyway. Those horses' asses I want to forget!"

I remember Dad telling me that he would make deals with first-year students who weren't doing well, telling them, "If you don't sign up for Spanish II next year, I will pass you this year with a D-."

Though Dad had retired, Mom continued to see her regular customers in her beauty shop. Hutchins Funeral Home merged with Jones & Rich and became Jones, Rich & Hutchins Funeral Home. Mom continued to be "on call." With her full social calendar, shopping trips with her sisters and friends, her volunteer work, and all she did for her family and friends, she hardly seemed to slow down at all.

Mom and Dad, 1975,
One of the best pictures of the two of them.

Cooking and Rules

Retirement never slowed Dad down either. Mom had plenty of projects for him to do around the house. Whenever anything needed to be painted, wallpapered, replaced, or fixed, he did it. The house became his job 24-7. He only stopped long enough to cook dinner.

He was "Mr. Mom." Every morning it was "up to Shaw's" to get groceries. An arrangement evolved where Shaw's stored his food, and he picked it up each day "nice and fresh." After lunch he would start a project and before you knew it, it was time to start cooking dinner. When Mom and I went shopping, Dad loved to have time for himself. When Mom was out she couldn't hound him about something that needed to done. At the end of the day he enjoyed being surrounded by family. We would sit at the dinner table, discussing everything from world events to whatever had happened to us that day.

Each day at exactly 4pm, Dad would place the infamous dishtowel over his shoulder and start dinner. His cookware was a collection of old Napoli Restaurant pots and pans along with some Mom picked up at auctions. One could tell what was for supper by what pot he was using. All his pots and pans were scrubbed clean and kept in perfect condition. Most of the flatware was from the Napoli Restaurant and there was a certain spoon we had to use when we ate Pasta "Fasul" [fagioli]. He trimmed his chicken and meats on an old wooden cutting board. He swore, "You don't ever submerge wood in water. You just wipe the damn thing down!" It's a miracle that we didn't get some type of ecoli.

He loved throwing leftovers together to make a frittata, or he might just pile it all on his plate. If we turned our noses up at leftovers, he made us something different while he would have a plate of mounded, mixed-up, week-old food enjoying every last bite. Many times I saw him eat something right after scraping off the mold—particularly cheeses. "After all, what do you think blue cheese and gorgonzola are?" he would ask. When one of us said, "I'm not eating that!" He would say, "Ah! You don't know what it is like to go without! If you were hungry enough you would eat it!"

There were a few rules that Dad lived by in his world of food and cooking:

1. In a restaurant always order the "Special of the Day." They have stocked up on the ingredients in expectation of serving more, so these specially priced meals are generally fresher.

2. To give any type of soup great flavor, fry a few cloves of sliced garlic in a few tablespoons of olive oil. When the garlic is golden brown, discard it. Let the olive-oil-flavored garlic cool and then add to any soup broth or base. "Delizioso." [Delicious]

3. Wash all vegetables well by placing them in a big bowl of water to flush out any dirt and grime. Always cook them slowly with plenty of seasonings.

4. It is cheaper to cut up a whole chicken yourself rather than pay for the butcher to do it. "The more 'they' have to handle it, the more I dislike it." Even the grandchildren watched in awe as he meticulously trimmed the fat off any meat or chicken; he would hold the knife at just the right angle with his right hand, a paper towel in his left hand to better grip the meat or chicken.

5. Properly refrigerated food is good all week. "Whoever heard of throwing food away just because it has been in the refrigerator for four days? When I was in Italy, we didn't even have a refrigerator and we kept cured meat hanging in the kitchen for weeks along with vegetables, bread, and chicken buried underground. If the bread or cheese got a little moldy we would just cut it off. We never died!"

6. Pasta water had to be well-seasoned with at least a heaping tablespoonful of salt. Dad was not all that wild about al dente pasta; he liked it cooked through. He claimed that if you did not cook it until the middle was soft; it would swell in your stomach and make you seem fuller than you actually were.

7. Never throw leftover food away. There were times when Dad would cook a meal, call us to the table, serve us what he cooked, then be back at the stove cooking up a little frittata for himself with any leftovers. He kept using leftovers night after night until they were completely gone.

8. He would always drink the juice left over from cooking spinach or any vegetable because all the nutrients were in the juice.

9. Dad never ate salads or fruit salads outside of the home. He claimed that they were "handled too much" and deemed them unsafe.

10. Clean your plate and the bones. I would get really worried that Dad would choke while gnawing on a chicken bone or pork chop bone. He claimed that it was good for one's teeth. If you left too much on the bone, you were deemed "wasteful." When the grandchildren were young he would be upset that they would leave so much meat on the bone, so he would take their pork chop or chicken bones and chew on them himself.

11. My mother never picked up any piece of chicken or pork chop with her fingers. She would use her fork and knife. Dad would go insane watching her. "Look at her! Ah...pick it up for Christ's sake! What are you afraid of? Use your hands. Get in there!"

12. If you don't have the opportunity to purchase fresh fish you are better off buying fresh frozen fish. The fishing boats clean, rinse, and freeze the fish as they catch it.

13. Keep your cooking area clean. "If you go into a restaurant and you see that the chef's apron is dirty with spills of food, and he has used his apron to wipe his hands, leave! If he is that messy with his appearance, just think how he is when he cooks your food."

14. Dad's Motto: "Eat like it's your last supper. For you never know, it just could be."

Sporca!

When dinner was done, Mom always liked to wash the dishes because Dad was stingy with hot water and dish soap. They would race to the kitchen sink in their effort to do the dishwashing. He would complain, "You're too wasteful! You let the water run constantly! Get outta here! I'll do them!" Mom would reply, "What a guy!" Dad would nudge her aside and start washing dishes. As he rinsed them and placed them onto the dish strainer, Mom would pick up a plate, inspect it for cleanliness and, if Dad had missed anything, walk over and slide it back into the dishpan. Dad would give her a rotten look, then shake his head and say, "What the hell is wrong with you? For Christ's sake, use the towel and wipe if off! You're too damn fussy!" This went on every night unless I stepped in. If I did them Dad never said a word.

He was a man of simplicity, never wanting or needing too much. After his childhood in Italy and here, he thought of running water as a luxury. Our running joke was to rush up to him as he went upstairs to take a bath, all of us shouting in astonishment, "Are you taking a bath, Dad?" He would turn to us and say, "Yeah! What's it to you?"

Mom would then yell, "It's about time you sporca!" (One who is dirty.) With a sheepish grin on his face he would climb the stairs and disappear. Later he would come down in his clean wife-beater tee shirt and boxer shorts, the shorts pulled way up high over his waistline. As he approached the last couple of steps he would look over to see if anyone was in the living room looking at him, and if he had someone's attention he would smile and break out in a little Italian dance step.

Every morning he spent an hour washing up in his bathroom in the cellar. It was simply amazing that he never once had body odor. His favorite deodorant was Tussy and when Mom could not find it for him anymore he switched to Old Spice Deodorant, with a little splash of their cologne on his face after he shaved.

He liked Dickie pants in blue, brown or khaki. He wore flannel shirts in the winter and cotton shirts in the warmer months. He wore his pants for such a long period of time the sheen and color wore off, or until Mom stole them to throw away. When Mom yelled at him to throw away his old clothes, he yelled back, "What the hell do you care? You're not wearing them!"

Mom would retort, "What are people going to think of you with those old clothes on?"

"Who the hell cares what people think!" he would say. "Ah, for Christ's sake, you're always worrying about what other people are going to think or say! It's none of their business! Never you mind!"

Mom would walk away mumbling, "Sporca!" (Dirty). Whenever she thought he was being unreasonable Mom would always say, "You're just like a woman!" That would send Dad into a sputtering, head-shaking, ranting, frenzy. "Ah! Go to hell! Va fanapoli!"

Sergio Franchi, Perry Como, Frank Sinatra, Dean Martin, Jerry Vale

Mom and Dad loved listening to their favorite singers, so Jim and I bought them a beautiful Panasonic Stereo System with huge speakers. Dad especially liked the tone of Dean Martin's voice, and he and Mom both loved Sergio Franchi singing in Italian. They would sit for hours listening to the many albums Jim bought for them. Jerry Vale's song "Al di la" would prompt Dad to join in singing in Italian. When Jim and I would go there for supper, Dad would be dancing around the kitchen, singing along with Sergio, Dean or Jerry while he cooked. It wasn't long before Angela was singing along with these records too. With the stereo, mealtimes took on their own routine: Dad cooking, singing and dancing, Angela singing with Papa as she set the table, Mom sitting in the living room, listening to the music as she read the paper, and Armand Jr. in the den playing his guitar. I was the one trying to get everyone together at the dinner table before the food got cold.

When Connie Francis would sing "Mama" Mom would sob, and soon Dad's eyes would be welling up. Eddie Fisher singing, "Oh My Papa", always brought my parents to a halt. Dad always cracked up while trying to sing along with Julius LaRosa's version of "Eh Cumpari".

Once they got the new stereo Mom could not wait to build a collection of her favorite singers. The stereo was off limits to the grandchildren and Mom tried to keep Armand Jr. from touching it. She didn't want him playing his loud music. He didn't when she was around, but when she wasn't home he would blast rock and roll. Mom and Dad never had anything as nice as that Panasonic Stereo. It still works, even surviving being knocked over by the cat.

Dad and His Music

During the first 20 years of Dad's 34-year career at Deering High School, he always conducted the music for the commencement exercises. In those days the graduating senior class had to learn to sing several songs for the ceremony, and Dad would spend hours directing their practices.

At the actual graduations he would appear in a tux with a white jacket. He would stand on his elevated platform, his back to the people, then signal with his baton for the senior class to enter as the orchestra played "Pomp and Circumstance." It was a moving sight as they marched onto the stage. Once they were in their places they sang "The Battle Hymn of the Republic."

When my cousin Tony's class graduated someone recorded their version of "The Battle Hymn of the Republic." Dad often played it on the stereo. He loved listening to it, saying, "Those kids did a great job! It sounds pretty damn good!" To this day I often wonder what would have happened if Dad had been able to stay at the Conservatory in Naples. He probably would've become a conductor.

Insomnia

Dad hardly slept at all. He never went to bed before 3am and he was always up at 7. Even after he retired he stayed up until all hours doing projects, paying bills or reading. He loved to read. Dad kept some of the Spanish books he had used in his early years of teaching, and I would often see him reading them. He often remarked that the older books had the best teaching techniques for learning a language. "Don Quixote" in the original Spanish was one of his favorites.

His books in Italian included his prayer book. As he got older, and had difficulty reading the print in his prayer book, he asked, "Nancy, is there any way you can blow this up for me? It is just too damn small!" I took it to work, enlarged the pages, and made him a new larger print version. You would have thought I'd given him a million bucks! He was so happy.

As children we were never aware of Dad's sleep habits, but once we hit our teens, and went out at night, it was pure hell. John was the first one to come in late and experience Dad's evil eye. We had curfews. If we did not come home by the designated time there was hell to pay, and it started the minute we walked through the door.

"Where the hell have you been?" he would ask John. "I told you to be home at 12pm! Don't you know that only bad things can happen to you late at night?"

"Relax, Dad!" John would say. "I'm all right!" Then John would go to his room, while Dad turned off the lights, muttering, "This staying out late is bad business. Nothing but trouble out there late at night! What the hell is wrong with these kids today?"

It only got worse. When John was 20, and moved back home from college, he would stay out until all hours, leaving poor Dad pacing, and watching out the kitchen windows for John's car. Sometimes John wouldn't show up until the next day. When he walked in the house Dad would flip out. "What the hell is wrong with you? You could have at least called, you moron! What could you possibly be doing out all night? You are looking for trouble."

John never let Dad get to him. He would walk away. Mom always went to bed at 11, and never got involved in these discussions.

When I was old enough to go out late, I was always conscious of Dad waiting up for me at the kitchen table. It was comforting to know that he was always there to protect me and to make sure I was all right. He wanted me to enjoy my life, but he also wanted no harm to come to me. I would often come in, sit down and have a cup of Sanka with him. We might discuss his latest project or watch the end of a TV program. He always picked up on the most intriguing facts in any newspaper story or television program. Dad had a way of turning everything into a lesson.

He had amazing energy and could get so much accomplished in

a day, but if he stopped and sat down for one second he would immediately fall asleep—probably because he did not sleep at night. My Mom, brothers and I were used to his falling asleep, but Angela was relentless in trying to keep him awake. "Come, Papa, and watch me sing and dance in the living room," she would say, pulling him by the hand, and sitting him in his green overstuffed chair. She would start up Mickey Mouse Club songs on the stereo, and walk around in a circle singing her heart out. Then she would look over and see that Papa had fallen asleep. "Papa, you're not watching me!" she would yell. "Wake up, please." If this didn't work she would turn the speakers up louder, shouting out the words. Then Dad would awaken and yell, "For Christ's sake, turn that damn thing down! I'm listening to you with my eyes closed!"

John Buys A Farm

John and Cheryl got married and bought a farm in Cumberland, about ten miles north of where Mom and Dad lived. John named the farm Tarantell Farm after the Italian folk dance "Tarantella". It had stalls for horses and it wasn't long before John had them full. He owned some of these horses, while others were boarding there. There was always work to be done and Dad was always willing to lend a hand.

Tarantell Farm, Cumberland, Maine

Burning the Field

One spring day John decided to get a permit to burn the brush on the 11-acre field behind the house and barn. It was the only way to clear it. He contacted several of his friends to help, and of course, he called Dad.

Dad arrived with gloves, shovel, and broom, ready to work. For some reason John thought that if he took a lit torch and ran around the outside perimeter of his property it would burn inward, making it easier to control. This seemed like a good idea until a wind kicked up, and the fire started moving out, not in!

As everyone ran around with shovels and brooms trying to contain the fire, the wind took over. After struggling for almost an hour, John's friends decided that he should call the fire department. John ran into the house to call, and when he came back out all his friends stood there waiting, except Dad. When John couldn't find Dad amidst the smoke and flames, he started to panic.

John ran around, yelling, "Dad? Dad?" He finally reached the back of his property and found Dad trying to control the flames with nothing but a charred broom handle stub. There was Dad stomping on the fire with his foot and saying, "Mannaggia il diavolo! [Damn the devil!] Jesus Christ! Cazzo! [Shit!] This is crazy!"

"Dad, give it up!" John yelled. "I had to call the Fire Department! It's out of control!"

"What the hell did you think you were doing?" Dad shouted. "I told you it wouldn't work!"

By the time John and Dad got back to the house the firemen were arriving. Once they put out the fire, the Chief wanted to know what went wrong. As John explained his technique, the Chief and his men just stood there, shaking there heads in disbelief. Dad paced up and down, muttering, "I told him it was bad business!"

Second Grandchild

On Father's Day, June 17, 1977, Jim and I celebrated another addition to the family, Adrianna Pizzo. My father called her Peppina, "Little One" and sometimes it was shortened to "Pep" or Peppy". Adrianna's olive skin and dark brown hair were the complete opposite of Angela's. Adrianna's temperament was different too. She was quiet, reflective and quite happy to just observe. She really didn't have much of a choice, with Angela taking charge of every toy and game.

Dad didn't waste any time teaching these two little ones to clean their plates and appreciate good food! It brought a smile to my father's face to see his young granddaughters finish eating their pasta fasul (pasta e fagioli), wiping the insides of their soup bowls completely clean with a piece of Italian bread. When they'd finished they would hold up their empty bowls and say, "There, Papa! I cleaned my bowl and you don't have to wash it!"

When it came time to sit down and eat as a family, there was no need to call my girls to the table twice. They loved to eat. To them dinnertime was exciting. Some of our best conversations took place at the dinner table and Angela and Adrianna were allowed to express their thoughts. One time Angela blurted out that she knew how to say broccoli in Italian.

"How do you say it in Italian?" Dad asked.

Angela put the fingers of her right hand together, held them up to the sky, and shook them back and forth, shouting, "Broccola, Papa!"

When we all cracked up, Angela said, "Is that right Papa!?"

My father choked on his food, laughing, when all of a sudden Adrianna's little voice chimed in, "Broccola! Broccola! I like dem!"

Armand Jr. Marries A Caterer

On May 5, 1978 my brother Armand Jr. married his childhood sweetheart, Lisa Marie Grassi, at St. Peter's Church. They were only 19, and Dad and Mom weren't completely happy about this youthful marriage. The newlyweds rented the Profenno house on Stevens Avenue in the Deering Center neighborhood. It was the house where my mom had grown up.

Lisa Grassi had a big heart, a warm personality and a laugh that was so contagious that just hearing it put a smile on peoples' faces. She was the first to help in a family emergency, the first to show up with a platter of food, and the first to crack a joke then laugh out loud as she reached the punch line.

Lisa grew up with nine siblings. Her father and mother, Louis and

Theresa Grassi, owned a variety store where Lisa and her siblings worked, cooking and selling Italian foods. Lisa's passion for cooking took her into catering. She started her own catering business shortly after she and Armand Jr. married.

Super Bowl Sunday

I often helped with Lisa's catering. Dad knew how hard it was to serve food in strange places, and he wondered if we should be doing this. One Super Bowl Sunday Lisa was hired to cater an event for fifteen Portland-area executives. They would watch the game on a big-screen television in a private room at a popular Portland restaurant called Horsefeathers. We planned to serve them a delicious Italian meal. The host was the then-President of the Guy Gannett Publishing Company, our cousin, John DiMatteo.

Lisa called me the day before, asking me to be there at noon. We would set out the food on the buffet table, then serve the hors d'oeuvres. Lisa said that if she needed me any earlier she would call me. Snow was forecast, and the weatherman had predicted that it wouldn't stop until late morning.

It snowed heavily the night before, and on Sunday morning I started to worry. I called Armand Jr. to ask if Lisa had gotten off all right. He said that she had headed out around 8 that morning. He hadn't heard from her, so he assumed everything was okay.

It was already 10am. Lisa had asthma, and I knew that if she was nervous or upset it might kick up. I decided to drive in and check on her. There was already 10 inches of new-fallen snow, so driving was treacherous. The snow banks were over five feet high, and snow was still falling. The sidewalks were covered, and there was no room to park. As I climbed out of my car and tried to pull myself up and over the huge snow bank, I noticed a bunch of stuffed mushrooms lying in the snow. It dawned on me that Lisa must have had to climb over the snow bank to get all of her equipment and food inside by herself. I thought to myself, "This is not a good sign!"

As I went in and climbed the stairs, I called out "Lisa? Lisa?" There was no answer. Then as I entered the dining room, I saw her lying on the floor, struggling to breathe. Between shallow breaths she managed to say, "I had to climb over the snow bank (gasp!) to bring in all of the equipment and food (gasp!) and lug it up those friggin' stairs! (gasp!) The mushrooms bit the dust! (gasp!) There was nothing I could do about it once I started to fall (gasp!) and they went all on the sidewalk. (gasp!)" Despite her gasping she ended her story with her infamous cackle, "Yuk, Yuk, Yuk."

I ran down to the front entrance, and picked up all the mushrooms. That way no one would stumble upon them and wonder what the hell happened. I took off my coat, and went to the kitchen. To my astonishment, I realized that Lisa had planned to cook everything in this rented room's kitchen. There were only two working burners on an ancient electric stove!

I'd always tried to get Lisa to cook as much as she could at home because you never knew what kind of a kitchen you would find at the job site. For some reason, she never heeded my advice. Now I went back, grabbed her by the arms, and literally dragged her into the kitchen. Between puffs on her inhaler, she told me what to do.

Starting without even knowing what dishes she'd planned on, I had two hours to prepare the entrees, antipasto, dessert, and hors d'oeuvres minus the mushrooms! I was running around like a crazy woman, climbing over Lisa as she lay in the doorway, and cooking everything with two burners and one small oven. I got it all done by noon.

I managed to change from my white apron to a black cocktail apron in time to greet the guests. I took their coats, then ran back to the kitchen to grab the hors d'oeuvres. When Lisa felt better she set up the buffet. Every time I crossed her path, I would say something like, "It's a good thing I love you so, because I wanted to kill you an hour ago!" Or, "Next time you need someone to help you, count me out!" She would just give me that laugh of hers.

When I told Dad he shook his head, saying that not preparing the food ahead of time was "bad business" "For Christ's sake," he said, "you don't even know how the equipment in the kitchen works! You guys are nuts! I hope you learned a lesson?"

THE WEDDING RECEPTION

Shortly after surviving the Super Bowl Sunday disaster, Lisa called to ask me to help her with a 150-guest wedding reception. "I can't do it without you!" she said. I took the challenge.

The reception was in a large empty room over a fitness club. It was starting at 4pm. We got there early in the morning, and, once again, Lisa did not prepare any of the food at home. As she started setting up for the buffet table I asked her where the food was. "I have to put together the cold-cut platters and salads," she said. "The only food we have to cook is the chicken fingers."

I went looking for the kitchen. After searching around, I asked an employee, only to have him look at me as if I had two heads.

"We don't have a kitchen up here," he said.

"Then where is it?" I asked.

"We don't have a kitchen anywhere," he replied.

I wanted to run out the door. When I told Lisa, she said, "Don't worry, I brought my mother's Fry Daddy just in case they didn't have an oven. We can use that to cook the chicken fingers."

I foresaw another stressful event.

After hunting down a couple of extension cords, I sat on the floor of a little storage room, frying up dozens of chicken fingers, a few at a time in the Fry Daddy. Every half hour or so Lisa would come in and ask, "How's it going?"

"Just dandy!" I would reply. "This really sucks!"

As she turned to walk away, I heard, "Yuk, Yuk, Yuk!"

Later, when Lisa realized how difficult these jobs were, she limited herself to smaller venues, and recruited Armand Jr. to help.

Grandchild #3

On April 10, 1981, Armand Arnold Polito, III was born to Armand Jr. and Lisa. Dad and Mom were ecstatic to finally have a grandson. Dad liked carrying on the family name with the "III." Now Dad and Mom had three grandchildren, two girls and a boy, and they were always available to take one or all of them for an overnighter. They did this most often on Saturday nights so we could go out for the evening.

The Grandchildren: Angela Sabia Pizzo, Armand A. Polito, III and Adrianna Pizzo

My brother John nicknamed him "bruiser." Armand III was a big, easygoing kid. He loved to be around his cousins Angela and Adrianna. Having a boy around was totally different for them. They didn't know how to play the way he played: rough and tough. This kid would do anything others were doing, and he ate whatever came along. He never asked questions.

His mother had diabetes and asthma, and on several occasions when she was hospitalized, Little Armand spent weeks at my house. I never had to call that kid to dinner twice. Once I started cooking he was right there. Once the table was set Little Armand was in his chair gripping his utensils. He was happy to eat. One time when I was serving at the table, I asked Little Armand if he liked mushrooms.

"No, Aunt Nancy. I don't wike them," he said.

As I passed out mushrooms to the others, Angela said, "Mom, Little Armand is crying."

"What's the matter, dear?"

Barely lifting his head, he pointed his tiny finger at the mushrooms on Angela's plate. "I didn't get any of doze!"

We all burst out laughing.

This kid was remarkable. He would eat anything, even if he didn't like it.

Thanksgivings

In 1982 my cousin George DiMatteo decided that the Profenno/DiMatteo clan should get together to celebrate Thanksgiving Day at a Mason's Hall. One of the men who worked for George's construction company was a Mason, and he offered to rent us a place. These gatherings might have as many as eighty relatives attending, and while we've used several different facilities over the years, these Thanksgiving dinners have become a tradition.

Each year three cousins cook three huge turkeys all night on Thanksgiving Eve. They wrap them tightly and bring them to the hall in mid-morning of Thanksgiving Day. Everyone has their role. Cousin Mike (Profenno)True's wife, Judy, always prepares the squash and cream cheese potatoes, while cousin, Jeannine (DiMatteo) Wilson makes her infamous sausage-and-sweet-potato stuffing. Aunt Rose brings her homemade cranberry jellied salad. Jan also makes creamed onions, and I cook the vegetables there at the hall.

My cousin Jan (Profenno) True and I, arrive first at 10am. We turn on the heat, get the coffee perking, and start the vegetables. One by one the different families arrive bringing their specialty dishes. Dad always asked that we give him the giblets, and he would cook them with some Italian sausage, green peppers, and hot pepperoncini. The few who loved this concoction kept a close watch on Dad until it was done, then scooped up a bowl of goodness with a slice of Italian bread. Dad cooked this for years until he read an article saying you should not eat the organs of any animal because that's where diseases strike first. That was the end of giblets.

Some of our cousins attend the traditional Deering/Portland High School Thanksgiving Day football game at 10am. We always wait for the game to end. The sports fans roll in around 1pm, then we partake in our turkey dinner. When everyone's there I bang a spoon on a pan to get everyone's attention. Once they quiet down cousin, Cammie Profenno says a short Thanksgiving Day prayer. Everyone cheers, then they form lines on each side of the long buffet table where the food is set out.

The Dessert Table

The dessert table presents us with the most competitive event of the day. Anyone can bring whatever they want, adding to the standard fare. The desserts are lined up strategically, each with its name written out in front. Usually there are a few pumpkin and apple pies, but we give the most attention to the most mysterious dishes. Some favorites are my Italian cookies, batches of brownies, Jan's chocolate layer cake, cousin, Betsy (Profenno) True's chocolate fudge and chocolate cream pie, and cousin Kevin (Profenno) Hutchins' wife, Betsy, always makes her shortbread cookies laced with chocolate chips and one end dipped in melted chocolate with walnuts.

Intermission

While we digest our turkey dinner we talk, joke and drink wine. Mike True brings a ping-pong table, and the playoffs get started before dinner. Dispersed around the room people play bridge or cribbage, or catch up on family news. The children run around inside and out, always giggling. Around 3:30 we play a few rounds of bingo with prizes of movie passes, movie rentals or a gift certificate from the ice cream parlor. Sometimes there's a piano, and choruses of "Ole Sole Mio" and "Come Back to Sorrento" fill the hall.

Cousin Jeannine brings in a batch of sugar cookies cut out into Thanksgiving shapes for the younger children to paint with food coloring and top with colored sugar and sprinkles. Usually, one whole table is covered with newly decorated cookies adorned with way too much frosting and sprinkles to ever dry.

THANKSGIVING ITALIAN STYLE

The evening meal chefs are the DiMatteo side, taking over at 4pm, preparing the Italian feast to be ready by 6pm. Cousin Joey Reardon loves to make his specialty, calamari. Cousin Peter (DiMatteo)Wilson was a fisherman and always got a great catch the previous day. With that he would create his favorite fish dish as a surprise. Cousin Michael (DiMatteo) Reardon loves to make delicious meatballs, while Cousin John DiMatteo might make Veal Parmesan, Chicken Cacciatore or Lasagna. Over the years some of the dishes have changed, but it's always Italian.

At 5:30 cousin George DiMatteo brings in a six-foot loaf of Italian bread on a wooden plank. He has this baked to order at Botto's Bakery. George and his wife, Carolyn, cut the loaf open and assemble condiments and Italian cold cuts on top of it. This strategic assembly of meats, pickles, onions, tomatoes, olives, lettuce and cheeses takes over a half hour. They put the top back on and cut it into serving pieces. When they're done it's a supreme masterpiece of a sandwich.

The Garage

As a lesson in construction the vocational school up the street contracted out their students to build garages for people in the neighborhood. These garages sold for far less than ones built by professional contractors. Dad was all for helping students learn and saving a buck at the same time, so he decided he would replace our old one-car garage with a new one-and-a-half-car garage.

John wanted to save the roof of the old garage, all in one piece. He planned to build a new frame for it, and use it on his farm. He thought they could support the roof with an old staging on wheels while they knocked down the garage walls. He figured he could keep the roof up in the air long enough to back his flatbed truck underneath it. It worked pretty well as they tore down the first three sides, then they prepared to knock down the last one. As John and Dad stood under the roof, checking it out, Dad yelled, "It doesn't look safe! Get the hell outta there!"

"Dad, it's all right!" John insisted. "Calm down!"

Dad ducked out from under the roof, "I am not going to stand underneath that damn thing! It just doesn't look too safe to me! Jesus Christ! It could let go any time!"

All of a sudden the staging collapsed, pinning John underneath. Dad ran around the heap of rubble yelling, "John, are you all right?"

"Dad!" John shouted. "Call the rescue! I can't move! I'm pinned down!"

Dad ran inside to make the call.

Mom and Angela were pulling in from a shopping trip when they saw the rescue and fire vehicles parked in front of the house. Mom jumped out of the car, saw the collapsed roof and Dad, but didn't see John. "Oh My God!" she screamed. "John? John?"

From beneath the rubble came a muffled voice: "I'm okay Mom!"

It took at least ten firemen to lift the roof off John. When they dragged him out, they saw a large gash across his shin, and his leg looked twisted.

They asked John why he'd thought the plan would work. Dad was angry with himself for letting John talk him into it. He kept saying, "I told you it would not work!" They took John to Mercy Hospital. X-rays showed the leg wasn't broken, but he needed 24 stitches to sew up the gash.

For two weeks Dad and John made trip after trip to the dump in John's pickup truck, getting rid of all the remains of the garage. Once the land was cleared, Dad had cement floor poured for the new garage so the vocational students could deliver the garage. Dad was so happy to have a new and bigger garage. This one had a side door, plenty of space for his car, staging, the planks of wood used with the staging, his lawn mower, snow blower, snow tires, gardening tools and a small work bench.

Dad Gets Ripped Off

A few years after Dad got the garage he'd filled it with every household tool and garden/snow device he could find. One day when he went to get the car out to go "up to Shaw's," he came running back in the house, yelling, "Son of a bitch! God damn bastards! I gotta call the police. Someone broke into the garage and stole the tires off the car and took the battery!"

The garage's side door and main door had both been locked. Dad couldn't believe someone could jack up the car, then strip it of tires and battery, without anyone in the house hearing or seeing anything. It turned out the crooks had gone where no one could see them, through the garage's rear window. How they got everything off the car and out the back window in the dark without one of the neighbors hearing was beyond us.

The police did nothing but take the information. Dad was furious, and decided to "fix those bastards!" He bolted steel grates across the rear window, and across the window on the side door. He put two huge padlocks on the outside of the side door, and one on the front of the garage door. After that it was always a pain to get anything from the garage. We had to get the key from Dad every time. In the winter the locks would freeze, sending Dad back inside for one of his six cans of lock defrost in his basement workshop. "God damn it!" he would mutter. "That damn lock is frozen! Son of a bitch!"

Normajean, Chris & Racehorses

John and Cheryl divorced in 1980. John kept Tarantell Farm. He continued boarding horses, and began buying racehorses. In 1982, when Jen Vanderwerth, one of the owners of a horse John boarded, got pregnant she asked Normajean Forbes if she would exercise and ride her horse for her. John met Normajean and her son Christopher and all three have been together, running the farm, ever since. With Normajean and Chris's help, John has had several racehorses. Some of the most notable are: Jo's Best, who he co-owned with Dr. Ernie Vandermast, Harry Hustle, co-owned by John and Mike Murray, John and Chris's Hour Glass, and Predetermined, owned by John and Kelly Case. There have been many others.

The racehorses are hard work, but they've also provided many years fun for the whole family. We would all go out to Scarborough Downs Racetrack to see John's horses run. When they would win, Dad, Mom, Armand Jr. and Dad's brother, Uncle Angelo, were the first ones to run out and have their pictures taken in the winner's circle.

Dad got a kick out of the notoriety that came with being father to an owner of racehorses. He would walk up to a window, place a bet, and hear someone say, "He's the father of the owner of Hour Glass." Inevitably these people would jump in line behind Dad to hear which horse he was betting on.

Before each race, John would drive the sulkie around the track, warming up his horse. As he would drive past Mom and Dad standing at the fence watching all of the horses warm up, people around them would scrutinize every move, thinking that John must be giving a coded tip to his parents. Dad would hear people say, "Did you see

how that driver looked over at his parents? He's gonna win tonight!"
Or "I think he nodded at them to give them a clue!" They wouldn't
have believed that neither Dad nor John ever knew who was going
to win a race. All they knew was whether the horse was in its best
shape, and how it compared to the rest of the field—the kind of information a savvy race fan might pick up from observation, personal
knowledge, or even the racing form.

Over the years Tarantell Farm was home to its share of special
animals. John and Normajean rescued an abused donkey named
Ernie J. Parsons. Then there was Windsor Dancer or "Danny," a
black Welsh Stallion pony John got from the people who sold him
the farm. There were three African geese named Isabel, Chester and
John who were so attached to John they would attack anyone that
came close to him, a big white rabbit named Polito, two pigs named
Cheech and Chong, several dogs named Taint, Rocky and Zoe, and
several cats named Scooters and Max. Normajean, John and Chris
have owned many riding horses. All of those animals that have
passed on are buried up in the back corner of the farm property.

Christmases through the years

Though we had all moved out of the house, and had children
of our own, we still kept the same Christmas morning ritual, driving
to Mom and Dad's. We would all be there at their Christmas tree by
11am. As soon as we arrived at the Washington Avenue house, we
walked up the three steps into the kitchen, to hear Dad greeting us,
dishtowel thrown over his shoulder, as he sang what we knew as
his favorite tune. It wasn't until after he died that we discovered that
this tune that he always danced around and hummed was one that
he wrote himself at the Conservatory in Naples, titled: "Oh Quorida
Senorita."

For 44 years we kept up this tradition, along with its preparations. On the first Sunday in December, the three grandchildren,

Angela, Adrianna, and Armand III, and I would meet at the house to set up and decorate the artificial tree. Once we arrived Dad would go up to the attic and pass down box after box of Christmas decorations. To make carrying easier, each box was tied up with either an old belt or a piece of clothesline rope. Dad had a system, so no one could open the boxes until he came down into the living room. There he would assess the situation, determining what was in each box. He would make everyone stand back as he carefully untied the belts, clotheslines, and other bindings that only he could untie. Armand Jr. and Armand III were left-handed which Dad saw as a handicap. Dad would yell out to Armand III, "Get away from there! You can't untie that box, you're left-handed! It will never work! Here! Let me do it!"

THE BIG WHEEL

One Christmas, when Angela was almost two years old, Papa and Mammie bought her a Big Wheel. It was under the tree when we arrived at their house. Angela loved that Big Wheel so much that she would ride it around the house for hours, making a circle from the kitchen through the dining room, living room, hallway and back into the kitchen. The Big Wheel had a device on the underside of the back wheel that made a clicking noise when you peddled it. Two weeks passed, and one day when we arrived at Papa and Mammie's, Angela ran into the den to get her Big Wheel. Moments later she rode it into the kitchen, screaming, "Broken! Big Wheel broken!"

When I looked at Dad I saw him trying to sneak out of the room. "What did you do to her Big Wheel?" I asked.

He grinned and said, "Ah! I fixed that damn thing! It made too much damn noise!"

Angela ran over to Papa grabbing his legs and looking up at him and said, "Papa, fix it!"

Dad melted inside when he saw her little face. He picked her up, saying, "Come on. Papa will fix it!"

Off they went, Big Wheel in tow, down the cellar stairs to Papa's workshop. Fifteen minutes later they emerged from the cellar with the Big Wheel fixed, and a big smile on Angela's face. Dad looked at me and said, "There, are you happy now? For Christ's sakes! Now everyone can stop fussing!"

Mom piped in, "What a guy!"

BAGS OF GIFTS

Mom and Dad took to buying items for all of us throughout the year. They knew exactly what type of deodorant, shampoo, soap, or toothpaste each of us liked. After the personal items they would buy pens, pencils, whiteout, potholders—anything you could think of—or items they came across while shopping at Marden's Salvage Store. After collecting these goodies, on December 1st, Dad would set up a card table down in my mother's beauty shop where the two of them would spend their nights wrapping. When we arrived on Christmas morning there would be ten or more huge bags lined up in front of the fireplace, each with a big bow, and a tag with a name. It took us hours to go through these gifts. We were always amazed at how personal each bag was, and how much thought they'd put into each gift. They must've spent hundreds of dollars on each bag, and then they'd wrap a few extra gifts and put them under the tree. They certainly spoiled us!

When we first got there, before opening our presents, Dad would have a big bowl of donut holes on the kitchen table, along with Sanka coffee. We would all greet each other with "Merry Christmas" and a big hug. Then we had coffee and donut holes at the kitchen table. Dad would run around the kitchen, joining in on all the stories, laughter and banter, while he prepared the Christmas dinner.

In our Christmas morning ritual we all had our assigned places: Mom on the couch, Dad taking the big green hassock in front of the fireplace, John perched nearest the dining room so he could steal Italian cookies between gifts, and Armand Jr. on the floor along with all the grandchildren. When we were all settled, Dad would pass out trash bags and steak knives. The knives were the only tools we used on wrapping paper and tape. Even the grandchildren used them. When I questioned Dad about giving young children knives, he would wave his hand and say, "Hell, its Christmas. They will be all right!" Then he would add, "Just be careful kids!"

It always took more than an hour to open the gifts. It was complete chaos, with boxes, tags, and crumpled wrapping paper flying. Dad got irritated when we threw paper, "Hey! Stop throwing that shit! There are trash bags everywhere! Use them!" As soon as he said it John or Armand Jr. would let fly balls of wrapping paper aimed directly at Dad's head. We would all crack up, and Dad would have a hard time keeping a straight face. " You horse's ass!" he'd say. "You're all nuts!" We moved as fast as we could, because Dad did not want to waste too much time on gifts. To him Christmas dinner was the important part.

Dad's Gifts for Mom

Every Christmas Dad came up with a new and special gift for Mom, one that required his unique touch even when she was opening it. He would work on her gift for weeks in his basement workshop. When the time came on Christmas morning he was always afraid she would somehow blow the surprise. He would get up from his hassock, lean over and tell her how to open it. This usually involved several steps.

One such gift was a huge mechanical Santa with a bag around its shoulders that Dad had filled with money. Another was a box rigged so when Mom lifted the cover, it exploded with lots of elastics tied tightly around bills. This made a loud noise as if something alive was inside. One year he gave her a pen packaged inside several boxes, each smaller than the last, much like a Chinese box. When she finally got to the pen she said, "So!" But that wasn't it. He gave her instructions to take the pen apart to reveal a $100 bill inside. One year it was a mechanical Santa sleeping and snoring (like Dad) in a little bed. Under the blanket Mom found a $100 bill.

Still another gift came in a huge box. When Mom opened it she found a helium balloon Santa that rose to the ceiling, money trailing beneath it. Another was a Santa head that shook and played Jingle Bells when you clapped your hands. One was a box with a tab that she pulled revealing 100 one-dollar bills taped end-to-end, wrapped around an empty toilet paper roll. One more was a Christmas ball that chirped loudly like a bird. Dad had successfully struggled to get the ball apart and hide money inside. Mom loved that chirping bird Christmas ball, and from then on she hung it on the tree every year. When you turned it on it never stopped chirping, which could be annoying.

These gifts were events, and it took time and effort for the presentation to come off the way Dad planned it. His main goal was to surprise her. She loved a good joke or a big surprise. When she opened one of these, Dad was the one laughing loudest. The rest of us always stopped to watch Mom's reaction. We never knew what was up Dad's sleeve.

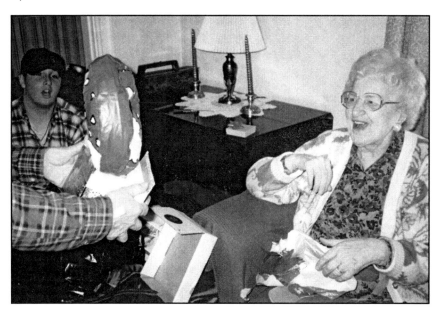

1995, Mom looking surprised as Dad shows her how to open up one of his Christmas gifts. Mom never opened any of the gifts Dad wrapped for her. He always stated, "There's a right way and a wrong way to open the damn thing! I'll do it!"

CHRISTMAS DINNER

When Dad prepared the Christmas meal I always helped. Two weeks before we would decide what to have, then we would make a list and go shopping. Dinner was usually Italian fare, like lasagna, meatballs, sausages, marinated mushrooms and Dad always made his infamous rice pilaf. This was one of his best dishes. Even if Mom wasn't feeling well, she could always eat rice.

After many years of the same Christmas dinner, I suggested some different entrees, and Dad was ready to try some. One time I wanted to use a recipe calling for deboning whole roasting chickens, leaving the drumsticks and wings intact, and stuffing the deboned bird so it looked as if the bones were still in place. Dad did a masterful job of carving and deboning, and I watched in awe as he cut, trimmed, and literally turned the chicken inside out. The stuffing was a mixture of breadcrumbs, eggs, spinach, onions, and parmesan cheese. When these two chickens arrived on the table, Dad carved through the whole bird. Everyone was amazed that there were no bones. It was an incredibly appealing presentation and Dad took great pride in his creation.

I always made the desserts. Every year it was Italian cookies, anise toasted and anise filled and frosted and Ricotta Cheese Pie. Dad never liked desserts that were too sweet. He wanted something dry that he could dunk in his coffee. He loved it when I would surprise him with Struffoli or Cenci (Rags or Bow Ties).

PULL THE TRIGGER

After finishing his junior year at the University of Maine Orono, Dad came home for the summer to have an ulcer operation, recuperate and enjoy the celebration of his sister Angie's (Angiolina) wedding.

The stress of college life added with his struggle with the English language and the change in the type of food he was not accustom too, took its toll on Dad's stomach. Even many years after his surgery Dad would occasionally have discomfort if he over ate.

He knew his limitations, but there were times after a huge Thanksgiving, Christmas or Easter dinner, his stomach was on overload and he was extremely uncomfortable. Dad would get up quietly from the table and head for the basement. One of us would yell to him, "Dad, where are you going?" He would stop at the top of the stairway, turn and state, "I am going down to "pull the trigger!"

We all would continue our conversation at the dinner table, patiently waiting for Dad's return. When he would join us again, he would say, "There, that did the trick! I had to get that God damn stuff out of there! It was way too heavy! That last brownie put me over the edge! Let's have a cup of coffee!" Then he would stop and look around at all of us and say, "What?"

Mom would look at him and shake her head, "What a guy!" Dad would reply, "The trouble with you Isabel is that you are too damn dainty! You don't know how to take care of yourself! There's nothing too it, for God's sake! You would rather suffer!"

Even the grandchildren knew what "pull the trigger" meant. They knew that Papa was very uncomfortable and it was his way of taking care of business.

I remember whenever John, Armand Jr. or me were sick with the flu or had a severe stomachache, Dad would make sure he was there to help us through it. Knowing how most kids dislike throwing up, Dad would state, "Get it up! Don't keep all those germs inside! Your body is telling you to throw it up for Christ's sake! Let it go! You will feel a hell of a lot better when that stuff's out of there!"

As we were hurling our guts out, Dad would be talking us through it, "That a boy! Keep it coming! That's it girlie, you're doing great."

Sometimes Dad would help us along. In other words, give us a special drink of warm water with a little salt in it. That alone would make us gag. We soon learned not to drink anything other than a glass of flat gingerale when we were ill.

New Year's Eve Parties

When my parents were in their early 60s, Mom decided that, instead of going out for New Year's Eve, she wanted to have a party at home. This became an annual event. She would plan it for weeks, inviting family and friends. Dad would make a list of the necessary food, soda and liquor, but Mom always waited until the last couple of days before she made her list. It drove Dad crazy.

Her preparations weren't terribly complex, but she gave Dad plenty of orders, delegating many important tasks. Knowing exactly how she wanted the house, I always helped set things up. It was easy for me because I'd been the one vacuuming, dusting and cleaning for so many years. I'd cleaned for Mom even after I got married. Dad and I always planned everything out just the way Mom wanted it.

When New Year's Eve came Dad and I spent all day getting the house ready. We'd bring the folding chairs up from the basement, set up a mini-bar at the kitchen counter, arranging the cold cuts on the glass platter, put out dishes of peanuts and candy, and set up the dining room table with Mom's beautiful Quaker Lace tablecloth. The only thing that Mom did herself was polish her antique silver candle sticks and silverware. No one else could do that to her specifications. God forbid there be water marks for this perfectionist! On everything else she directed. By three o'clock she'd be lying on the couch exhausted, while Dad and I finished up.

After Mom rested she would disappear upstairs, and take over two hours getting herself ready. Finally she would make her grand entrance down the stairs and into the kitchen. Dad would look up and smile, saying, "Wow! Lady! You look very pretty! That's a nice!" Mom really knew fashion, and what looked good on her. Dad loved her style. They were the perfect complements for one another.

As family and friends arrived Mom came to life, entertaining everyone with jokes, and games with prizes. The party would go on until two or three in the morning. As soon as the last person had left Mom would have to lie down. Dad would say, "Isabel! Go to bed! I will take care of everything." Dad and I would spend hours cleaning and putting everything away. When Mom got up the next morning the house was back to normal. No one would have ever known we'd had a party.

Dad's Home Remedies

When Dad was at the University of Maine he took a course in first aid. He could cure a common cold, flu, cut, splinter, stomachache, sore throat, ingrown toenail and anything else we complained about. The following are examples of his expertise in the medical field:

Alcohol: He used this to sterilize the instruments he used when "operating" on his children and grandchildren. He stopped pimples by dipping a Q-tip in alcohol and dabbing it on the spot. "Dry them the hell up!" he said. Alcohol also stopped the itch from mosquito bites, and if you used it diligently, it would take care of a little sebaceous cyst on your body or even your face. If it didn't work it was because, "You don't know what the hell you're doing! You didn't give it time! Ah, you gotta keep at it, for Christ Sake!"

Splinters: The moment you mentioned that you had a splinter Dad dropped everything, and went down to his private bathroom. He would return with a Russell Stover box filled with matches, needles, a magnifying glass and surgical tweezers so sharp they could cut through skin. With the needle in one hand and a match in the other, he burned the tip of the needle to sterilize it, then examined the splinter with his magnifying glass. Taking his time, he picked and pried, while we squirmed in intense discomfort. "Stop moving!" He would yell. "For Christ's sake! I almost got it!" Once the splinter was out he would display it to us, saying: "There you go! All done! Christ's sake look at that thing!"

Sore Throats: At the first sign of a little scratchiness in your throat Dad would be right there with salt and warm water. He would say, "All you have to do is gargle with a little warm water with a teaspoonful of salt a couple times a day." We would always complain about how the bad taste made us gag even more. Dad would reply loudly, "Go ahead, suffer! What the hell is the matter with you! Ah, you don't know how to take care of yourself! There's nothing to it!" Finally the patient would stand over the kitchen sink while Dad mixed his little concoction. We'd struggle to gargle the way he directed. "Just let it go down your throat a little and then start gargling. Just do it!" We cried that we couldn't do it or that it tasted bad. Dad would walk away in disgust, waving his arms, saying, "The hell with you, then! Suffer!" He also told us to wrap a scarf around our necks to keep our necks warm, but we never did.

Ingrown Toenails: When Mom got an ingrown toenail Dad fixed her up with his special trick. He would slowly push a tiny piece of cotton up under the nail, making a space between the nail and skin, relieving the pressure. He would add one small piece of cotton after another, pushing it with the head of a needle. At one time or another we all had this problem, and Dad's cure worked like a charm. A few days later the nail would start to grow up over the cotton, easing the pressure and stopping the pain. "Now, don't cut your toenails down around the edges," he would say. "That's what causes ingrown toenails. You need to cut them straight across. Watch that closely and if you need to have more cotton added in a few days, let me know."

Stuffed Up Nose: Dad was always filling the bathroom sink with warm water and sucking it up his nose to clear out his sinuses. The thought of it repulsed John, Armand Jr., and me, and we refused to do it. He would fill a bowl with warm water, mix in salt, and tell us to cup our hands and suck it up into our noses. When we put up a big stink he would say, "What's the matter with you? Ah, it's nothing! Do you want to breathe or not? Go ahead, suffer!"

Another remedy for stuffy nose was to stick a Chapstick up your nose to coat the inside. According to Dad, it would help clear your stuffy nose and make you sleep better. He had a special Chapstick just for his nose. One day Angela asked Papa if she could use some of his Chapstick. When she reached for it in his bathroom, he said, "No, not that one. That is the one that I use for my nose." Angela said, "Nose? Why would you put it up your nose, Papa?" Dad explained, "It keeps moisture up there; helps you breathe better; and the inside will never crack."

Abscessed Tooth: Dad once went to the dentist for an abscessed tooth. When presented with the option of a root canal, crown, and a huge price tag, he decided to think about it. The dentist could not understand how someone in that much pain could "think about it." Dad came home mumbling, "I never heard of such a thing. He wants me to spend all this money on a root canal and crown and all I have is an abscess! He's nuts! I'll get rid of it myself!" He figured that if it was an abscess then like most abscesses you need to draw the infection out. He rolled up some gauze tightly, soaked it in a solution of Epson Salt and very warm water, placed it on the gum where the pain and abscess were. Every hour he took the gauze out, re-soaking it with Epson Salt and warm water. He went grocery shopping with that lump of gauze in his mouth. After 24 hours he saw a lump developing on the gum, the skin broke and fluid and a little blood seeped out and the pain was gone. He never had a problem with that tooth again.

He did the same thing to another tooth later, and got the same result.

Extraction: Dad used to grind his teeth so loud at night I could hear him through the bedroom wall. He ground them like that for so many years that he loosened his back teeth. His dentist recommended the removal of one of Dad's back molars before it created worse problems. The dentist told Dad that an oral surgeon would have to extract the tooth. He refused to pay an oral surgeon to pull a "God damn tooth" that he could pull himself. Night after night I saw Dad sitting at the kitchen table, his handkerchief wrapped around his fingers, as he worked on getting the tooth out. Finally, after weeks of seeing him perched in the same position at the kitchen table, he got out the pliers, and wrapped black electrical tape around the end so the metal would not hit his silver filling. I ran out of the room screaming for Mom. When we all ran back in we saw blood all over his handkerchief. Dad smiled, saying, "Here you go!" He threw the tooth on the kitchen table, rinsed his mouth out at the kitchen sink, drenched a piece of gauze in whiskey, put it in his mouth, and bit down hard to stop the bleeding. He then sat down to read the paper. As we stared in awe, he looked at us and said, "What? What's wrong with you?"

Cuts and scrapes: Whenever someone got a cut or a scrape the bottle of peroxide came out of the kitchen closet. Dad made you stand over to the sink as he poured the peroxide over your cut. He said the bubbling peroxide meant that it was disinfecting the wound.

When I was eight or nine years old, I was playing with a friend, Linda Foster, two houses down from Arbor Street. Her grandfather had hung a swing from a branch in the backyard. I'd pushed Linda high in the sky then she told me it was my turn. Linda pushed me up really high, and I just kept on going. I sailed up, taking the swing and branch with me. When I crashed, the branch stuck in my shin, tearing my skin wide open. I ran home crying, blood running down my pant leg. In the house Dad had me take off my pants and lay my leg over the toilet bowl as he poured the peroxide. As I screamed and cried I heard my mother say, "Maybe we should take her to the doctor for some stitches? It looks pretty deep!" My father would not hear of it. "She will be alright," he said. "I will take care of it." My leg bled for days. Every night Dad would take off the artistically applied bandages and gauge, pour peroxide over the wound and, re-dress it. It took weeks to heal. I still have the scar to prove it.

New Skin: Dad would get little cuts from dry skin around his fingernails, especially in winter. These hurt whenever his fingers got wet, often opening and bleeding. This made cooking and washing dishes painful. One day he discovered a product called New Skin. It burned like hell when applied to an open wound, but Dad loved it! Whenever we complained about a cut or crack on our hands he would take out the little brush attachment (like the one in a nail polish bottle), then shove the brush into the cut to coat it. We would wince at the sting, and he would say, "Ah, what's the matter with you? Go ahead and suffer then!"

The Grandchildren's Relationship

Six months after Angela was born in 1975 Dad retired. This opened up a whole new side of him that none of us had ever seen. This was when our Dad became our children's "Papa," forming special relationships with each of his three grandchildren, offering support, guidance and assistance in their lives. He became their mentor.

MUSCILLE, MUSCILLA

In the late afternoons or evenings, when his beard had grown out a little from his early morning shave, Dad would take a grandchild on his lap, facing him. Amidst the scents of supper cooking on the stove, he would take the child's little hands in his, lift them to his face, passing the open palms over his whiskers as he slowly chanted, "Muscille, Muscilla." Gradually he would speed things up, all the while saying, "Musce, Musce, Musce, Musce." All three grandchildren laughed out loud at the feel of his beard and the sound of his voice. It was something he'd done with me when I was little. I never knew if the words meant anything. I didn't have to.

Sleepovers

The three grandchildren, Angela, Adrianna and Armand III, stayed overnight at Papa and Mammie's house many times. My mother was inclined to make her grandchildren work for her. The girls might polish her antique silver candlesticks or silverware, or dust the mahogany furniture, or set the table for meals. Armand III might be helping his grandfather fix something down in the workshop, or paint a fence, or change the oil in the lawn mower, or rearrange Papa's collection of wood. When working with Armand III, Dad watched him closely because, like his father, Armand III had the "disadvantage" of being left-handed. When work was done for the morning, Dad would take Armand III up the street to Steve & Renee's Diner for a hamburger.

In the summertime the grandchildren often stayed over during the week. Every day at noon they would watch "I Love Lucy" while eating peanut-butter-and-jelly sandwiches, or ham-and-provolone on a sub roll, microwaved just enough to soften the cheese. Once in a while Dad would feed them hot dogs. He would boil these in a little water and place the rolls in a strainer over the hotdogs, and cover them with a towel to steam them. The kids loved them that way.

Watching Television

Dad let them watch some TV. Adrianna would sit in between his legs on the floor, with Angela on the "Big" gold pillow next to them. They would laugh hysterically at "The Honeymooners," and Dad would let them stay up and watch Johnny Carson before a midnight snack of toast or cereal. In the morning they ate Rice Krispies and Dad would let them dunk their toast in his Sanka coffee. If it was nice out, they would do outdoor projects in the garage or the garden. If it rained, they worked in the house, or went down to the workshop to help him with one of his projects. In the kitchen a television faced the stove. Dad sat there in a chair, watching while he cooked. Adrianna would sit on his lap and he would fall asleep as they watched "People's Court."

Whenever Dad sat in his favorite chair in the living room, Angela and Adrianna climbed all over him, combing his wavy hair, placing clips, headbands and barrettes all over his head. He would doze off then come awake asking Angela how long it had been. He was always keeping an eye on the supper cooking in the kitchen.

He always started supper by three, delegating small tasks, such as setting the table or peeling carrots, to the children. When the time came he always stopped everything and said, "Hey! I gotta get supper started. Andiamo! [Let's go!]"

ORIGAMI

There were few toys at my parents' house, so the kids brought toys with them. My father got creative when entertaining his grandchildren. For hours they would watch him folding paper, transforming it into a horse-drawn wagon, or a witch flapping her arms up and down, or spinning wheels on a paper stick, or a camera that flipped open revealing a picture. Adrianna thought that camera was really going to take her picture, and she still has it to this day.

One day Angela asked him, "Papa, don't they call that origami?"

"Yeah," he said, "I think so. But, all I know is that I had no toys to play with as child in Bovino, so my friends and I used to make our animals and things out of paper."

GROCERY SHOPPING

The quaint little sun porch, with its table against one wall, and a desk and overstuffed chair along the other wall, was the place where the grandchildren loved to play. In the winter months the afternoon sun shone through the windows, making it warm. With the table as a counter, a Fisher Price cash register, and Monopoly money, Angela, Adrianna and Armand III would set up a grocery store. They used the on/off switch on the reading lamp as the store pager and microphone (press the button and speak into the top of the light to page for a price check). They had a Fisher Price shopping cart, and even a stack of paper bags for the groceries. Dad let them come through to the kitchen into the back pantry for the groceries, and from there it was on to the sun porch for check out, payment and bagging. This kept them busy for hours, allowing Dad to nap in the living room until it was time to start supper, or until a fight broke out.

TOOTH PULLING

One day after shopping with my mother, I came back to their house to find Angela screaming about her loose bottom front tooth. Dad had convinced her to let him pull it, but then, feeling scared, she'd decided not to go through with it.

Dad would not give up. He was determined to "Get that damn thing out of there!" He talked her into letting him tie thread around the tooth so she could pull on it any time that she liked. When I came into the house, Angela cried, "Mommy, I don't want the thread on my tooth any more and Papa can't get it off! I don't want to pull it today! I changed my mind!"

As I peered into her mouth I saw that my father had tied strong navy blue nylon thread so tight that the thread had slipped down under the base of the tooth near the gum. The thread came out over her lip and hung down the front of her jersey. A quick glance told me there was no way to cut the thread off without leaving the piece wrapped around the bottom of the tooth. I knew she would have a fit if she had to go to school the next day with that blue thread around her bottom front tooth. Dad stood behind me, bending down to see what was going on.

Looking at him over my shoulder I said, "You need to do something about this! And I don't mean talking her into pulling it! Do you understand?"

Dad looked me in the eye. "I'll take care of it." He shifted his gaze to her and said: "Angela, come here dear. Papa wants to see if he can get the string off for you."

Angela came over to him, saying, "Papa, don't pull it. Promise?"

Leaning over him, I whispered in his ear, "Get it outta there, now!"

In one quick motion he grabbed the end of the thread and pulled. Angela's mouth was wide open. The first sound she made was a scream. She started to cry, then, realizing that the tooth was out, she started to calm down. She saw the tooth dangling in front of her. My Dad swung it back and forth in her face saying, "Ah, stop your crying! It's all over! Here's your tooth!" He turned to me and said, "All that fuss for nothing!" Then he walked away to cook dinner.

DRAWING

Dad would sit for hours with Angela and Adrianna, playing a drawing game that he'd invented. Someone would start by drawing a mark on a piece of paper (always the back of a piece of junk mail, or an envelope he saved just for them). When you lifted your pen/pencil off the paper your turn was over. The next person would take the pen/pencil, and add to the drawing. Those who were playing could not talk about what they were trying to draw, or try to influence the other players in any way. Gradually a picture formed. Before you knew it, the picture was complete, with everyone's contributions adding up to a whole image.

Dad drew his infamous Rose and Indian drawing for all of us. Every time he introduced his techniques for drawing a rose, we all would try to duplicate his. None of us accomplished this, but it was fun trying.

WALKS TO WENDY'S

When Angela was four, Dad would walk her up to Wendy's Restaurant. At two-years-old Adrianna was too little to make the trip, so Angela and Papa would sneak out of the house. Holding hands they would slowly walk a little over a quarter of a mile to Wendy's. On the way they would sing out about whatever caught their attention. Dad saw that someone lost a button so he would start singing, "Somebody lost a button, a button, a button. Somebody lost a button, I wonder who it is." Then Angela would look around for something to sing about. This continued all the way there. They would walk back on the opposite side so they would have something different to sing about.

Cooking & Eating

Angela, Adrianna, and Armand III all learned how to make sauce. Whenever Dad heard people say that they cooked their sauce all day long like their grandmothers use to do, he'd comment, "They don't know what the hell they are doing! You don't have to cook the sauce all day. The only reason it took all day, for Christ's sake, was that they had to cook it in a pot hanging over an open fire! Those people are nuts! The longer you cook the sauce the more bitter it becomes. A couple of hours and it is done! Remember that kids!"

The best part of making sauce was sautéing the onions in olive oil until they were nice and brown. You would then take them out with a slotted spoon, and put them in a bowl to cool. After Dad put the rest of the ingredients into his Napoli Restaurant pot, he would bring the sauce to a slow boil. He then left the sauce to cook slowly. That was the time to make an onion sandwich. The grandchildren could hardly wait to sink their teeth into this sandwich. Dad would slice a couple pieces of Italian bread, put a piece of provolone on top of each bread slice, then mound the sautéed onions on top. He would pass these out to whoever wanted some. As they ate Dad would tell his stories of Italy. To this day when I make Dad's sauce, I always save the onions for my girls.

The grandchildren could watch and learn how to make sauce and meatballs, but Dad never let them do it themselves. No one could touch the food he was cooking, nor could they roll the meatballs out. "One person makes the meatballs," he would say. "Too many hands rolling is bad business and not sanitary." With the cooking of each meal came a story, "You know, we never had meat when I was a kid. Meat was for a very special occasion like Christmas or Easter. What little meat we got throughout the year was usually scraps that the Duke did not want, and he would have the servants pass it out to the town's people. Those little scraps were ground up very small and used to make meatballs. It wasn't enough for any one person, but my mother would mix it with stale bread and oil and make little balls with it. She would then place it in sauce to cook the balls up."

At this point Angela would pipe in, "Hey, Papa, that's how they became meatballs!"

"Yes, that is what we call meatballs. And today people make a meal of it. But, back when I was a child it was a way of stretching what little meat we had available."

When the dinner was cooked and it was time to eat, Dad did not waste time getting the hot food to the table. Leaving the kitchen with a dishtowel slung over his shoulder he would go from room to room calling us, "Hey, supper is ready. Let's go! Andiamo! Chi tarde arriva, male allogia!" (One who delays their arrival, has poor lodging.) In other words, if you come late to the table you may end up with nothing left to eat. Even the grandchildren knew that when supper was ready, supper was ready! Jumping up into their chairs, and digging into the wonderful meal, they sometimes started singing. Whenever one of them started singing while seated at the table to eat, Dad would say, "Quando si mangia, non si canta; si combatte con il diavolo." Meaning, "When one is eating, you don't sing, because you are fighting with the devil." And one could choke.

CHICKENPOX

When Angela was seven and Adrianna was five they both came down with the chickenpox. It happened a couple of days before the weekend when Jim and I were scheduled to chair the St. Joseph's Church Fair. Mom and Dad insisted we leave the girls with them so we could do our work for the fair.

Angela was the sicker of the two. Dad was up with her half the night. Her itching kept her from sleeping. To relieve the itching Dad had her sit in a bath tub filled with Aveeno, then at 2am he took her downstairs to watch horse racing on tv. He tried making a game of picking the winners. He tried talking to her—anything to keep her mind off scratching herself. When I called to check in on the girls he said to me, "Adrianna is fine, she hardly has any pox. But Angela, that poor kid is loaded!"

Stella Doro, Hydrox, Fresca & Ice Tea

The grandchildren all knew Papa did not like anything too sweet for dessert. The only cookies he would buy were Stella Doro. Stella Doro made a two-pound box with a little window on the front so that you could see what kind of cookies were inside. Dad despised the ones with green and pink frosting. He would scrape off the colored frosting before he would eat the cookie. He also disliked the star cookie with its chewy, sticky pink center. He would dig that out with his knife before he ate it. The star would only get eaten if it was all that was left.

Every night after dinner, he would send either Angela or Adrianna into the cold pantry to retrieve the box of Stella's. The three of them would sit there having fun with all the different cookies. Adrianna sat to his right. In a signal kept secret from me (because I always knew he was trying to shed a few pounds), Dad would tap his finger on the table as if requesting a card in blackjack, and that told Adrianna to get him a Stella. She would make sure I was not watching, then grab a Stella out of the big box, and slip it under his cupped hand next to his plate. Dad would peek at the cookie and either nod to her or shake his head in rejection.

Adrianna knew he disliked the colored, frosted cookies, so she would purposely give him one of these. Dad would look at it, make a face and shake his head in rejection. She then would repeat the process, usually with something he liked. When he liked her selection he would give her a wink.

Sometimes Angela, Adrianna and Armand III would beg for cookies other than Stella's, "Papa, can you get us some Oreos? Or Chips Ahoy?" Dad would say, "What's a matter with Stella Doro?"

"We just would like something different once in a while."

"I will see what they have up to Shaw's."

Once in awhile Dad would come back with some Chips Ahoy or a box of Hydrox. He refused to pay the price for the Oreos. Hydrox were "just as good!" and he always made the kids laugh by calling Hydrox "Clorox."

Fresca was his soda of choice. It wasn't too sweet and it quenched his thirst. He also liked to roll the Rs as if he was speaking in Italian or Spanish. After years he gave in and bought Pepsi, but only to please the grandchildren. He never liked the high price of soft drinks, so he took to buying Salada Diet Ice Tea. Mixing it with frozen concentrated lemonade, he devised a recipe that kept everyone happy.

The Zipper

Dad had to undergo an ulcer operation upon finishing his junior year of college. The incision started about five inches above his belly button and went four inches below. During the surgery they removed his belly button and after the incision healed he was left with a thick, irregular scar caused by keloidosis (excessive tissue growth). It was brownish red and almost a half-inch wide. When I was a child Dad would always say it was his zipper. He told me he could unzip it, get in there, move things around, and take out anything he wanted.

When the grandchildren would stay over they would see him walking around in his underwear and ask him to tell them how he got his zipper. "Well….years ago I had to have an ulcer operation. So, I told the doctors, 'If you're gonna cut me open, you might as well put in a zipper in case you have to ever go back in, or I have to get in there to do some work.'"

He claimed that, at the same time, he'd asked "That the odor be taken away when I farted." Yeah, right! Dad would stand at the kitchen sink washing dishes, and purposely let one rip. Mom would immediately yell at him, "Sporca! (You pig!) One of these days you are going to shit yourself! Tu sei Puzza! (You stink!)" Dad wouldn't even turn around. He would just keep washing dishes. We could see his shoulders shaking as he laughed. Then he would turn to us wearing an innocent look. "What? What's the matter with all of you?"

We would all talk at the same time, "You just farted and it smells! Don't act like you don't know what we're talking about!"

"Ah, you're all nuts!" he'd say. "I don't smell anything! Mine don't stink since my surgery!"

Angela, Adrianna and Armand III experienced Dad's gas attacks when they went with him "up to Shaw's" to pick up groceries. He would let five or six loud ones rip, and keep walking as if he had nothing to do with it. This would have the kids giggling. "Papa! That was loud!" they would say.

"Ah, for Christ's sake it's normal! Everybody does it! You can't keep that inside, you'll die! That's bad business!"

Driving

Dad never liked driving. If we were going anywhere off his normal routes Mom drove. He hadn't even gotten his driver's license until he turned 34, and he only did it because he knew we wouldn't be living across the street from Deering High School forever.

Mom had a lead foot, but Dad was the one holding up traffic as he stuck to the speed limit (or sometimes went even slower). Cautious to a fault, he always drove a little to the right, next to the gutter. When coming up on a red light or stop sign he pumped the break early, then pressed it hard to come to a complete stop. If Dad was at the wheel every stop was a jolt forward, followed by a lash back into our seats. He wasn't easy on passengers.

If Dad was going up town Portland, driving up Congress Street was out of the question—too busy. In my senior year of high school, when I was working at Porteous, an uptown department store, Dad would take backstreets up, park on a side street, then walk to Congress and wait for me across from Porteous. The journey home took forever as he took all the side streets back to our house. Going far out of the way to avoid Congress Street never seemed to bother him.

During my senior year of high school Dad arranged for a friend who taught Driver's Ed at Deering High School to give me a few lessons. After just one lesson the teacher told my father, "Armand, she is ready to take her test."

"Are you sure?" Dad asked, obviously stunned.

"Yes, she is ready. She did a fine job," the teacher replied.

Maybe I was ready, but Dad wasn't. I sent in for my license test date and a few weeks later Dad drove me to the Steven's Avenue Armory for my test. As I got out of the car Dad said, "I hope you fail. Good luck!" As I watched him walking away, shaking his head, I was devastated and determined at the same time. As I went through the test I kept glancing at Dad nearby. He kept shaking his head and rolling his eyes.

Driving out of the parking lot all I could hear in my head was Dad's voice saying, "I hope you fail!" I did everything that the tester told me to do, and I did it all rather well. After fifteen minutes or so, I drove back into the Armory parking lot to see Dad waiting in the same spot. I got out of the car and ran over to him waving my passing grade. "Dad! I passed!"

He looked up and said, "Good job, dear!"

Looking into his eyes I asked, "Why did you tell me that you hoped I would fail?"

Walking back to the car he waved his hand, saying, "Ahh.....I knew you would pass. Let's go! You drive!"

When they went to a shopping plaza, if Mom was driving, she would drive to the front of the lot looking for a space close to the door, pull in fast, put the car in park, and jump out. She would already be in the store while Dad was still in the passenger seat, assessing the parking space and stewing about the other cars. When Dad drove he looked for parking spots far from the other cars. Mom would climb out sputtering, "For God's sake, can you get any further away? What a guy!" She would hurry away angry, as if she weren't even with him. In the store when it was time to leave, Mom would say to Dad, "Go get the car." His reply would be, "Ah…for Christ's sake! Can't you walk, girlie? You got two feet!"

Pump Three Times

There were rituals to starting Dad's cars. When he let you take his car he would watch from the sun porch to make sure you were doing everything right. First, you had to adjust your rearview mirror so you could see behind you, then you would put the key in the ignition, step on the gas three times, wait about a minute, then turn the key and pump the accelerator really fast at the same time. Once the engine "fired up" you had to rev it a few times to "get the gas pumping," and you had to wait a few minutes to make sure the car was "warmed up." It was a real pain in the ass but we all knew what we had to do if we wanted to drive his car.

Plastic Covers/Blankets

Mom and Dad covered the inside upholstery of every car they ever owned with plastic, blankets, or beach towels. They seemed to be in constant fear that the seats would get dirty. When you climbed into the backseat inevitably the blankets would slide off. Even though you were already sitting there, you still had to fix it. They were probably this way because they grew up in a time when a car was a luxury. You had to take good care of this expensive investment. It was meant to last. Their cars did last, usually for ten years or more.

Dad never liked anyone kicking the back of his seat while he was driving, "Stop kicking!" he would yell. "Your shoes are dirty. Put your feet on the floor. Fix that blanket back there. Isabel will have a fit if you get the seat dirty."

Fender Benders

Whenever the grandchildren went with Papa on a trip "up to Shaw's" he would park far away from the other cars. There he would teach them how to use the letters on Shaw's front sign to locate the car. He would figure out which letter the car was lined up with, and that way he could find the car when he came back out. Adrianna was with Papa when he had a couple of "fender benders." He might back into one of the cement guardrails, or a cart left in the parking lot. He would start swearing "Jesus Christ. I didn't even see that damn thing!" On one occasion he tore off the metal strip from the side of the Dodge Diplomat. Instead of getting his mechanic to glue it back on, Dad pulled out his electric drill and screwed it back on permanently.

CAN MY PICKLE OR COOK MY POTATO

Sometimes, during vacations from school, Papa would pick up Angela and Adrianna to take them back to his house. They always thought it was funny that he took side streets the whole way. One of the streets he used was Canco Road, home to the Central Maine Power Company. The sign on the building read: "CMP" in huge letters. When my brothers and I were little, Dad would always say CMP stood for "Can My Pickle." When the grandchildren came along, he changed it to "Cook My Potato." Whatever he called it, we always giggled.

He wouldn't let the grandchildren turn on the AM radio because it distracted him. Whenever he came to a stop sign they would chant softly, "Go, go, go, go…" then louder, "Go, Go, Go, Go." Finally he would go, then he'd say, "Alright, alright! Settle down!"

With Dad at the wheel it was slow going. People would pass him all the time and he would say, "Ah, for Christ's sake! What's your hurry? Go ahead, break you neck!"

"Mom?"

In the fall of 1984, while going to vote, my Mom hit her shin on the edge of the car door, getting a bad bruise. This trauma led to an ulceration and many visits to the office of a vascular doctor. She'd already had bad circulation in the leg, and the doctor warned her that another blow to that area could result in her loosing it.

The last part of her healing involved having her leg fitted with an elastic stocking at Blackwell's Medical Supply Store. They made a mold of her leg and used that to make the stocking. A week or so later Dad took her in to pick up the new stocking. They showed him how to put it on her foot, and roll it up her leg for a perfect fit with no wrinkles. Once it was on they told her to leave it on for as long as she could stand it through that first day. When she wanted to remove it, Dad would roll it off.

Mom kept the stocking on into the evening. Jim, Angela, Adrianna and I had dinner at Mom and Dad's that night. Mom complained about an ache in that leg, and said she would have Dad remove the stocking after dinner. She thought it was a little too tight. Jim, the girls and I left around 8. At 10 Dad called me, saying, "Nancy, something is wrong with your mother. She was sitting on the couch knitting and she asked me to remove the stocking because it was really painful. I knelt down and rolled it down over her leg to take it off. It was so tight it left a big indentation just below the knee where the stocking ended. Within a few minutes I asked her a question and she was just staring blankly into thin air. She isn't moving or talking." I told Dad I would call an ambulance and come right over. I knew she probably was having a stroke.

In the Mercy Hospital emergency room I noticed her glazed expression. She could not speak to me. They did a scan checking for a stroke, then told Dad and me she hadn't had one. They said we could take her home.

Knowing that she needed medical attention, I immediately went ballistic. I called the emergency doctor over to my mother's bedside, lifted the white sheet they'd draped over her, and pointed to her blue left shin. "If I take my mother home in this condition, with her unable to speak, not knowing anyone, and with you not even telling us what's wrong with her, and if she gets up without us knowing, and falls on that leg, I will sue you. Her own doctor has warned her that she must never even bump that leg or she will loose it. That's how bad it is."

The doctor looked down at my mother's leg, and walked away. When he came back he said that they would admit my mother for observation.

I told the doctor my thoughts on what had happened. I figured that the tight stocking had blocked the blood flow in her leg causing a clot. I thought that when the stocking was removed, the clot traveled to the brain, causing her to have a stroke. He disagreed, saying a clot would've traveled to her heart first, killing her.

It was going on 2am. There was nothing else Dad or I could do. I reassured Mom that she would be all right and that we would be back in the morning.

The next morning Dad and I went back to the hospital to check on Mom and as we approached her room I could hear someone yelling. We peered into her room. A doctor stood over her holding up a pen. "What is this?" he snapped at her. "Can you tell me? Can you? Follow this object with your eyes." He grabbed her foot and said, "Can you move your leg?" He fired questions as if he were a prosecutor cross-examining a criminal. She lay there, petrified, with no escape.

Walking into the room, I asked the doctor, "Who are you?"

"I'm Dr. Pazzo,[1]*" he said. "I'm a neurologist—"

"Get away from her and stop yelling at her," I said. "In fact, get out."

He turned to leave, and stopped at the doorway to say, "Your mother has had a stroke. And she will never walk or talk again. And she is blind in her left eye."

I replied, "Get out!"

Leaning over my mother, I quietly comforted her and told her that she would be okay. Holding her left hand in mine, I asked her to squeeze my hand as hard as she could. She did. Taking her right hand in mine, I asked her to do the same. She squeezed it just fine. Moving to the foot of the bed, I asked her to lift her right leg. She did.

What the hell was that doctor talking about? I wondered.

I spoke to Mom very slowly, asking if she knew where she was.

---

1   * Not his real name

She couldn't tell me. She couldn't get any words out. Her speech was a garbled mumble. She couldn't even say my name.

Finally, a nurse came in. Dr. Pazzo must have said something to her because she asked, "Is everything all right?"

I told her what I'd seen Dr. Pazzo do, then gave her the essentials of my mother's case, starting with the bump on the shin. I then told the nurse my thoughts about what had caused the stroke—the too-tight stocking, the blood clot, and the probability that it had hit her brain. Unlike the emergency room doctor from the night before, she didn't dismiss my ideas.

"That's exactly what happened," she said. "I am sorry to say you will never get a doctor to agree with that diagnosis, but I would agree with you that it did somehow happen."

Dad and I brought Mom home a few days later, but she would never fully recover. Even with months of speech therapy she was unable to communicate clearly. She still had most of her strength on her left side, so physical therapy got her up walking, but her life had changed drastically. So had ours.

No More Hairdos

Doing hair was over. Her career as a cosmetologist ended. I took over her "on call" job doing hair for the Jones, Rich & Hutchins Funeral Home. It was if someone had cut Mom's hands off. She was losing her special relationships with her customers. On Saturdays, Mom's two sisters, Aunt Rose and Aunt Angie came over, and I would do Mom's hair along with theirs, but otherwise the shop stood empty.

On those Saturdays, as I shampooed and set Aunt Rose and Aunt Angie's hair, Mom would go upstairs and get us all tea and English muffins. This was the one time she could socialize, and at least watch someone else perform her beloved art of hairdressing. This was the one event of the week that interested her. For the next ten years Dad kept her license up to date, hoping that someday she might practice again. Every Friday night he mopped the floor and cleaned and straightened the shop in preparation for its one remaining function: the Saturday visits of my aunts.

WIPE YOUR HEAD

Mom's stroke limited her communications skills, and sometimes she spoke in opposites. One day Angela and Adrianna came in, and Mom said: "Wipe your head."

"Okay Mammie," each of them said. "I wiped my feet."

Her inability to make her thoughts known made it impossible for her to tell Dad or us what she wanted or needed. Her helplessness became a source of severe depression, anxiety and paranoia. Dad struggled to figure out what she was saying. He did all he could to get her what she wanted. We all did, but inevitably there were gaps.

GET HER A CLOE!

One Easter Dad and I were adding the leaves to the dining room table for dinner. Without warning Dad inadvertently pushed his end of the table towards me. The skin on my palm caught between the leaves and I got a little cut.

I was trying not to drip blood onto the carpet when Mom yelled, "Get her a cloe! Get her a cloe!"

I knew she was trying to say, "Get her a cloth!" But Dad didn't understand. "A 'cloe'!" he said. "What the hell is a 'cloe'?"

"A cloe, for God's sake!" Mom yelled again.

Instead of interpreting for Dad, I ran into the kitchen and grabbed a dishcloth.

When I returned Dad said, "Why didn't she say a cloth?"

As Mom walked away I heard her mutter, "Just like a woman!"

PARANOIA AND DEPRESSION

Mom took her frustrations out on poor Dad. Unable to process information properly, she misinterpreted some things and imagined others. She accused him of taking things from her pocketbook, moving furniture around, and sometimes she imagined that he was going to harm her.

How she could think up these things was a mystery that troubled us all. What was worse was her inability to change her mind. She believed these things. Though in our own minds we knew it was because of the stroke, in our hearts it was so difficult to see. The grandchildren had a particularly hard time witnessing her strange behavior toward their beloved Papa.

After the stroke Mom's stomach illnesses got worse. She accused Dad of trying to poison her with his meatballs. She would hold her stomach, point at her plate and say, "Those! No good!"

It was hard for all of us. We'd always known our Mom as being full of life, fun, and compassion. She'd always been funny. To see her retreat into herself, and become a stranger was hard to endure. As the effects of the stroke took their toll her friends stopped calling. She couldn't communicate with them on the phone, and visiting her put them in situations that they didn't know how to handle. As Mom got more and more trapped in a failing body, we felt as if we'd lost a limb. We tried to make life normal, but with Mom sealed off from us, nothing could be the same.

Sometimes Mom had to go through hospital stays so they could adjust all her antidepressants. One morning she thought that she saw her dead brother, Domenic, on television. She threw her coffee cup at the set. She insisted that there were "bits" (her new word for bugs) crawling all over the house. Dad was stealing her money. Whenever Dad answered the telephone she was sure he was talking about her.

One time she thought Dad was trying to kill her. She tried to escape by running barefoot into the middle of Washington Avenue. It was midwinter, and Mom was in her bathrobe. As Dad tried to stop her, she fell in the street. She was screaming at cars when a policeman who happened to be driving by stopped to help them. Dad was shaken and mortified. He'd always been a private person.

An ambulance took her to the hospital where they observed her again, and made more adjustments to her medication. It was hard for all of us, but worst for Dad. His wife, whom he loved above all others, was convinced that he was her enemy.

We all rallied around Mom giving our understanding and support. She insisted there was nothing wrong with her; it was Dad. As the years passed we settled for appeasing her. John, Armand Jr., Angela, Adrianna, Armand III and I would do whatever was necessary to make her happy and get her off our backs. As Dad bore the brunt of her hostility, we all tried to do what we could to make his life easier.

Mom could set the table, wash dishes, do some laundry and make a cup of tea for herself. That was about it. Most days she watched television and took a nap. Dad washed the floors, cooked all the meals, grocery shopped, vacuumed, cleaned the bathrooms and kept the house running. He ran the snow blower in winter, mowed the lawn in summer, and planted Mom's favorite flowers in the garden. His daily trip "up to Shaw's" was like a little reprieve when he could see friends and neighbors away from the pressures at home. When he got back he would tell Mom whom he'd run into. "Just like a woman!" she would say.

Donations

Dad loved donating "a little something" to certain organizations. He could not afford to send much, but he always sent something. Once in a while, as he sat at his desk in the sun porch opening the mail, I would hear him say, "I just sent them something. They must be really hard up." And he would put their request on the pile of unpaid bills. One organization sent him incredibly ugly ties. He figured he'd bought them with his "little something" donation, so he would wear them.

When one of us would say, "Dad that is a butt ugly tie!" he would walk away laughing, mumbling, "Since when do you design men's clothing?" And Mom would say, "What a guy!"

SALESIAN MISSIONS

Dad especially liked the Salesian Missions founded by John Bosco. Don Bosco (Italian for Father Bosco) gathered priests and lay people together to found a religious congregation within the Catholic Church. He named it the Salesian Society after St. Francis de Sales. St. Francis de Sales had been known for his kind gentle manner, a trait which Don Bosco wanted his Salesians to imitate. Don Bosco chose Mary, Help of Christians as their patroness. His mission was clear and simple: to be a friend – a friend to kids who were poor, abandoned, or otherwise at risk. In doing so Don Bosco and his followers aspired to be friends to Christ.

The Salesian Missions published little handbooks of inspirational prayers, and sent them out along with a letter and a donation form. Dad loved these little books. He had a stack of them on his bedside table and enjoyed reading them at night before bed. They would also send Christmas cards, Easter Cards, all-occasion cards and the infamous address labels. Dad would keep them all on his desk, and use them when he could.

FRANCISCAN MISSION ASSOCIATES

The Franciscan Mission Associates is a spiritually-based organization that helps missions worldwide. It promotes interest in the missionaries and their people by providing information about them. It concentrates on the Franciscan Missions of Central America, and Franciscans working in the inner cities of the U.S. and Canada. It helps missions on every continent.

They sent Dad brochures showing children who lived, abandoned and tortured, in horrific environments. Dad read all of it from cover to cover, then put the request on top his pile of bills. He would soon send "a little something" to help them out.

PINE TREE SOCIETY FOR HANDICAPPED CHILDREN & ADULTS

The Pine Tree Society for Handicapped Children & Adults provided Maine's disabled population means and opportunity to improve life for them and their families. Dad received the following letter from their Executive Director:

March 16, 1993

Dear Mr. Polito,

This is a thank-you letter or perhaps we should call it a letter of congratulations.

Please note: This is not a letter asking for a donation of any kind.

In reviewing our records recently, we discovered what a wonderful and generous person you are. You may not realize it, but over a 22-year period, you have made 64 contributions to help handicapped children and adults in Maine. This extraordinary string of gifts amounts to $226.00, a truly remarkable sum.

There are not many people in Maine who have such an impressive history of loyal support and you have our deepest admiration. We just want you to know that your spirit of generosity has not gone unnoticed.

We repeat: This is not an appeal for a gift....it is just a THANK YOU, pure and simple!

Sincerely,
William F. Haney
Executive Director

This brought a big smile to Dad's face. He was pleased with himself, but he could barely believe he had been contributing for so long. He was proud of this personal note of thanks from the executive director.

Harvest Fair

For over ten years on the first weekend in November Dad and I volunteered to work in the kitchen for the St. Joseph's Harvest Fair. We introduced a two-day event with lobster rolls, fish chowder, meatball sandwiches, peppers and sausage sandwiches, pizza and hot dogs. Dad and I started the sauce for the meatballs and pizza a few days ahead. Our volunteers were devoted to helping us make the kitchen a big hit. Rudy, Big Joe Tuttle, Cousin Jean Wilson, Martha Concannon, Mike Murray, and numerous others stood by our side all that time.

Big Joe Tuttle was tall and had a big voice. "Fire up on those meatballs!" he would yell. "Let's go! Are we serving people today or tomorrow?"

We all had our assigned stations and duties, which helped when things got chaotic. I would loose track of time, but when I stopped to take a breath, I would always see Dad at his meatball sandwiches station working his ass off. The last year that Dad and I worked that kitchen he was 81 and still going strong.

CHRISTMAS PAINTINGS

When I decided that I was going to help decorate St. Joseph's Church altar for Christmas, I asked Dad for some advice. What could "we" do that was different? What could "we" do well? Notice the "we" in both questions. Once I asked Dad, I wasn't fool enough to think I could go it alone.

Dad took over and immediately he had a brilliant idea. He suggested that we paint two huge pictures on white window shades, one for each side of the altar. Afterwards the window shades could be rolled up and stored. He'd already found two beautiful pictures from Christmas cards he had saved. One was a little boy holding a staff as he knelt in a field looking up at the Star of David. The other was of Joseph and Mary in the manger. Both looking down at the baby Jesus lying in a bed of hay.

We bought two heavy-gauge white window shades and began our project. For weeks Dad and I spent every spare moment bent over these shades, drawing the pictures. It was hard drawing to scale from the small cards. We worked at his house. I would stay late, drawing, then return the next day to find that he'd been up all night working on them. When we had the drawings done, it was time to paint.

We draped each shade over the dining room table, laying old sheets underneath to catch any spills. Dad hung lights from the chandelier and brought in a couple of standing lamps with extension cords running everywhere. We had all of our paintbrushes, acrylic paints, drop cloths and every other tool that might help. Our work made it dangerous for anyone approaching the dining room table.

If Mom even entered, Dad would yell, "Hey! Watch out! Get the hell away from here! You're going to knock something over!" When Mom finally got a peek, she was amazed. "That's beautiful," she said. Then she pointed to the sky. "What's that?"

Dad turned his head and stared at her. He was stooped over, brush in hand, painting. "What the hell are you talking about?" He stood up, went around to her side of the table, and leaned in close to see what she was saying. "What?" he asked.

"That! The color?" Mom said.

Dad bit his lip, turned and went back where he was working. "You don't know what the hell you are talking about," he said. "Hey, haven't you got something to do?" Turning to look at me, he said, "For Christ's sake! When did she become an artist?"

When we finished the paintings the people at church hung them on the two huge columns on each side of the altar. A photographer took a picture. The altar was decorated with poinsettias, along with the paintings and red banners. The photo would be used on the church's Christmas cards that it would sell to parishioners the following year. It was a beautiful picture.

At Mass on Christmas morning I stared up at our paintings. After all the hard work, long hours and backaches, I could still look back knowing how great a joy it had been, doing this project with Dad. I never could have done it without him.

Camillo's Bakery

Jim and I had separated in 1985, and Jones, Rich & Hutchins Funeral Home offered me a 3-day-a-week job in their office. I was also doing hair "on call," working some evenings at the funeral home's wake services, so I was able to make ends meet. As a single mom with two children, what would I have done without my Dad's help? God bless him. He would drive to my house and pick up Angela, Adrianna, and Picco, our Maltese dog, after school, then take them back to his house. There he would help them with their homework, teach them how to cook, play games with them, or just let them chill out and watch television. Dad was there to keep them safe and make it all work for me.

After Jim and I divorced in 1987, my cousin, Kevin and I started an Italian bakery named after our grandfather, Camillo Profenno. Camillo's was located across from where I lived on Stevens Avenue, next to the house where my mother grew up. With his bucket of tools in tow, Dad was the first to come help us paint and get ready for opening day.

Around this time Dad's doctor said Dad's blood was low, so he sent him to see a hematologist. I remember asking Dad what they were checking his blood for. "Nothing! My blood is low! That's all!" The doctor scheduled a bone marrow test to be done at Maine Medical Center. A week later, after he returned from another visit to the hematologist, I asked him what they discovered. "Nothing! She is going to keep an eye on me! Ahhhhh! For Christ's sake stop asking questions!" And I did.

Camillo's Bakery was an experience. After staying up most of the night baking and preparing for opening day, I noticed my eyes had gotten swollen, red and itchy. Just my luck, I was allergic to the flour dust in the Italian pastries, cookies and breads. I tried goggles, but my sweat steamed them up so I could not see anything. Kevin and I had to hire someone to do my prep work.

My sister-in-law, Lisa, ran the storefront. She was in charge of making coffee, and keeping stock of baked items and paper goods. We hired her sister-in-law, Sarah Grassi, to prep the baked goods, so all I had to do was stand at the ovens and bake them off all day. Lisa's mother, Theresa Grassi, came in every morning and made the muffins. Lisa's sister, Donna Hutchins, relieved Lisa at 3, working the front until closing. We worked well together and had the best time. The bakery business is one of the hardest; you need to reach out to many different communities. Right from the start we had to put a lot of money into advertising, yet, with the major supermarkets putting in low-priced bakery items, we had to keep our prices low too. Although the food chain baked goods weren't homemade, they drew enough buyers to cut into our clientele.

Dad told me several times, "the food business is a tough job, Nancy. It is very competitive, long hours, and very hard work." But regardless of Dad's warnings, Kevin and I gave it our all. Running a bakery did have advantages. Living across the street made it convenient for my girls. Once they were up, dressed and ready for school, they would come in the back to the kitchen, sit at a small table in the corner, and eat their breakfast. That was my favorite part of the day.

Dad would pick them up after school and stop in at the bakery to buy a loaf of Italian bread. Sometimes during vacations Angela and Adrianna would work. Some mornings my brother, Armand Jr., came in after working the midnight-to-seven shift at the paper mill. He would grab a muffin and coffee before going to bed.

It was truly a family affair. Kevin's wife, Betsy sometimes helped bake, especially if there was a holiday coming up, and Normajean's son, Chris would work the front end on Saturdays.

I Love Lucy

We were always closed Sundays and Mondays. Because of my allergies the bread dough was made ahead of time, rolled it into loaves, and frozen in a large upright freezer in the corner of the kitchen. On a Saturday night this usually meant about 50 rolled loaves. One hot humid Saturday night Lisa and I were shutting the bakery down. As my sister-in – law, Lisa, and I were cleaning I said to her, "Did you put all the bread dough into the freezer?"

"Yup!" Lisa confirmed. "All set! They're all packed away."

We both walked out and said our goodnights. She went next door to my grandmother's house, where she and Armand Jr. lived, and I crossed the street to my home.

At four o'clock the following Tuesday morning I opened the door to the bakery, and smelled the pungent scent of yeast. It filled the whole building. As I got to the back kitchen area, I turned on the light, and my mouth dropped open in disbelief. I was staring at an enormous, molten, foaming mass of bread dough. It flowed from the freezer, spilling halfway across the kitchen floor. Lisa had packed the bread loaves so tightly that they had shifted, pushing the freezer door open. The temperature was at least 90 degrees. With thick, humid air, this dough was rising in an ideal atmosphere.

I called Lisa's house, "Get your ass over here to the bakery! I have something to show you!" When she saw it she could not stop laughing. "What the hell happened?" she asked, cackling, "Yuk, yuk, yuk."

The two of us grabbed trash bags and started stuffing pieces of dough into them. It was still rising. The more we pulled the more it grew. It reminded me of an "I Love Lucy" episode when she put too much bread dough in the oven and it overflowed across her kitchen. Lucy had nothing on us. We filled over 20 large trash bags, piling them at the back door to load in Kevin's truck. He could take them to the dump.

By the time Kevin arrived, the bags themselves were expanding across the floor as if there was something actually alive in them. We all grabbed bags, tossing them into the back of his closed-cab truck. We couldn't hang on to them. The bags had no firmness, or shape. It was like trying to pick up a half-filled water balloon when your hands are greasy. When we finally had the bags shoved into the back of the truck, we saw that they were still growing. As Kevin drove off he could hardly see out the side or back windows.

ANNIE OAKLEY

Sharing Camillo's Bakery building was Pat's Meat Market. Pat's had a big garbage dumpster in back. Lisa and Armand Jr.'s driveway ran down the side of the bakery emptying into the parking lot behind our building where the dumpster sat. More than once Lisa had seen rats climbing out of the dumpster. She was determined to kill them. One morning she came in with a shotgun. She came back to the kitchen, and rested the shotgun by the open screen door. "Let me know if you see that damn rat going under my porch!" she said.

Once in a while Lisa would come back to the screen door, and look out towards her back porch. All day she watched for that damn rat. Finally she saw it. Lisa flew by me, grabbed the gun, and fired right through the screen. I screamed, then started laughing hysterically. "Damn it!" she yelled. "I missed it!" Then she looked at the huge hole in the screen. "Oops!"

At that moment we both heard the bell on the front door. Someone had entered the bakery. Lisa leaned the gun back up against the door, and walked out to tend to the customer. I peeked around the doorway to the front, and yelled, "Hey! Anne Oakley? You couldn't open the screen door first?" Lisa cackled, "Yuk, yuk, yuk!"

CAN I HELP YOU?

When customers couldn't make up their minds, it drove Lisa crazy. One day I was stocking the day-old shelf when a lady came in for six muffins. As the woman pointed to muffins in the showcase, Lisa politely pulled them out and put them in a box. When the woman had selected six muffins, Lisa said, "Is that gonna do it for you, M'am?"

"Nooooo…" said the woman as she looked at the rest of the muffins in the case. "I think instead of that cranberry, I'll take a blueberry. Oh…is that date nut? Maybe I will take one of those. Hmmm….I do like bran though. You have a great selection of muffins."

I saw Lisa force a smile as she made the substitutions. When the box was full she slid the case door closed, saying, "There you go. Is that it for you?"

"Mmm..." said the lady, "Maybe I will take a cranberry. People seem to like cranberry."

Again Lisa reached down. Again she slid the showcase door open. Again she put the cranberry muffin in the box. Lisa closed the door and walked to the register.

"Wait," said the lady. "I only want six muffins, so you can put back one of the blueberry."

I watched as Lisa stopped, took the blueberry muffin out, and set it next to the register. The lady paid, turned, and walked out. As soon as the door closed, I saw something fly through the air and smack against the inside glass of the door-- the blueberry muffin. From behind the counter Lisa looked at me, but addressed the now-absent woman. "There's your f.....g muffin! That bitch! She f.....g drove me crazy! Yuk, yuk, yuk!"

SHOW AND TELL

One morning a little boy on his way to school came into the bakery. He set a big brown bag on the floor near the door, and as he walked back and forth in front of the two big pastry showcases, he kept glancing back at it. Detecting a foul odor, Lisa leaned over the counter to check out the bag. It was wet and fluid was seeping out of it. "What's in the bag?" she asked.

"It's for show and tell," he said.

"But what is it?"

"It's a dead skunk. Wanna see it?" said the little boy.

"I don't think so. Could you please take it outside for me, because it really stinks."

"Sure, lady!"

ANISE

Lisa's sister-in-law, Sarah Grassi, would come in to Camillo's early in the morning to start preparing the traditional Anise Italian Cookies made with pure anise flavoring. Sweet and aromatic, anise contains a liquorice-like component. Most anise winds up in baked goods, such as Italian Biscotti and Pizzelles. In the summer when the bakery's front door and windows were open, the smell of anise filled the neighborhood, drawing in many passers-by.

One warm summer day I heard Lisa's cackle, and went out front. She was bent over behind the counter, laughing her ass off.

"What's so funny?" I asked.

She looked up with tears in her eyes, barely getting her words out. "Some guy just came in and said, 'I can smell your anus from across the street. And it smells real good!"

"I told you!"

Camillo's Bakery produced all natural, mostly Italian, homemade pastries. This proved to be expensive. Most people could have cared less about homemade, and were more concerned with price. After several years of allergies, and the headaches of competing with the chains, Kevin and I decided to sell. Dad was glad for me. "Nancy, I told you," he said. "The food business is one of the hardest industries to work in. At least you now know what it is like and you can move on to something better for you and the girls."

I decided to take the summer off to enjoy being with Angela and Adrianna. The new bakery owner kept the business going for a year before selling. Pat's Meat Market already occupied the other half of the structure, so Kevin and I also sold the building and my grandparent's house next door to Pat's owner.

1990-2001

After recuperating from the bakery for a summer, in October 1990, Angela and Adrianna's orthodontist, Dr. Thomas Stegemann, hired me as the front desk receptionist, assistant, financial manager, and insurance processor. I did this for three offices. Dad was so pleased that I was well and had a good dependable job. As he put it, "Now, you can settle down."

For the next eleven years John, Armand Jr., Angela, Adrianna,

Armand III, and I continued the family gatherings at our parents' home. Dad never slowed down. He still mowed the lawn, ran "up to Shaw's" every day, cooked all the meals, ran the snow blower through the huge driveway, and shoveled the front and back stairs.

Dad in his 80's up on a staging caulking and painting the gutters of the house. When I asked what would happen if he should fall, his reply was, "Ah…I got it under control. I got this rope tied around my waist. If I fall I will just hang in mid air!"

LONG, LONG, TIME!

One of the three orthodontist offices that I worked from was in a business complex called Northport Professional Plaza up the street from Dad and Mom's house. The complex had a drive-thru street from Washington Avenue to Allen Avenue, which was a great little short cut avoiding the huge intersection at Washington and Allen Avenues. This was a good way to get to Shaw's Shopping Plaza without all the traffic. One day I looked out the window to see my Dad's Dodge Diplomat cutting through there. Just seeing his small visage behind the wheel of that huge car made me smile. He was still avoiding the traffic, just like he always had.

At eleven each morning I called Mom and Dad from work to see if they needed anything. Working less than a half-mile up the street, most days I had lunch at their house. Most days when I arrived Dad was already "up to Shaw's." Often he didn't get back until after I left. I knew this meant he'd run into some of his many acquaintances. Other times he stopped at CVS Pharmacy to pick a prescription for Mom.

One day, when he wasn't there as I left, I told Mom, Dad was sure to be along shortly. At about 2pm she called and said: "Nancy? Long, long, time! I don't know!" I knew exactly what she meant. Dad had not come home. I told Mom that I would go look for him.

I left quickly and started driving his route, cutting through the Northport complex. I must have looked like a bobble-head doll looking this way and that for him or his car. Reaching the end of the complex I drove across Allen Avenue to the back entrance to Shaw's parking lot. I knew better than to look for his car anywhere near the store entrance. He would never park his beloved Diplomat where it might get bumped or scratched. Finally I found it! I took the next space, ran into Shaw's, and thanked God that I hadn't seen any ambulances.

By this time Dad was in his mid 80s, and he'd shrunk quite a bit. He always wore a blue baseball cap pulled down tight on his head. Shaw's aisles run vertical, and that made it a little easier. I could check each aisle with a glance, then move to the next one. Still, after searching several aisles, I was weary. Then I reached the aisle with the over-the-counter drugs. About ten feet down, with a shopping basket in one hand and a notebook in the other, stood Dad. He wore his infamous baseball cap, and his glasses had slid down to the tip of his nose. Hunching over, he was shaking his head, and I could hear him swearing, "Mannaggia il diavolo!" [Damn the devil]

Running up to him, I said, "Dad? What are you doing? Mom called me at work because she was worried that you had been gone so long!"

"Ah! For Christ's sake, I am trying to find your mother's vitamins! They keep moving them on me!" Dad had his usual list on his notepad.

Grabbing the notepad I read the name of the vitamins, took a quick look around, and grabbed them off the top shelf, "Here they are! Right here!"

"Oh! For Christ's sake! How the hell am I suppose to reach them way the hell up there? Give me those damn things!" Grabbing them from my hand, he turned and headed for the checkout yelling, "I gotta get outta here. Your mother is going to be worried."

I just stood staring after him. It didn't occur to him that Mom called me herself (a minor miracle), or that I had left work to come to find him. He didn't say "thank you" or anything else that might indicate that anything odd had happened. I was back at work before he even got out of the checkout line at Shaw's, so I called Mom to let her know he was on his way. "Thank God!" she said. "What a guy!"

You Horse's Ass!

After watching Dad's neurotic care of his automobiles, one might have thought that I would have learned how to take care of my own cars. Over the years I'd bought several used ones from John's various friends. In these cars I'd managed to break down on roads all over southern Maine. One fine car was a used Sable I drove for six years. One day I heard a ticking noise under the hood. It seemed to get louder, driving me crazy. I was driving several co-workers to lunch when one named Katie said, "Nancy, when was the last time you had the oil changed? You know, if a car is low on oil it can seize up the engine, and it usually will start ticking before that happens."

I thought for a second, then replied, "I never have. I was waiting for the oil light to come on, then I would add some." Everyone in the car broke out laughing.

After work that night I went to my Dad's, and asked him to help me check the oil. I didn't have to ask twice. He always jumped at the chance to help any of us kids.

We went out to the garage where Dad got an old rag to wipe the dipstick. Out in the driveway, we opened the hood, and Dad pulled out the dipstick. He wiped it, pushed it back in place, and waited a few seconds. When he pulled it out he gave the dry stick a skeptical look, then, grunting, he shoved it back in. When he pulled it out the second time there was still no oil, not even down at the tip. "You horse's ass!" he yelled. "There's no oil in this damn car! What the hell are you thinking? You're lucky that the whole damn car didn't seize up and ruin the engine! That's bad business for Christ's sake!" I just stood there, not saying a word.

He walked into the garage and came back out with a quart of oil. "That's bad business," he mumbled. "She could have ruined the whole damn car!" Shaking his head he uncapped the quart can, slipped the funnel into the hole, and poured in the oil. When he was done he said, "Now, just wait a few minutes for it to soak in. Then we will test it."

As we waited he stewed, and shook his head. "What is wrong with you?" he asked. "Don't you know better than that?"

"Dad," I said, "I just thought that the oil light would come on and then I would add some oil."

Reaching down he pulled out the dipstick, wiped it off, and pushed it back into the slot; after waiting a few seconds he pulled it out again. After going through the same motions, with the same results, he said, "For Christ's sake, it isn't even showing that I added that quart of oil!" Pushing me out of the way, he walked back into the garage, his head shaking more rapidly, as he mumbled, "Mannaggia il diaviolo! I don't' understand how anyone can be so stupid?"

As he came back with the second quart of oil he said, "This is it girlie! This is all I have!" After adding the second quart of oil, he looked at the stick and said, "There! At least it is registering on the stick, but it is still too low. You go up to the filling station and get another couple of quarts now! You are one lucky girl you didn't kill the engine. I gottta finish cooking. Go!"

GRADUATIONS

Angela graduated from Deering High School in 1993, and Adrianna did the same in 1995. My father was so proud of their accomplishments, and enjoyed attending both graduations from the school where he'd taught at for 34 years. He would read the programs from beginning to end, noting all the top students and award winners.

In 1997 Angela graduated from Bates College and Dad, Adrianna and I drove up to Lewiston for the day. Mom stayed home with Armand Jr. As I sat next to him on the front lawn of Hawthorne Hall, Dad paid rapt attention to every detail. It reminded me of how amazing he was, all the more so for his 86 years of life, guidance, love, and devotion to his family. He was simply astounding. When the graduation ceremony was over Dad was anxious to congratulate Angela's classmates Erica Nappi and Rob Blood, and to chat with John Lambert, a high school friend of Angela's who'd driven up that day. Dad was interested in every aspect of education. He was excited for his grandchildren's futures, and for their friends.

SNOWPLOWING

While at work one winter day, the mother of one our patients told me how her husband, Don Sawyer, was busy plowing that season's snow. When I mentioned that I thought snow blowing might be getting to be too much for my 80-something father, she said Don would gladly come by and plow Dad's driveway.

That evening, when I told Dad, he wasn't happy. "You know, it won't get done right! Those plow guys end up destroying the lawn, driveway, and bushes. They are always in a helluva hurry!"

"Dad," I said. "All you have to do is give him a diagram of your driveway and tell him where you want him to plow the snow."

"I don't know, Nancy. I just don't like the idea."

"But Dad, I really think it is way too much work for you to keep doing it yourself."

"How much does he charge? It's probably outrageous!"

"Dad, he only charges $20.00, and he'll shovel off your front stairs too."

"Not the God damn front stairs! He will ruin them! It costs me a fortune to get those bricks fixed!"

"Dad, let's give him a try. If he doesn't do a good job, then you can go back to doing it yourself."

"Ah…all right! But, if he ruins my lawn or those stairs I am going to be pissed!"

So Don Sawyer got the diagram Dad had meticulously drawn, with complete plowing and shoveling directions. I convinced my father to not pay Don then and there; I would send him a check and Dad could reimburse me. I wanted it that way because the plowing really cost $30.00. I was afraid that Dad would balk at the price, so I made up the difference.

Arriving at the house after a storm, Dad said, "Don't send Don a check. I already paid him. What the hell, I can pay him when he comes here! That way you don't have to bother send it to him and you can save the stamp."

The minute Don pulled into the driveway, Dad would start running from one window to the other, monitoring the work. Don did such a great job that when he showed up Dad would break his neck to get out there before Don left, to thank him and pay him $20.00. Sometimes Dad stood at the doorway to do this. "Great job, Don," he would say. "Thanks!" Then I sent another $10.00 in the mail. Dad never found out.

Still I often pulled in after a storm (and after Don had plowed and shoveled) to find Dad breaking up ice, or up on top of a huge snow bank at the end of the driveway, removing snow like he was "king of the mountain." I swear, I could not keep that man from doing strenuous work!

WAL-MART - 1999

One Sunday afternoon while shopping at Wal-Mart with Adrianna and me, Mom lost her footing and tripped over the wheel of her wagon. When I tried to break her fall we both went down. Mom could not move her left leg. A nurse who was there in the store stayed with us until the ambulance came. Adrianna took my car back to the house to get Dad.

At the hospital x-rays showed that Mom had broken her left hip. She would need a hip replacement. I worried about the anesthesia. I told doctors about her stroke, and convinced the surgeon to use a spinal. They did the surgery that afternoon. Dad, Adrianna and I sat and waited.

Finally the doctor came out saying everything had gone well, and we could see her in the recovery room. As we rounded the corner, there Mom lay being tended by a nurse. As soon as Mom saw us she said, "It was wonderful! Beautiful!" She was higher than a kite!

Her recuperation went miraculously well. Once she gained some strength they released her to a local nursing facility for five-to-six weeks of rehab. Dad and I quickly realized that Mom wasn't going to like nursing facility food. Who would? We took her home. Each week a physical therapist came to help her regain her mobility, and twice a week a nurse came to help with bathing.

Mom was never one to exert herself physically, so none of us were surprised when she resisted strength training and exercise. The physical therapist was supposed to help her build up the muscle around the replacement. Mom exercised with a half-hearted, under-the-breath laughter, and a continuous roll of her eyes. She seemed to take it as a penance.

Mom could not use stairs without help, so we moved her bed down into the living room and Dad's bed into the den. They were there on the same floor near each other. Dad had a terrible time adjusting to having his bed in the den. He didn't like sleeping on the first floor. "If someone breaks in, you don't have a chance in hell of doing anything because you're on the same floor as the predator! You can't leave the windows open in the summertime because someone can easily stand right out there and break in! It's just bad business!"

Mom claimed that the hip replacement ruined her leg, and she couldn't walk or stand for any length of time. Whenever I took her for her yearly checkup at the orthopedic surgeon's, he would come in the room and say, "Hi Isabel. How are you doing?" She would point at her leg and snap, "Lousy! It's no good!"

The doctor always took an x-ray, studied it, and said, "Everything looks good, Isabel. I will see you next year." As he left Mom always looked at me, saying, "He's no good." I would try to explain that her leg was fine, and the problem was that she never built up its strength with exercise.

When we got home, Dad would always ask, "How did your mother make out at the doctor's?"

"The doctor said that her leg looks good," I would answer. "He says there's nothing wrong with the surgery, and he wants to see her next year. The problem is that she complains to the doctor that her leg is 'no good,' as she puts it, but he can't understand what the problem is because everything looks fine."

Dad would shake his head. "The problem with Isabel is that she wants a pill for everything! God forbid she has to do anything to help herself!"

AIR CONDITIONER

Dad always turned off all fans and air conditioners at night. Even on a 90-degree day it was a struggle to get him to turn them on for more than a couple of hours.

Getting the air conditioner in and out of the window each year was a big, tightly controlled process. Only Dad could do it right, and he made no bones about letting you know that. "Get outta the way! You don't know what the hell you're doing! There's a right way and a wrong way! Move!"

Dad used an old, wheeled television stand with a board lined with a rug remnant on the top, and pieces of wood crisscrossed underneath. Once he had the air conditioner on this thing, he could wheel it to and from the front hall closet, bringing it out for the summer, then wheeling it back in for the winter. He could easily slide it on and off the sill.

In summer, once he had the air conditioner up to the window, Dad would take all day getting the window prepared. He'd bring a pail of tools, duct tape, foam, plastic bags, and all different sizes of wood from his workshop, then line the sill of the window with protective planking. He would then shove pieces of foam and plastic bags into any air holes to keep the bugs out. He would wedge little bits of wood underneath to balance it, then seal it with duct tape all around to stop smaller bugs.

He brought the fans down from the attic one at a time, strategically placing them so the air circulation was just right. Once all of the cooling equipment was in place, Dad took charge of turning them off and on. "Don't touch those. I have them all set up in the proper positions."

It was bad to have a fan or anything blowing on you. Dad positioned everything so, no matter where you might sit, no air blew directly on anyone.

Things One Just Knew

FRIDAY NIGHT DINNER

For over 50 years it seemed written in stone that on Friday night Dad would cook "pasta fasul."[Pasta e fagioli] If you asked him what he was cooking for dinner on a Friday, you'd get a cocked head, furrowed eyebrows, and a look of general disgust, as he replied: "What's wrong with you? What do I always cook?"

Dad saved old Sanka jars to pack up pasta fasul for Angela's trips back to school. Whenever Armand Jr. and his girlfriend, Linda, stopped by on Sunday, a Sanka jar of pasta fasul left with them. The jar was wrapped tightly in an old bread bag with an elastic band to prevent leakage. Dad then put this in a tightly knotted Shaw's plastic bag. Sometimes he even would staple the damn thing.

Disassembling all this was a chore, but when you sat down to a big bowl of Dad's piping hot pasta fasul, it was well worth it.

THE BACK ROOM

Whenever Dad heard one of us say we were going downstairs to get a screwdriver or some other tool, he'd say, "You just wait a minute. What the hell are you looking for? Don't go touching everything. I'll go with you!" And he would run down the cellar stairs, racing into his little back room where the tools were. From that moment on your project was in Dad's hands. He decided how it would be done. It was hopeless to ask him questions or to state any ideas you might have about what you were doing. His answer was inevitable: "No, that will never work! I'll show you how to fix the damn thing! Move! Let me have it!"

Once Dad had a project it could take all day. There might be sojourns up to Paris Hardware for a certain size nut or bolt, and there were always numerous trips up and down the cellar stairs, for rulers, tape, scissors or whatever he needed. A project might require days or even weeks, but he got the job done. When Dad was finished he would present it to you, saying, "There! How's that? I'll tell ya the way that thing was made it would never had lasted a year! That's a hellava notion."

THE ATTIC

No one went up to the attic to get anything. If you mentioned you wanted to look for something up there, Dad would say, "You can't go up there. It is too dangerous with that heavy damn door! It will fall on your head and kill you. I will have to go up. What the hell do you need up there anyway?"

The attic door was in Armand Jr.'s bedroom. That door opened to stairs. A bulkhead-type door that weighed a ton lay over the head of the stairs. Even using both hands, it took plenty of strength to step up while pushing that door. Once you reached the top step and the door was perpendicular to the floor, you hooked the rope loop onto a large nail, holding the door in place.

To come back down you unhooked the loop, then slowly descended the stairs, holding the door above you. The bulkhead door followed your every step until you reached the bottom. At that point the door lay flat over your head. Once Armand Jr. went up without telling anyone. As he came back down he almost knocked himself out when he lost his grip on the door and it fell on his head.

When he arrived in the kitchen, and told Dad how he got the lump on his head, Dad said, "That's bad business. You could have killed yourself! I told you not to go up there without my help. That will teach you!"

THE LAWNMOWER & SNOWBLOWER

We had the old push lawnmower for quite a few years before Dad finally broke down and bought a gas-powered mower. He wouldn't let anyone else use the damn thing. Armand Jr. was in his twenties before Dad let him mow the lawn. Even then Dad followed him, checking his every move.

Mom, John, Armand Jr. and I pooled our money to surprise Dad with a snow blower. Either we got him a damn snow blower or he would have a heart attack shoveling! We knew he would never buy it himself. John called it "the Herman" because that's "Armando" in Italian, French and Portuguese, and he stenciled "Herman" across the front of the gears. No one ever touched "the Herman" but Dad.

Dad was meticulous about snow removal. He always blew the snow away from the end of the driveway so he would have enough room to maneuver his big Dodge Diplomat when he turned in from the street. Turning in from busy Washington Avenue was a nightmare. Dad always turned wide to avoid the curb, but he didn't want to risk going up on the lawn. To do that he had to clear the snow back and away from both sides of the driveway. Though the car had power steering, Dad always drove it as if it were a bus, gripping the wheel at the ten and two o'clock positions, turning a little at a time.

BOXES

Someone always needed a box to wrap something, and/or send something. If you mentioned that you needed a box, Dad would run down to the basement where his stockpile of boxes lined one side of the cellar wall. If a box had a cover and was in "good condition" he saved it. Whenever he emptied one, he'd say: "You never know when you might need a box of this shape and size." Then he would save it. There were Russell Stover boxes, Haven's candy boxes, boxes that had held blank checks from the bank, shoe boxes, jewelry boxes, the boxes watches came in, and all gift boxes—all fitted neatly inside of one another, then stored inside larger boxes from the grocery store, then stacked along the cellar wall. We all knew where to go when we needed a box.

SAUCE

When Luigi's stopped producing sauce commercially, Dad made Luigi's sauce at home. Every couple of weeks the smell of sauce cooking met you at the front door. It was heart warming. Dad orchestrated the whole process, laboring over the sauce for a couple of hours. It was his labor of love, and it produced marinara sauce that was simply the best. His recipe made over a gallon of sauce. He poured this into Sanka jars and froze it. "Leave an inch at the top," he would say, "because when it freezes it will expand and you don't want the glass jar to break." He washed and cleaned empty Sanka jars, put a napkin inside "to keep moisture from settling into the jar and to absorb any odor," screwed the covers on, then saved them in a small box in the pantry.

Whenever someone tasted Dad's sauce, they would inevitably say, "That's the best sauce I have ever tasted!" Whenever Dad heard someone rave over his sauce it brought a smile to his face. He would say, "I don't care what type of pasta you cook. The sauce makes the dish!"

2002

Easter Sunday

Ever since Mom's stroke she'd suffered from depression, blaming poor Dad for all of her illnesses. After her stroke she was never truly happy. I always watched her closely for signs of her depression, for she could spiral down fast, slipping into a confrontational mindset that led to bizarre behavior.

On Easter Sunday of 2002 I noticed that Mom was not herself.

When Dad called the next day, saying she was being unreasonable I was not surprised. He didn't know what to do with her, so I drove over. I saw that she was indeed experiencing paranoia, blaming Dad for things that were completely untrue. When she was in this state her words came out clearly.

"He touched my thing!" she said pointing to her pocketbook.

"I moved it to set the table for breakfast!" Dad yelled.

"It's the true! He's awful!" she said.

She would describe some ridiculous situation, leading Dad to defend himself. "What the hell are you talking about?" he said. "You're nuts! I had to move it out of the way!"

Rather than stand there and listen to this, I calmly told Dad to leave the room, and let me deal with Mom. I could see that she was not in a good place mentally, so I contacted her doctor. He said I should bring her into the hospital to be evaluated.

Mom stayed there for a couple of weeks while they adjusted her antidepressant medications. It was a difficult time for her. Mom depended on her family to understand her wants and needs. Because the doctors and nurses weren't sure how much she really understood, they had a hard time communicating with her.

By this time Dad was 89, and I did not feel comfortable leaving him alone at night, so I stayed with him. Working, checking on Mom at the hospital, and Dad at home, then staying at Dad's at night, was exhausting. The best part was sitting with Dad in the living room at the end of a hectic day. The two of us would watch television, totally exhausted.

I would find a history program that interested him. He would watch, and say, "Can you turn it up a little, dear?" I would turn up the volume a little louder. A few minutes would pass and he would say, "A little more please. I can't really hear it that well." I would turn it up so loud that my head would hurt. "That's good, dear," he would say. I would think: *Oh, my God! He is sitting three feet away from the damn thing and he can't hear it!*

My Aching Back

About the second week Mom was in the hospital, I came home to find that Dad had changed some of the storm windows over to screens. I told him he should have waited for me to help him. He said he'd hurt his back trying to open one of the windows. He'd complained of lower back pain for years, but we'd never thought much about it. He never named a cause, and we just figured he had a bad back.

That evening as he climbed into bed he let out a scream of pain. Running into his bedroom I asked, "What is wrong?" Half on the bed and half off he exclaimed, "Oh my God! My back is killing me!" I got him on the bed and tried to make him comfortable. I said that he must've done something to it.

The next day I called his doctor who sent Dad to Mercy Hospital for an x-ray. It looked as if he had a small fracture, so the doctor sent Dad to a specialist for a bone density test. Once they looked at the test and another x-ray, they said he did have a small fracture and that his bones were very brittle. As Dad explained it to me, "I am loaded with Osteoarthritis." They prescribed a medication to help make his bones stronger and sent him on his way. With his middle wrapped in a wide bandage held snug with Velcro, Dad could move around without too much pain.

A few days later Mom was released from the hospital with new medication. As I drove her home I tried to explain all that Dad had endured, but she didn't fully realize how severe the fracture was, and how much it had slowed him down, until we walked into the house. When she saw him hobbling to the stove, and lifting the teapot in his shaky little hands, she started crying. It was if lighting had struck her in the side of the head. She ran over to help him, but he said: "Leave me alone. Get outta here! I can do that myself!"

Her response was, "What a guy!"

THE HEMATOLOGIST

Over the next few months Dad's back seemed to get a little better. Maybe it was a little less painful or maybe he just never complained. But his hearty appetite had diminished, and he said that everything tasted metallic. He looked gaunt and pale. In January Dad had seen a hematologist about his anemia, and he had an appointment to go back to her in July. I drove him there, and went in with him so I could ask her exactly what was going on.

As I sat in an examination room with Dad across from me, the doctor came in and asked him, "Well, Armand, how do you feel?"

Dad just shrugged.

I asked, "What is wrong with him?"

"It's his multiple myeloma," she said.

"His what?" I demanded.

"I've been watching his anemia all these years," she said, "and his levels started to climb in 1999. I noticed that they were higher in January. That's why I wanted to see him in six months."

I hadn't heard about this, and I was stunned. Apparently, Dad had been diagnosed with a deficiency of immunoglobulin G, one of the five major types of antibodies affecting the immune system. It was called an IgG deficiency. They'd tested the immunoglobulins (antibodies) in the blood to find certain autoimmune diseases or allergies and certain types of cancer such as multiple myeloma. I don't know whether Dad knew what the doctor was testing him for. All I know is that he never said a word to any of us. He transitioned to multiple myeloma in 2002, cancer of the bone marrow.

The doctor said Dad could undergo chemo tabs to help bring back his appetite. As she said these things I looked over at Dad. He gazed out the window, seemingly uninterested in our discussion. He seemed to be leaving it up to me. I decided we should try a round of chemo tabs to see if it would bring back his appetite. If he ate, maybe he would feel a little more like himself.

As we left with prescription in hand, I asked, "Dad, did you hear what the doctor was talking about?"

He looked up at me. "Yeah! Let's go home. Your mother is by herself."

We never discussed his illness again. I picked up the chemo tabs and gave him the five-day supply. I felt awful giving him those pills, but I was desperate to help him regain his appetite.

Through the rest of the summer Dad gained a few pounds, but he still had little interest in eating. By September the doctor had him at Mercy Hospital Oncology Department every week for intravenous injections to help boost his blood. A few times he needed blood transfusions which took up half his day. The first time I dropped him off for one of these the nurses told me that it would be at least four hours. They would call me at work when he was finished. After two hours I called the hospital to check on him. They hadn't even started yet. He had an uncommon blood type, and they were still tracking down the right blood. The nurse said he wouldn't have to wait so long next time because they would arrange ahead of time to have his blood type on hand.

It was after 5pm when I picked him up. Dad sat in a big recliner chair waiting for me. I asked him how it went.

"Not bad," he said. "Boy, it sure took a long time. They didn't do anything with me all morning, something about waiting for my blood type."

"Dad, did you eat anything?" I asked.

He looked at me as if I had two heads. "No. They brought me something to eat, but I only wanted coffee. You know I would not eat that kind of stuff!"

The Big Move

In December 2001 construction was started to have an addition placed on the back of my house so Mom and Dad could move in with me. By March 2002, the contractor was giving me the runaround. He used what money I gave to him for personal purposes, failing to pay the subcontractors. The lumber company, window-supply company, and the excavator were calling me for payment. Then the contractor disappeared.

I hired another contractor, and by October, 2002 I was finally able to move my parents into my house. The day they moved in was emotional for all of us. Dad didn't understand that he would not live in his beloved house ever again until we brought in his bed and set it up in their new bedroom. Still wearing his jacket, Dad sat down on the bed, lowered his head, and cried.

I went over and hugged him. "It's all right Dad," I told him. "This move is the best for you and Mom. And, if you remember, we have been talking about moving for more than a year."

He looked up at me and said, "I know. It just came so fast. I am going to miss my home."

The next minute I turned to find Dad trying to help Armand Jr. carry in a bureau. As weak as he was he was trying to do as much as he could to put less work on all of us. Dad never mentioned missing his home again.

Dad's 90th Birthday

On November 22nd, 2002 we celebrated Dad's 90th birthday. I cooked a big meal and we all gathered to enjoy being together as a family, and to honor Dad. He did not eat much but we still joked around like always. We sang happy birthday, read Dad's cards for him, and Dad remarked on how he was the first one in his family to reach 90 years of age.

Angela and Adrianna had gone on line at the Ellis Island website and purchased a print of the ship, the *Taormina*, that had brought Dad to the United States 82 years earlier. We were all excited to see his reaction to this picture.

Dad took his knife and began to meticulously cut away at the taped sides, working slowly so he would not rip the wrapping paper. Once the paper was off he held the picture up in front of him and said nothing. Angela piped up, "Papa? What do you think of that picture? That is the boat that you came on from Naples to America." Dad turned to her with the most disgusted look on his face and said, "What the hell do I want that picture for? That was the most horrific three weeks of my life. I was so sick!"

Placing the picture on top of the hassock in front of him, he moved to the next gift. We all just stared at each other in disbelief. We'd all been convinced that he would love that picture of the *Taormina*. We were blown away by his reaction. We all made the best of it, and the party continued. We knew this was his last birthday, and we were determined not to let a picture ruin it.

As I passed Armand Jr. coming back from the kitchen he said,

"Well, we all blew that one didn't we? He really was upset!" John asked, "Whose idea was that?"

Cousin Cammie wrote the most beautiful card:

"Dearest Uncle,

I am so fortunate to be truly blessed. Not only do I have an uncle who fulfilled that family role so well, but I also have an uncle who helped guide me in my professional career from high school onward. You have been a great teacher and mentor to me and have made my life a wonderful adventure. For this I will be forever grateful.

As you start your tenth decade, I wish for you the best possible happiness and peace.

Lots of love,
Cammie

Angela and Adrianna's birthday card read:

Happy Birthday Papa!

How incredible – 90! Quite an accomplishment. You are a remarkable person, Papa...a fun loving grandfather...and our favorite teacher and mentor. We strive to be like you every day (we have learned your stubbornness already!) We only hope that someday we will be as wise, compassionate, sensible, and crafty as you! We love you Papa,

Love,
Angela & Adrianna

Thanksgiving 2002

The week before Thanksgiving I approached Dad while he was sitting, reading the paper, in his favorite overstuffed green chair in the living room. "Dad," I asked, "do you think you would like to go to the hall for Thanksgiving this year?"

With his glasses hanging on the tip of his nose, he never looked up. In a weak voice he said, "I always do, don't I?"

It was bittersweet to know that it was my father's last Thanksgiving. He sat with Mom at the end of one of the long tables. He barely ate anything, and I could only imagine what he was thinking. At one point during the afternoon social time, I asked him if he wanted a cup of coffee. He said he did. When I brought it to him he said it tasted terrible. Trying to please him I drove to a nearby Dunkin Donuts to get him a fresh brewed cup. When I returned with the coffee and he took a sip of it, he immediately made a face, "For Christ's sake, you know I hate naselnut coffee!" Firing back at him I said, "First of all, it is not naselnut it is hazelnut! And second, you don't have naselnut. It is regular coffee!" Needless to say the coffee sat untouched in front of him all afternoon.

Christmas 2002

Christmas had us all feeling the same as we had at Thanksgiving: another last holiday with Dad. I tried to do all the same things we'd done at their house, setting up their four-foot fake tree, and decorating it and the house with all of their ornaments and decorations. A week before Christmas I set the two of them up at the kitchen table wrapping presents while I was at work.

Dad was so weak he needed a walker to get around. His main complaint was that he could not swallow very well. On one of his visits to the Oncology Department I told the nurse about Dad's difficulty with swallowing. She looked in his mouth and said he had thrush, a yeast infection (Candida) that causes white patches in the mouth and on the tongue. In severe cases it travels down the esophagus. An illness or medical situation can make Candida infection more likely in people with diabetes, HIV infections, or cancer. Dad's thrush was so bad that he could hardly swallow his beloved cup of coffee without choking, and running to the sink to vomit up sputum that looked like white foam. The nurse made a call to the hematologist, who prescribed a drug to clear the thrush up.

By this time Dad was losing weight fast. He slept all the time, and barely ate. For the first time in their 60 years of marriage Mom was trying to take care of Dad. She tried to help him dress in the morning and undress for bed at night. He resisted her, saying, "Leave me alone. I can do it myself. Why are you fussing over me so? Haven't you got something else to do, for Christ's sake?

During Christmas break, Angela came home for the holidays. I asked her if she would cut Papa's toenails for he complained that they were very long. I said that if she could speak to him about his illness, it would be good to see what he was thinking. With reluctance, she entered the living room carrying a plastic pan of warm water, towels, and toenail clippers.

Sitting on the floor in front of Dad, she started soaking his feet and talking to him about his cancer, "Papa, do you know that you have a type of cancer of the blood?" There was complete silence. "Papa, you were there when the doctor told my Mom about your illness, right?"

Very quietly, without looking at Angela, he said, "Yeah."

"Well, do you have anything you want to talk about?"

Still silent.

When Angela finished and came back into the kitchen, I asked her, "What did Papa say?"

With a bewildered look on her face she said, "Nothing. He did not want to talk about it."

"How could he not talk to you if you asked him a question?"

"Mom! He just would not talk to me! He said he is spending a lot of time in the past instead of the present."

We all gathered at eleven on Christmas morning for coffee, donut holes, and to open up our presents, just like in the past. As always it was chaos, with all of us crammed into my small living room. The wrapping paper flew, hitting people in the head. Dad tried to control the trash bags and made sure everyone had a knife. Some were opening their gifts and trying them on right then and there. Every time Dad opened a gift we would stop to see his reaction. Over the years Dad always had a comment on his gifts, but this time he was quiet about them. "That's nice. Thank you. Nancy, who gave this to me?" he would say as he placed a present on the floor next to his chair. I could read Dad like a book. His eyes said it all. He knew this was his last Christmas.

After opening our presents we gathered around the dining room table for our Italian Christmas dinner. Dad sat at one end with Mom beside him.

He started saying, "You know, I have been thinking about Bovino all week long." His voice started to crack, "You know I never went back after I left the Conservatory in Naples." There was complete silence in the room. Everyone stopped eating and looked up at Dad. "It is a beautiful place high on the mountain top."

I jumped in with, "I know Dad, remember? Angela, Adrianna and I were there in 2000. It is a beautiful place and remember all the pictures we took and all the relatives we visited?"

Dad became quiet as we changed the subject to something less tense and stressful. We all glanced around looking at each other for we knew what he was thinking about.

While my Mom, Angela, Adrianna and I cleaned up, Dad sat in his green chair. The boys were in a heated discussion about "something stupid," as I would always call it, in the kitchen. When the dining room table was clear, I put the coffee pot on and brought out the Italian cookies and ricotta cheesecake. Grabbing a small plate and placing a few biscotti on it, I took it to Dad in the living room. "Dad, I brought some cookies for you," I said, as I placed them in front of him on top of a hassock that was directly in front of him, then I headed back to the kitchen.

Armand Jr.'s girlfriend, Linda, was sitting in the living room with Dad. A few minutes later she came out to the kitchen to tell me, "You know, when you brought the cookies into your Dad, he waited for you to leave and he turned to me and said, 'I won't need those where I am going.'" She continued, "Nancy, I started to cry. I had to get up and leave the room, oh my God!"

February, 2003

As Dad got weaker and weaker he wanted to sleep more and more. He wasn't in any pain, just tired. If it wasn't for the immensely irksome thrush, he would have slept the rest of his life away.

On the morning of Wednesday January 29th, my day off, I had someone from Hospice coming to the house to help Dad wash and get dressed. We were bringing them in to help us through the last days of Dad's life.

When the nurse arrived she asked, "Does your father know he has cancer?"

"I think so," I said. "None of us ever talked about it or mentioned it to him. It is a silent understanding between all of us and Dad."

When I took her to Dad and Mom's bedroom, Dad was not in bed. He had gotten up and was standing in the bathroom in front of the sink, preparing to wash up. He was so thin and frail he could barely lift his head up to see who was standing in the hall. The nurse introduced herself, "Hi, Armand, my name is Cindy. I am here to help you wash." I was standing behind Cindy and Mom was behind me.

Dad lifted his head up very slowly and with his very weak left hand waving up in the air, said; "Nobody washes me, I'm Italian!" And he slammed the bathroom door in our faces. I turned to Cindy and said, "There you go. See ya! Case closed! Tutti bene! [All Good!] We are done!" Cindy asked me if she should stay awhile to see if he changed his mind. I told her, "You got to be kidding me? He is not going to let anyone help him. He even gives my mother a hard time."

Cindy left.

That afternoon, as I tried to get Dad to eat something or drink a cup of coffee, I noticed that he was having even more difficulty with the thrush. I called the hematologist and begged her to do something so he could at least take some liquid. She did not want to have him admitted to the hospital because there wasn't much she could do, but I insisted that he go in, hoping they could give him intravenous medication to try to clear the thrush up.

THE HOSPITAL

I took Dad to Maine Medical Center where they admitted him to the Gibson wing. He was placed in a private room just outside of the nurse's station. He cooperated with the nurses as they got him into bed. Once he was settled he admitted to being more comfortable. They started the IV antibiotic, administered fluids, and hooked him up to machines to monitor his blood pressure and heart rate. He got IV morphine for the pain.

For the first time in months I felt as if he was in much better hands. It wasn't that Mom and I weren't doing everything possible, but Mom still needed help and monitoring herself. Between my job, running home, cooking, cleaning, hospital trips, laundry, and making the decisions for them, I was exhausted. To see Dad relatively safe and secure made so much difference.

Dad was glad to have a private room, his own bathroom, television, couch and table. It looked like someone's living room with a bed in the middle. Once Dad seemed a little more relaxed, I told him that I would be back with Mom after work the next day. I said he should rest and let the medication do its job. He turned to me. In a barely audible whisper he said, "Thank you Nancy. I feel so much better now. This bed is so comfortable and soft." I kissed him goodbye and left.

For six days Mom and I visited Dad every day. On days when I worked we went early in the evening and we went twice a day on the weekend. On one visit, one of the nurses told me that my father had disconnected all of his IVs, and climbed over the bed rails. They'd found him in the bathroom. I wasn't surprised.

On Wednesday, February 5th, the seventh day, as I pushed Mom's wheelchair towards the door to Dad's room, we ran into the doctor coming out. We stopped. Mom peered through the doorway at Dad. The doctor told me that Dad could go home the next day, but she confided that he probably would not last more than a week. She said he would not be in any pain; he would just be very tired, and want to sleep.

Mom and I went in and found my cousin Cammie sitting next to Dad, talking with him. Cammie explained, "You know Nancy, your Dad just drank a full cup of coffee that I got in the cafeteria." I looked at Dad and said, "Wow! I bet that tasted good Dad?" Dad whispered, "Damn right."

After visiting for an hour or so, I went over and sat on the edge of Dad's bed, "Dad, you are coming home tomorrow. What do you think about that?" He just gave me a strange, vague look. I kept making conversation but his look bothered me. I kissed and hugged him goodnight. Grabbing the back of Mom's wheelchair, I said, "Goodnight Dad. See you tomorrow."

As I pushed my mother down the long corridor I kept picturing that look in his eyes. It burned through my mind over and over. What was that look for? I'd never seen that look before. What was he trying to tell me? All the way home I was silent. Had I failed to read what was on his mind? Once in the house I became restless. I paced back and forth still thinking about that look. I loved this man, my father, and I did not want to lose him. He'd always been there through troubled times, giving me a shoulder to lean on, or an ear to bend. Whatever I might be, his work, love, and understanding had made me a better person.

At eleven that night the telephone rang.

Italian words one would hear Dad muttering to himself:

The Italian language has a smaller number of words compared to the English language. To compensate, many Italian words have multiple meanings.

Addio – Good bye

Andiamo – Let's go!

Arrivederci – Goodbye

Aspetto – Wait/hold on

Basta – Enough!

Cacazza- Cock

Cafone – Bad mannered one

Capatosta – Hardhead

Capisce? – Do you understand?

Cazzo – Shit! (Also means cock, prick, penis, pecker & dick)

Che Cazzo – What the f…

Che se dice?- What do you say?

Chiacchierone- Chatterbox, mouthy, blabber, know it all

Ciao – Hi, hello, goodbye, see ya

Citrullo- Cucumber/ large, lumpy, dense, blockhead

Comare –Godmother (slang)

Compare – Godfather (slang)

Cosi Cosi – So, So

Culo – Ass, buttocks, fanny

Cucuzza –Pumpkin, squash (as in use ones head)

Faccia – Face, look, expression

Fa freddo – It's cold

Fesso – Stupid,Silly, foolish

Fresco – Fresh

Goomba- Old friend/ companion/associate

Grazie mille – Thanks a lot

Mama Mia – My mother

Mangia – Eat

Mannaggia il diavolo – Damn the devil

Mezza e Mezza – Half & Half

Mi Dispiace – I'm sorry

Moppina – Mop/dish cloth (slang)

Non rompere I coglioni! – Don't bust my balls!

Paesano – Villager, peasant, *(used in speaking to another Italian living in the U.S. that also came from humble beginnings)*

Pazzo- Crazy, insane, lunatic, nuts

Pisciare – Piss, pee

Puttana – Prostitute

Puzzo – Smell, stink, stench

Puzzolenti – Little stinker

Schifo- Disgust, grossness

Sfatcheem- Shit face

Sporca – Dirty, nasty

Stata zitto! – Be quiet, shut up!

Stronzo – Asshole, someone who is a real bastard

Stupido – Stupid one

Tu Sei Pazzo- You're crazy!

Tutti Bene – All good, All done

Tutto stutto- Very crazy – in disarray

Va fanapoli – Go f……..yourself in Naples

Va fanculo – Go f…. yourself

Yio – Hey boy?

CPSIA information can be obtained at www.ICGtesting.com
Printed in the USA
265975BV00006B/30/P